UNDERSTANDING FLORIDA LEGAL ETHICS

A Review of the Rules of Professional Conduct and disciplinary cases of the Florida Supreme Court

Jason C. King

This publication is designed to provide accurate information in regard to the subject matter covered herein. It is sold with the understanding that the publisher is not engaged in the rendering of legal, accounting, or other professional services. If legal advice or other expert assistance is required, the service of a competent licensed professional should be sought. The author is not a member of the Florida Bar.

No copyright is claimed in the text of statutes, regulations, rules, and excerpts from court opinions quoted within this work.

TABLE OF CONTENTS

ABOUT THE AUTHOR

Jason C. King was born in Lakeland, Florida in 1979 to Edith and Stephen King. His parents moved to southwest Florida when he was 12 years old. He graduated from Cypress Lake High School and went on to attend college at Edison State College. He graduated with a bachelor's degree in Criminal Justice Administration in 2008 from the University of Phoenix. Jason then pursued his lifelong dream of attending law school and graduated from Ave Maria School of Law in 2012. Jason has been in the legal field for over fifteen years working as a paralegal and law clerk for law firms in various areas of the law including family law, real estate, general civil litigation, personal injury and criminal defense. Jason is not a member of the Florida Bar.

Jason C. King

TABLE OF CITATION

Jason C. King

INTRODUCTION

While studying for the Multistate Professional Responsibility Exam (MPRE) I noticed that I could not find any books that provided an emphasis of the Florida Rules of Professional Conduct. I became acclimated to the case study method in law school and could easily learn a Rule or theory of legal reasoning with a case example. After my search turned up only a few resources I decided to write my own book on Florida legal ethics and research cases involving these Rules and the real world application of them. I have always had a passion for the law, and now writing about it fulfills a deeper understanding and appreciation of it.

The Florida Rules of Professional Conduct establish the foundation of the lawyer client relationship and provide an understanding of how important this relationship becomes. This text will explore several important Rules within the Rules of Professional Conduct and review Florida Supreme Court cases of disciplinary proceedings interpreting and enforcing these Rules.

At the end of the 2014 fiscal year, The Florida Bar reported there were 98,922 licensed Florida attorneys. The Florida Bar opened 6,293 investigative files and filed 993 disciplinary cases that resulted in 391 discipline orders. 61 attorneys were disbarred, 129 were suspended, 61 received public reprimands, 44 received admonishments and 51 were placed on probation during the fiscal year. The Florida Bar Discipline Statistics are supplied in the appendix for further review. If these lawyers had a better understanding of their professional responsibility, perhaps they could have avoided the breach of trust that led them to injure their own client or violate the Rules subjecting them to discipline. After investing four years for an undergraduate degree, three years in law school and another year studying and taking the bar exam, one should be careful in the practice of law and possess a complete understanding of the Rules of Professional Responsibility.

Jason C. King

CHAPTER 1
A LAWYER'S RESPONSIBILITIES
THE PREAMBLE

A lawyer's responsibilities are multifarious. As the Rules of Professional Conduct identify in its preamble a lawyer "is a representative of clients, an officer of the legal system, and a public citizen having special responsibility for the quality of justice." The Rules further define the role a lawyer is expected to fulfill.

A lawyer is expected to be a skilled advisor to his client. He is to offer informed understanding of the law. A lawyer is expected to communicate to his client the implications of his client's legal rights and obligations based on the client's factual situation.

Not only is the lawyer required to advise his client, but also to be an advocate for his client when necessary. Should negotiations fail or be unavailable, the lawyer should zealously advocate for his client in the appropriate court of law. As a negotiator, the lawyer must utilize his skill and knowledge to obtain the most beneficial result for the client using honest dealings.

A lawyer also has a duty to the tribunal. A lawyer may not bring or defend a matter or issue unless there is a basis in the law or facts of the case that is not frivolous. The lawyer is under a continuous obligation to be candid with the court. This includes disclosing material facts to the court and legal authority known by the attorney even if it is contrary to the client's position. A lawyer may not misrepresent the facts or the law to the court.

Finally, a lawyer must not only operate in his profession with dignity and honesty, but he must do the same in his personal life. It is not enough to merely practice law ethically. As a lawyer, one must be ethical. Under the Rules, a lawyer who engages in conduct involving dishonesty, fraud, deceit, or misrepresentation, whether in the practice of law or in his personal affairs, is subject to discipline.

In *Young v. Hector*, 884 So.2d 1025 (3rd DCA, 2004), the Court reminded counsel that "[i]n fulfilling his or her primary duty to a client, a lawyer must be ever mindful of the profession's broader duty to the legal system; this broader duty to the administration of justice and the judiciary cannot be forsaken in the name of zealous advocacy or self-interest." *Id* at 1028.

The Court also ordered the attorney and client jointly liable for the opposing party's attorney's fees and costs.

This case provides both an example of an attorney being overzealous in the representation of his client and misleading the trial court by re-arguing the attorney fee award that had already been upheld on appeal.

Young v. Hector, 884 So.2d 1025 (3rd DCA, 2004)

The former husband, Robert S. Young ("former husband"), seeks review of the trial court's order on appellate costs and attorney's fees. We reverse.

In June of 2003, this Court partially granted certiorari in favor of the former husband, finding the trial court had exceeded its jurisdiction in freezing certain trust account proceeds. A few months later, this Court granted the former husband's motion for attorney's fees, and remanded to the trial court to fix the amount of the fees. The former wife, Alice G. Hector ("former wife"), then filed a petition to withdraw the mandate and challenged the propriety of the award of appellate attorney's fees to the former husband. The petition to withdraw was denied.

Thereafter, the trial court conducted a hearing on the former husband's motion for attorney's fees. The former husband's expert witness testified that the reasonable number of hours expended by the former husband's attorney was 75.3 hours, and that the $300 per hour rate was a reasonable hourly rate. Thus the expert witness opined that the reasonable amount of the fee award would be $22,590.

No expert witness testified on behalf of the former wife. However, notwithstanding the mandate, the former wife's counsel again argued against the former husband's entitlement, raising the same issues argued on appeal and in her petition to withdraw mandate. In apparent agreement with the arguments made by the former wife's counsel, the trial court determined the reasonable hours to be 15 hours (instead of 75.3), and awarded attorney's fees of $4,500 (instead of $22,590). The trial court also awarded expert fees in the amount of $1350 and awarded costs only for the filing fee in the amount of $250.

The former husband then filed the instant "Motion For Review of Order on Appellate Costs and Attorney's Fees", and a "Motion for Attorney's

Fees" with this Court. The former husband essentially argues in this proceeding that the trial court was misled into revisiting the attorney's fees entitlement issue, and erred in reducing the reasonable attorney's fees by $18,900 and in awarding only the filing fee for costs. We agree.

We see no reason why the former husband was not awarded the full amount of costs including charges for preparation of the record. The trial court's order which awarded an unreasonably low amount of attorney's fees and costs, is not supported by the record. Therefore we remand with instructions to increase the award of appellate attorney's fees to $22,590, and to increase the award of costs to $488.

With regard to the attorney's fees incurred in the instant action, we grant attorney's fees in favor of the former husband and against the former wife, based upon the need to file an appeal made necessary by frivolous claims brought before the trial court.

The former wife's counsel argued to the trial judge that it was improper to grant fees which were clearly proper, and re-argued issues which had already been denied by this Court. By so doing, the trial judge was plainly misdirected and misled. No possible view of the law would sustain the former wife's counsel's arguments which led the trial judge to the incorrect result that the former husband was needlessly forced to appeal.

We remind counsel that, especially in the area of family law, great care should be taken to reduce emotional strife and to avoid vexatious and needless litigation. This Court will not hesitate to impose sanctions against parties and their counsel where unnecessary fees are incurred in response to frivolous positions and claims. In *Visoly v. Sec. Pac. Credit Corp.*, 768 So.2d 482 (Fla. 3d DCA 2000), this Court assessed attorney's fees against the appellant and appellant's counsel finding that the issues raised on appeal were neither supported by the record, cogent argument, nor pertinent legal authority. We granted attorney's fees in favor of the appellee for the unnecessary litigation costs incurred in being forced to defend a frivolous appeal.

Here, we are asked to grant a motion for attorney's fees in favor of the appellant for the unnecessary litigation costs in being forced to pursue appeal. Although Visoly differs procedurally from the instant case, the same basic principles regarding ethical responsibilities and responsibilities for payment of attorney's fees apply.

. . . . .

In fulfilling his or her primary duty to a client, a lawyer must be ever mindful of the profession's broader duty to the legal system. This broader duty to the administration of justice and the judiciary cannot be forsaken in the name of zealous advocacy or self-interest. It is simply unacceptable for an attorney to misdirect a trial judge to achieve a result that is clearly erroneous. This Court will impose sanctions not only to deter those who would pursue appeals which clearly lack merit, but also to deter those who would argue unsupported positions that are clearly contrary to appellate mandate.

Here, counsel for the former wife, even in the responses filed in the instant proceeding, continued to argue and re-litigate matters already determined non-meritorious and which should have been finally concluded by this Court's mandate.

These arguments were contradicted by the record and established case law. Accordingly, the former wife and her counsel shall be jointly responsible for the attorney's fees incurred by the former husband in the instant action based upon their conduct both in the trial court and in this Court.

Reversed and remanded with instructions.

Questions for Discussion

1.   Would it have made a difference if Young's client was the one demanding this course of action? Why?

2.   What did Young do to mislead the trial court?

Jason C. King

CHAPTER 2
COMPETENCE
RULE 4-1.1

Rule 4-1.1 requires that a lawyer "provide competent representation to a client." This competence is explained to include "legal knowledge, skill, thoroughness, and preparation reasonably necessary for the representation." Whether a lawyer is competent to handle a specific legal matter is determined by several factors.

The Comments of the Rule suggest that the competency required varies depending on the legal matter to be address; it further states that competence can be attained in many ways. A newly minted lawyer may obtain the requisite competence by study and review of the law and precedent, by association or consultation with a lawyer with established competence, and even co-counseling of the matter with an experienced lawyer.

Competence is the ability to analyze the specific facts of the case, identify the issues therein and understand how the law applies to them. Black's Law Dictionary defines it as "A basic or minimal ability to do something; qualification." I suggest that in regarding to a lawyers competence, it means much more. As the Comments continue, they identify other requirements of competency which include the ability to "inquiry into and analysis of the factual and legal elements of the problem" but also "adequate preparation" which means not only knowing the law but reviewing the facts of the case and having the capability to utilize such skills on behalf of the client. Taking a first look at the client file 15 minutes before the hearing is never adequate preparation, though one may be well informed of the law. Additionally the Rule requires the lawyer to maintain competency. This requires the lawyer to keep well informed of the law and changes thereto. This also means continuing study and attending continuing legal education (CLE) courses as required.

In *The Florida Bar v. Springer*, 873 So. 2d 317 (Fla. 2004), the Court disbarred an attorney for violating Rule 4-1.1 in that he failed to provide competent representation and continuously lied to his client about the status of the cases. Springer was hired to defend the client in a partition action in the state of Georgia. Springer never filed a motion to appear *pro hac vice* and never appeared for trial. Springer lied to the client about the status of the case even after the final judgment against the client was entered. Springer prepared but never filed a motion to set aside the final judgment and continued to make excuses to the client. In another matter, Springer also misrepresented the status of 24 foreclosure cases. Springer went as far as creating fraudulent certificates of title causing serious problems to his client in the future sale of these units. Finally, in a third matter, Springer lied to his client about obtaining a garnishment for the collection of a judgment when in fact none existed.

The Bar recommended disbarment and the Referee stated "Springer's multiple incidents of incompetent action followed by lies, then more lies to cover up the deceit, demonstrated "a defect, if not an absolute absence, of honesty, integrity, and ethical judgment." The Court agreed and Springer was disbarred from the practice of law and not eligible for readmission for a period of 5 years.

The Florida Bar v. Springer, 873 So2d 317 (Fla. 2004)

FINDINGS OF FACT AND RECOMMENDATIONS OF GUILT

The Florida Bar filed a six-count complaint against Springer. At a disciplinary hearing, The Florida Bar and Springer stipulated to detailed facts which the referee adopted as the facts of the case. Based on these facts, the referee issued a report containing the following recommendations as to each count.

COUNT I

Howard Mitchell hired Springer to defend him in a real property partition action in Georgia brought by David Centa. While Springer was involved in the case, from December 1997 to November 2000, he never filed a pro hac vice motion or a notice of appearance with the Georgia trial court; thus, Springer did not file any documents with the court during the case. Springer did communicate with the plaintiff's counsel, who informed Springer of the trial date set by the court. However, Springer did not appear at trial. The jury found in favor of the plaintiff Centa, and the court entered judgment against Mitchell. Even after the court entered judgment, when Mitchell asked about the case Springer told him "it's going to be fine." Springer prepared but did not file with the court a motion to set aside final judgment. He repeatedly lied to Mitchell, telling him that hearings had been scheduled on the motion and then postponed. Mitchell did not recover the value of his interest in the property, which he alleged was about $29,000.

On count I, the referee recommended that Springer be found guilty of violating the following Rules Regulating the Florida Bar: rule 4-1.1 (a lawyer shall provide competent representation to his client); rule 4-1.3 (an attorney shall act with reasonable diligence in the representation of his client); rule 4-1.4(a) (a lawyer shall keep a client reasonably informed about the status of a matter and promptly comply with reasonable requests for information); rule 4-5.5 (a lawyer shall not practice law in a jurisdiction where doing so violates the regulation of the legal profession in that jurisdiction); rule 4-8.4(a) (a lawyer shall not violate or attempt to violate the Rules of Professional Conduct); rule 4-8.4(c) (a lawyer shall not engage in conduct involving dishonesty, fraud, deceit, or misrepresentation); and rule 4-8.4(d) (a lawyer shall not engage in conduct in connection with the practice of law that is prejudicial to the administration of justice).

COUNT II

The Camelot Condominium Owners' Association, of which Howard Mitchell was president, hired Springer in 1993 to handle foreclosures of timeshare condominium units whose owners failed to pay their maintenance fees or taxes. In March 1998, Mitchell asked Springer about twenty-four foreclosure cases which had not been finalized. Springer gave Mitchell falsified copies of certificates of title to the twenty-four timeshare units, all dated April 9, 1998. Springer misrepresented to Mitchell that the twenty-four foreclosures were final. Mitchell sold some of the units to new owners, but in April 1999, Mitchell discovered that the certificates of title were not recorded and that the foreclosures were not finalized. The sales of units based on Springer's falsified certificates of title resulted in Camelot's having to resolve cases of multiple owners claiming the same unit, creating additional legal expenses and potentially harming Camelot's reputation.

On count II, the referee recommended that Springer be found guilty of violating rule 4-1.1 (competence); rule 4-1.3 (diligence); rule 4-1.4(a) (communication); rule 4-8.4(a) (violation of Rules of Professional Conduct); rule 4-8.4(c) (dishonest conduct); and rule 4-8.4(d) (conduct prejudicial to the administration of justice).

COUNT III

In December 1995, Howard Mitchell hired Springer to pursue a breach of agreement claim arising from Mitchell's sale of a house to Garland and Mary Cunningham. Springer failed to file a claim against the Cunninghams. In March 1999, Springer falsely told Mitchell that he had obtained a garnishment of Mr. Cunningham's wages. In August 1999, Mitchell learned of Springer's negligence in this and other cases, and Springer signed a letter admitting his negligence and promising diligence in the future. Despite his promises, in April 2000, Springer falsely represented to Mitchell that he was following up with Mr. Cunningham's employer to enforce a garnishment, when there was in fact no judgment to support a garnishment. In December 2000, Mitchell fired Springer and Springer withdrew from the case. In January 2001, Mitchell filed pro se a motion for default that Springer had drafted and successfully obtained a default judgment against the Cunninghams.

On count III, the referee recommended that Springer be found guilty of violating rule 4-1.1 (competence); rule 4-1.3 (diligence); rule 4-1.4(a) (communication); rule 4-8.4(a) (a lawyer shall not violate or attempt to violate the Rules of Professional Conduct); and rule 4-8.4(c) (dishonest conduct).

COUNT IV

In January 2000, Howard Mitchell hired Springer to pursue a breach of contract claim arising from the failure of Randy Baron and Jennifer Wall to pay Mitchell for construction work on their home. In February 2000, Springer filed a claim of lien, but the defendants filed a motion to dismiss because the complaint failed to allege certain elements of an oral contract. The court gave Mitchell fifteen days to respond. Springer failed to respond, and the court granted the defendants' motion to dismiss.

Over the next several months, Springer told Mitchell he was filing papers and scheduling hearings to reinstate the case, which he did not do. In October 2000, Springer filed a new complaint. Baron and Wall counterclaimed. Springer failed to answer the counterclaim, and the court entered a default judgment against Mitchell. In December 2000, Mitchell fired Springer, and Springer withdrew from the case.

On count IV, the referee recommended that Springer be found guilty of violating rule 4-1.1 (competence); rule 4-1.3 (diligence); and rule 4-1.4(a) (communication).

COUNT V

In November 1997, Howard Mitchell hired Springer to file a lien against C & D Printing for failure to pay Mitchell for construction work. Over the next several months, Springer did nothing substantive on the case but told Mitchell that he had filed a complaint and that a hearing was scheduled. In August 1999, Mitchell learned of Springer's negligence in this and other cases, and Springer signed a letter admitting his negligence and promising diligence in the future. In September 1999, Springer filed a complaint but misnamed C & D Printing as "Cee & Dee Printing." In February 2000, the clerk of court issued a notice of intent to dismiss for failure to obtain service. In May 2000, Springer lied to Mitchell, saying he had obtained a judgment and was attempting to enforce collection. In October 2000, Springer filed an amended complaint and C & D Printing filed a motion to dismiss. In January 2001, Mitchell fired Springer and Springer withdrew from the case.

On count V, the referee recommended that Springer be found guilty of violating rule 4-1.1 (competence); rule 4-1.3 (diligence); rule 4-1.4(a) (communication); and rule 4-8.4(c) (dishonest conduct).

COUNT VI

In 1998 Camelot filed a lien against timeshare unit owner Richard Baserap for failure to pay maintenance fees and taxes. In November 1998, Baserap filed suit against Camelot alleging illegal lockout and challenging the amount of the lien. Springer timely filed an answer and affirmative defenses for Camelot but then failed to comply with a court order regarding discovery.

The court entered a judgment of liability in favor of Baserap. Springer settled the case for $18,000 without Camelot's consent. He paid the $18,000 from his own funds and told Camelot about the settlement after the fact.

On count VI, the referee recommended that Springer be found guilty of violating rule 4-1.2(a) (a lawyer shall abide by a client's decision whether to make or accept an offer of settlement of a matter); rule 4-1.3 (diligence); and rule 4-1.4(a) (communication).

RECOMMENDED DISCIPLINE

At the disciplinary hearing, the Bar sought to have Springer suspended from the practice of law for two years followed by a two-year probationary period and a mandatory review of his practice by the Law Office Management Assistance Service of the Florida Bar (LOMAS), as well as payment of the Bar's costs. In his final report, the referee recommended that Springer be disbarred from the practice of law and be required to pay the Bar's costs. The referee found in aggravation that Springer had committed multiple offenses and demonstrated a pattern of misconduct. The referee stated that Springer's multiple incidents of incompetent action followed by lies, then more lies to cover up the deceit, demonstrated "a defect, if not an absolute absence, of honesty, integrity, and ethical judgment." In mitigation, the referee found that Springer had a cooperative attitude during the proceedings and showed remorse. In evaluating the mitigating factors, the referee found that Springer's cooperation and

remorse did not "rise to the level of a valid basis to outweigh the harm of Respondent's actions." The referee concluded that Springer "has not and cannot meet" the Bar's standards of professional and ethical responsibility, and "thus is not qualified to practice law and represent members of the public."

CONCLUSION

Arthur James Springer is hereby disbarred from the practice of law in the State of Florida without leave to apply for readmission for five years. The disbarment will be effective thirty days from the filing of this opinion so that Springer can close out his practice and protect the interests of existing clients. If Springer notifies this Court in writing that he is no longer practicing and does not need the thirty days to protect existing clients, this Court will enter an order making the disbarment effective immediately. Springer shall accept no new business from the date this opinion is filed until he is readmitted to the practice of law in Florida. We also enter judgment against Springer in favor of The Florida Bar, 651 East Jefferson Street, Tallahassee, Florida 32399-2300, for costs in the amount of $3,313.12, for which sum let execution issue.

It is so ordered.

Questions for Discussion

1.   When Howard contacted Springer regarding the Georgia matter, what should Howard have done? Referral? Why do you suppose Springer took the case?

2.   What could Springer have done to avoid violating the Rules of Professional Responsibility in the foreclosure cases?

3.   Why do you think Howard keep hiring Springer for new matters?

4.   Review the comments to Rule 4-1.1, do you think the Rules make clear what competence is? What does a new lawyer do to become competent?

CHAPTER 3
DELIGENCE
RULE 4-1.3

Rule 4-1.3 requires that a lawyer "shall act with reasonable diligence and promptness in representing a client." This short and powerful sentence is provided ample explanation in the Comments section. The lawyer must "pursue a matter on behalf of a client despite opposition, obstruction, or personal inconvenience to the lawyer and take whatever lawful and ethical measures are required to vindicate a client's cause or endeavor." This Comment sheds light on just how deep the lawyer's connection goes with his client. The lawyer must put his client's needs above his own.

The lawyer must become the navigator of the legal ship the client has chosen to set sail. While the client has the ultimate authority over the purpose of the voyage, it is the lawyer's duty to navigate the legal rocky reefs before them. Yet a lawyer must pursue his client's lawful interests ethically. This requires the lawyer to avoid offensive tactics and requires the treating of all parties, even the adversary, with dignity and respect.

This diligence also requires the lawyer to maintain his workload so that each client can be given the time and resources the lawyer needs to competently handle their matters. Furthermore, procrastination must be avoided. This can lead to cause the client unnecessary anxiety, and in some egregious cases to miss the statute of limitations deadline which eliminates the clients claim entirely.

In *The Florida Bar v. Whitney*, 132 So.3d 1095 (Fla. 2013), the Court found that Whitney's misconduct warranted a one-year suspension from the practice of law in Florida because Whitney had failed to act with reasonable diligence in representing a client.

Whitney was hired by a doctor to represent his girlfriend in an immigration matter because she was in the country illegally. The retainer agreement provided that Whitney would receive a flat fee of $15,000 and costs of $5,000. When Whitney was paid the monies, rather than placing any unearned fee or cost deposit in his trust account, he deposited the funds in his personal checking account "to pay his personal bills because respondent was experiencing financial problems at the time." Whitney later demanded an additional fee between $40,000 and $60,000. Whitney was later sued by his former client and also violated numerous rules of conduct during the litigation of that matter.

Whitney traveled to Brazil twice to allegedly check on the requirements of the client getting married in Brazil. The Referee found this to be somewhat suspicious and determined that, besides these two trips, Whitney took no further meaningful action. The Referee found that Whitney failed to act with reasonable diligence. The referee recommended a 90-day suspension from the practice of law and the Bar appealed. The Court accepted the findings of fact and increased the sanction to Whitney suspending him from the practice of law for one year.

The Florida Bar v. Whitney, 132 So.3d 1095 (Fla. 2013)

FACTS

....

A referee was appointed to hold hearings and provide a report to the Court. The referee made the following findings of fact and recommendations. On January 19, 2004, Dr. Hill hired Respondent to provide immigration and legal advice. At their initial meeting, Respondent was advised that Ms. de Oliveira, who was present at the meeting, was a native of Brazil and was in the United States illegally for the third time. Respondent was informed that she had received a letter from the United States Department of Justice banning her from the country for twenty years because of her two previous illegal entries into the United States. Respondent was further advised that Dr. Hill intended to marry Ms. de Oliveira, but that they were not engaged and Dr. Hill had only known her since November 2003 when she moved into his house.

Based upon their meeting, a fee agreement was executed, which provided for a flat fee of $15,000, plus a $5,000 deposit for costs. In the agreement,

Dr. Hill was referred to as the client. The fee contract provided that Respondent would represent Ms. de Oliveira "in regard to all matters pertaining to her immigration status" and that Respondent's obligations under the contract would terminate "upon decision of the Office of the Attorney General granting or denying permission for Leila Mesquita de Oliveira to reenter the United States." Dr. Hill provided Respondent with two checks, one dated January 26, 2004, in the amount of $10,000, and one dated February 6, 2004, in the amount of $9,365. Dr. Hill also paid directly for an airline ticket for Respondent to travel to Brazil. Respondent deposited the checks into his personal checking account, and used Dr. Hill's funds "to pay his personal bills because respondent was experiencing financial problems at the time."

In early 2004, Respondent twice traveled to Brazil to allegedly research the requirements for Dr. Hill and Ms. de Oliveira to marry in Brazil. The referee found that this information was easily obtained without leaving the country. Respondent also claimed that one of the trips to Brazil was to obtain information on rental properties for Ms. de Oliveira and to verify her Brazilian documents. Because the location in which Respondent indicated that he found a residence for Ms. de Oliveira was in an area other than where she lived in Brazil, the referee concluded that that trip was for a purpose other than for his client's case. In September 2004, Respondent took possession of Ms. de Oliveira's Brazilian passport, which she advised him was a falsified document, as well as other original Brazilian documents. The referee found that Respondent "took no further meaningful action with respect to Ms. de Oliveira's immigration matter."

Dr. Hill contacted Respondent in late 2004 or early 2005 after failing to receive any communication from Respondent since hiring him in January 2004. Respondent advised Dr. Hill that he had not initiated the process to have Ms. de Oliveira remain in the United States or to reenter legally so that they could be married in the United States. Respondent advised Dr. Hill that Ms. de Oliveira needed to marry Dr. Hill in Brazil, and that he would only proceed further after Dr. Hill paid an additional fee of between $40,000 and $60,000. Dr. Hill terminated Respondent's services and demanded a full refund of his fee and costs, as well as the return of Ms. de Oliveira's documents. Respondent denied Dr. Hill's request, stating that he had earned the fees and costs paid. Respondent failed to provide an accounting to Dr. Hill, and failed to timely return Ms. de Oliveira's documents. Ms. de Oliveira executed a letter dated February 22, 2005, demanding return of her original documents. Respondent did comply with the written request from Ms. de Oliveira, who returned to Brazil in or around April 2005.

In July 2005, Dr. Hill filed a civil lawsuit against Respondent alleging breach of contract, legal malpractice, and unjust enrichment. (Hill v. Whitney, Case No. 05–CA–5999). Dr. Hill was represented by attorney Bonnie Jackson and Respondent was pro se. The referee found that "[R]espondent engaged in a course of conduct where he was uncooperative in coordinating the scheduling of hearings."

In an order entered on December 12, 2005, the trial court directed Respondent to produce responsive documents on or before December 19, 2005. Respondent failed to comply with that order and failed to appear for his duly noticed deposition on December 21, 2005. At no time did Respondent contact opposing counsel or file a notice of unavailability for his deposition. Not until January 4, 2006, did Respondent produce the documents sought by the request for production dated September 20, 2005, and which were ordered to be produced by December 19, 2005. Respondent did not produce all of the documents sought.

On January 18, 2006, a hearing was held on Ms. Jackson's second motion to compel. Respondent was admonished by the court and advised to fully cooperate with discovery. At Respondent's deposition on January 27, 2006, Ms. Jackson learned of the outstanding documents when Respondent arrived with a client file containing documents that he had not previously produced pursuant to the request for production. Further, Respondent produced documents that were redacted without asserting an objection or otherwise indicating that a redaction had been made.

Respondent failed to produce Visa credit card statements or receipts that were responsive to Dr. Hill's first set of interrogatories and that the circuit court had ordered him to produce. Ms. Jackson sought such records to document the expenditures Respondent made in Brazil that had been allocated to Dr. Hill's cost deposit. In answering Dr. Hill's request for production, Respondent stated that he did not advertise, when, in fact, he had a website which was discovered by Ms. Jackson.

The referee found that Respondent testified falsely and deceptively at his deposition. While he testified that the name of his law firm was "Max R. Whitney, P.A.," Respondent failed to disclose that his website used the name "Max Whitney & Willie Jones Advogados Associados." Moreover, the business card provided to Dr. Hill reflected the name "Carvalhosa & Whitney Direito Internacional," while the Florida Secretary of State, Division of Corporations, reflects the firm registered under the name "The Law Offices of Max R. Whitney, P.A." and includes an address different than the one Respondent testified to during his deposition. In addition, Respondent testified falsely that the only pending litigation in which he was involved was a suit against him by U.B. Vehicle Leasing, Inc., relating to a dispute as to the mileage of a car. However, a mortgage foreclosure action had been filed against Respondent on November 1, 2004, and was pending at the time of the deposition. Respondent falsely testified that the mortgage on his home had not been in foreclosure. The referee found Respondent's failure to reveal the existence of the foreclosure action "particularly relevant to Dr. Hill's lawsuit given respondent's sworn deposition testimony on January 27, 2006, that he deposited the fees and costs Dr. Hill paid him into his personal checking account and used the funds to pay, among other things, the mortgage on his home."

Ms. Jackson served a motion for sanctions and motion for entry of default judgment against Respondent on March 31, 2006. The circuit court entered an order on May 30, 2006, granting the motion for sanctions and entry of default judgment, striking Respondent's defenses and awarding reasonable attorney's fees and costs to Dr. Hill. The circuit court found that "[R]espondent had 'willfully failed and refused to comply with previous order [sic] of this Court, failed and refused to participate in pretrial discovery and provided falsified documents' in the case."

On October 4, 2007, the circuit court entered a final judgment against Respondent in favor of Dr. Hill, including $20,000 on principal, which Respondent has remitted to Dr. Hill through Ms. Jackson. Respondent appealed to the Fifth District Court of Appeal, which upheld the final judgment but remanded for a determination of the correct amount of attorney's fees. See Whitney v. Hill, 1 So.3d 1157 (Fla. 5th DCA 2009). A Second Amended Final Judgment was entered on June 15, 2011. Respondent has not paid any of the additional $24,246 in attorney's fees, expert fees, and taxable costs awarded to Dr. Hill.

The referee recommended that Respondent be found guilty of violating Bar Rules: 4–1.3 (diligence); 4–1.4(a) (keeping a client reasonably informed and promptly comply with requests for information); 4–1.4(b) (explaining a matter to the client to the extent reasonably necessary to permit informed decision); 4–1.16(d) (upon termination of representation, a lawyer shall take steps to protect a client's interest); 4–3.3(a) (a lawyer shall not knowingly (1) make a false statement of material fact or law to a tribunal; (2) fail to disclose a material fact to a tribunal when disclosure is necessary to avoid assisting a criminal or fraudulent act by the client; (4) permit any witness to offer testimony or other evidence that the lawyer knows to be false); 4–3.4(a) (a lawyer shall not unlawfully obstruct another party's access to evidence or otherwise unlawfully alter, destroy, or conceal a document or other material that the lawyer knows or reasonably should know is relevant to a pending or reasonably foreseeable proceeding); 4–3.4(b) (a lawyer shall not fabricate evidence); 4–3.4(c) (a lawyer shall not knowingly disobey an obligation under the rules of a tribunal); 4–3.4(d) (a lawyer shall not make a frivolous discovery request or intentionally fail to comply with a legally proper discovery request by an opposing party); and 4–8.4(d) (a lawyer shall not engage in conduct in connection with the practice of law that is prejudicial to the administration of justice).

Although not expressly addressed in the referee's report, the referee did not recommend that Respondent be found guilty of violating the following Bar Rules alleged in the complaint: 3–4.3 (the commission by a lawyer of any act that is unlawful or contrary to honesty and justice, whether the act is committed in the course of the attorney's relations as an attorney or otherwise may constitute a cause for discipline); 4–1.1 (competence); 4–3.3(a) (a lawyer shall not knowingly: (3) fail to disclose to the tribunal legal authority in the controlling jurisdiction known to the lawyer to be *1102 directly adverse to the position of the client and not disclosed by opposing counsel); and 4–8.4(c) (engaging in conduct involving dishonesty, fraud, deceit, or misrepresentation).

With respect to Respondent's representation of Dr. Hill, the referee found the testimony of the Bar's expert witness pertaining to immigration law to be helpful. In addition, the referee found Ms. Jackson's testimony to be "forthright" and credible. The referee found Respondent's testimony "to be self-serving and, at times, contrary to previous testimony and/or statements." In addition, the referee found Respondent's testimony regarding the immigration matter to lack credibility.

. . . .

(B) Discipline

Based upon the rule violations found by the referee, the Bar argues that a one-year suspension is appropriate, rather than the ninety-day suspension recommended by the referee.

The referee found the following aggravating factors under Standard 9.22: (b) dishonest or selfish motive; (c) pattern of misconduct; (d) multiple offenses; (h) vulnerability of the victim(s); and (i) substantial experience in the practice of law. The referee found the following mitigating factors under Standard 9.32: (a) absence of prior disciplinary record; (g) character or reputation; and (k) imposition of other penalties and sanctions. In addition, the referee found as mitigating factors the length of time elapsing between the civil proceeding and Respondent's ability to avoid disciplinary action.

The referee recommended a suspension after considering the following Standards for Imposing Lawyer Sanctions were applicable: Standards 4.43 (Lack of Diligence [public reprimand]); 4.62 (Lack of Candor [suspension]); 6.12 (False Statements, Fraud, and Misrepresentation [suspension]); 6.22 (Abuse of the Legal Process [suspension]); and 7.2 (Other Duties Owed as a Professional [suspension]).

. . . .

Here, Respondent accepted a substantial fee from his client but did not perform notable work in furtherance of that representation. He also misused his client's funds by twice traveling to Brazil, once for no apparent case-related reason and once as unnecessary to obtaining the information sought. While the immigration issue may have been complicated, Respondent did not communicate that issue to Dr. Hill and Ms. de Oliveira. Next, with respect to the malpractice action, Respondent failed to produce documents, did not appear for his first noticed deposition, and offered frivolous responses to the interrogatories. Respondent has not paid the portion of the judgment awarding attorney's fees and costs in the malpractice action, and continues to refer to his conduct as negligent.

Based upon the facts in this case and established case law, we find the referee's recommended sanction of a ninety-day suspension unsupported and instead impose a one-year suspension.

Questions for Discussion

1. What was the first violation of the Rules that Whitney committed?

2. What would have been a reasonable fee for the immigration case?

3. Was it reasonable for the Whitney to travel to Brazil to research the requirements for the couple to marry there?

Jason C. King

CHAPTER 4
COMUNICATION
RULE 4-1.4

A lawyer must maintain an open line of communication with his client. The Client must be well informed of matters in order to make decisions regarding the representation. Under Rule 4-1.4, the lawyer has a duty to explain matters "to the extent reasonably necessary to permit the client to make informed decisions regarding the representation."

In litigation, the lawyer should explain to the client the strategy of reaching the client's goal and the likelihood of success and possible hurdles in the process. In the negotiation process, the lawyer should explain a proposed agreement, and its effects on the client's rights and responsibilities, before completing the agreement. As the Comments further note, the client "should have sufficient information to participate intelligently in decisions concerning the objectives of the representation…"

In *The Florida Bar v. Roberts*, 770 So. 2d 1207 (Fla. 2000), the lawyer was suspended for 91 days for failing to keep his client informed and failing to explain matters to the client to the extent reasonably necessary to permit the client to make an informed decision. Roberts also failed to return the client's telephone calls.

Roberts referred the family law client to another lawyer, without telling the client he was not affiliated, and the lawyer missed several court appearances. The client insisted Roberts continue representation and Roberts entered into a new agreement with the client. However, he failed to return numerous calls from the client leaving the client with no choice but to retain new counsel only a month before mediation. The Court imposed the 91 day suspension and required evidence of rehabilitation before being readmitted and a one year probationary period.

The Florida Bar v. Roberts, 770 So. 2d 1207 (Fla. 2000)

. . . .

The Florida Bar filed a complaint against Roberts alleging various ethical violations concerning his representation of a client in a dissolution of marriage proceeding. A hearing was held on June 11, 1999, and the referee made the following findings of fact.

On September 24, 1996, a client hired Roberts to represent her in a dissolution of marriage proceeding. After being served with a petition for dissolution, the client went to Roberts' office for a scheduled appointment and was informed that another attorney would be handling her case. Roberts failed to inform the client that this attorney was not affiliated with his law firm. Roberts did not have written permission from the client allowing him to refer her case to outside counsel. Moreover, when the referred attorney attempted to obtain the client's financial records from Roberts, he was informed that they had been misplaced.

The referred attorney thereafter failed to appear for two scheduled appointments and could not be reached. It was then that the client learned that he was not an associate of Roberts' firm. Because the client was no longer satisfied with her representation by the referred attorney, Roberts agreed to meet with her on January 14, 1997. At this meeting, Roberts attempted to return the client's retainer and advised her to hire new counsel. The client did not want Roberts to withdraw from the case because it had been four months since the divorce proceeding began. At this time, the client's financial records had still not been found. Roberts agreed to remain on the case, and an agreement was executed.

Roberts subsequently attended a case management hearing on April 28, 1997. Following this hearing, the client attempted on several occasions to discuss the hearing with Roberts and requested a status report. On May 12, 1997, the client was notified that mediation had been scheduled for July 16, 1997. On May 29, 1997, the client received a letter from Roberts informing her that he would be closing his law offices as of 4 p.m. on May 30, 1997, and referring her to a third attorney. The client then called Roberts and insisted that he handle her case at mediation. Roberts assured the client that he would remain on her case and represent her at the mediation. The client called Roberts several times between June 6, 1997, and June 23, 1997, to discuss the mediation; however, Roberts refused or failed to return her calls. The client then retained another attorney to represent her on June 23, 1997, leaving new counsel less than a month to prepare for mediation.

Based on this conduct, the referee found that Roberts had failed to keep the client reasonably informed of the status of her representation in violation of rule 4-1.4(a) of the Rules Regulating The Florida Bar and had failed to explain the matter to the client to the extent reasonably necessary to permit the client to make an informed decision, in violation of rule 4-1.4(b).

In aggravation, the referee considered Roberts' disciplinary history, consisting of: (1) a private reprimand on May 8, 1984, for neglect; (2) an admonishment on September 24, 1992, for "allowing kids to drink in his house"; (3) an admonishment on December 15, 1993, for failing to communicate; (4) an admonishment on January 20, 1995, for failing to comply with the Rules of Discipline concerning the supervision of a suspended lawyer; and (5) a ninety-day suspension on April 1, 1999, for lack of communication, failing to hold a client's funds in trust and collecting unearned fees. In mitigation, the referee considered the fact that Roberts was suffering from personal or emotional problems.

Based on these findings, the referee recommended that Roberts be suspended for six months and thereafter until rehabilitation is proven and upon reinstatement be placed on one year's probation. The referee recommended that the suspension run concurrent with that imposed on April 1, 1999.

Neither party contests the referee's findings of fact, and we find them to be supported by the record. See *Florida Bar v. Vannier*, 498 So.2d 896, 898 (Fla.1986). Therefore, we approve the referee's decision as to the violations of the Rules of Professional Conduct.

Roberts, however, challenges the referee's recommendation as to discipline and argues that it should not be approved because it is based on an improper aggravator. Roberts argues that the referee erred in making his disciplinary recommendation because the referee considered in aggravation Roberts' prior disciplinary proceeding occurring April 1, 1999. Roberts contends that because the conduct that was the subject of that proceeding occurred after the conduct in the instant case, the referee is precluded from considering it in aggravation. We do not agree.

We considered a similar contention in *Florida Bar v. Golden*, 566 So.2d 1286 (Fla.1990). In that case, Golden argued that the referee's disciplinary recommendation should not be followed because the referee erroneously determined that Golden had committed cumulative misconduct and a prior disciplinary offense. See *id.* at 1287. Golden argued that, at the time the misconduct under review occurred, he had not committed any prior misconduct because any prior misconduct was not subjected to discipline until after his conduct in the case under review occurred. See *id.* This Court held that cumulative misconduct is a relevant factor when determining the appropriate penalty in a disciplinary matter. See *id.* at 1287. The Court found that it was proper for the referee to consider the prior disciplinary proceeding, noting that cumulative misconduct can be found "when the misconduct occurs near in time to the other offenses, regardless of when discipline is imposed." *Id.* at 1287. Thus, the referee properly considered Roberts' misconduct that resulted in the prior proceeding.

Roberts' related argument, that had this been a criminal proceeding the referee would not have been able to consider the subsequent misconduct, is also without merit. This Court has held that Bar disciplinary proceedings are neither civil nor criminal but are quasi-judicial administrative proceedings to which many of the technical requirements of a criminal case do not apply. See *Florida Bar v. Vannier*, 498 So.2d 896 (Fla.1986).

Because the referee properly considered the misconduct that resulted in the April 1, 1999, suspension, cases cited by Roberts in support of a one-month suspension had that proceeding been removed as an aggravating factor do not apply. Considering Roberts' disciplinary history, we find that the referee's recommendation is reasonably supported by existing case law. See Florida Bar v. Fredericks, 731 So.2d 1249, 1254 (Fla.1999).

In *Florida Bar v. Brakefield*, 679 So.2d 766 (Fla.1996), and *Florida Bar v. Rolle*, 661 So.2d 296 (Fla.1995), this Court imposed a six-month suspension for misconduct similar to what occurred in this case. In *Rolle* the attorney was found guilty of violating rule 4-1.3 for failing to act with reasonable diligence in representing a client. 661 So.2d at 298. *Rolle* had two prior disciplinary actions. See id. In *Brakefield*, the attorney was found guilty of violating rules 4-1.1, 4-1.3, 4-1.4(a), 4-1.4(b), and 1.16(d) for various acts of client neglect. 679 So.2d at 769-70. *Brakefield* also had two prior disciplinary actions. See *id.* at 679. Thus, the referee's recommended discipline is reasonably supported by existing case law.

We here make the specific point that an attorney's consideration of his or her client's interests and communication with the client at reasonable times in response to the client's inquiries are a vital and necessary part of the attorney-client relationship. We expect and require this of members of The Florida Bar and will not hesitate to impose discipline upon Florida attorneys who do not fulfill these obligations to their clients.

In conclusion, we approve the referee's findings of fact. As to discipline, the referee recommended that Roberts' six-month suspension run concurrent with the ninety-day suspension imposed April 1, 1999. Such a recommendation, if followed, would result in an actual suspension of three months and require proof of rehabilitation prior to reinstatement. However, because the previous suspension has terminated, in order to effectuate the intent of the referee, we hereby suspend Roberts for ninety-one days, which will require proof of rehabilitation prior to reinstatement.

Accordingly, Larry B. Roberts is hereby suspended from the practice of law in Florida for ninety-one days and thereafter until he has shown proof of rehabilitation. Upon reinstatement, Roberts shall be on probation for a period of one year. The suspension will be effective thirty days from the filing of this opinion so that Roberts can close out his practice and protect the interests of existing clients. If Roberts notifies this Court in writing that he is no longer practicing law and does not need the thirty days to protect existing clients, this Court will enter an order making the suspension effective immediately. Roberts shall accept no new business from the date this opinion is filed until the suspension is completed. Judgment is entered for The Florida Bar, 650 Apalachee Parkway, Tallahassee, Florida 32399, for recovery of costs from Larry B. Roberts in the amount of $1,043.62, for which sum let execution issue.

It is so ordered.

Questions for Discussion

1. Why did the Court suspend Roberts for 91 days? Why not 90?

2. Why do you think Roberts accepted the case if he was simply going to refer it to another attorney?

3. How much time do you think the new attorney needed to prepare the case for mediation?

4. How do you plan on communicating with your clients? Telephone? Email? Will you give them your cell phone number?

CHAPTER 5
ATTORNEY'S FEES
RULE 4-1.5

A lawyer may not charge an unreasonable fee or cost for his services. Rule 4-1.5 lays the ground rules for determining whether a fee is reasonable. A fee is unreasonable if it is obtained by misrepresentation or fraud. Additionally, a fee is unreasonable if "after a review of the facts, a lawyer of ordinary prudence would be left with a definite and firm conviction that the fee or cost exceeds a reasonable fee or cost for services provided to such a degree as to constitute clear overreaching or an unconscionable demand by the attorney."

The time expended and hourly rate charged is not the only factor to be considered when determining the reasonableness of a fee. In fact, the Rule lists several factors to consider which include:

(A) the time and labor required, the novelty, complexity, and difficulty of the questions involved, and the skill requisite to perform the legal service properly;

(B) the likelihood that the acceptance of the particular employment will preclude other employment by the lawyer;

(C) the fee, or rate of fee, customarily charged in the locality for legal services of a comparable or similar nature;

(D) the significance of, or amount involved in, the subject matter of the representation, the responsibility involved in the representation, and the results obtained;

(E) the time limitations imposed by the client or by the circumstances and, as between attorney and client, any additional or special time demands or requests of the attorney by the client;

(F) the nature and length of the professional relationship with the client;

(G) the experience, reputation, diligence, and ability of the lawyer or lawyers performing the service and the skill, expertise, or efficiency of effort reflected in the actual providing of such services; and

(H) whether the fee is fixed or contingent, and, if fixed as to amount or rate, then whether the client's ability to pay rested to any significant degree on the outcome of the representation.

In *The Florida Bar v. Carlon*, 820 So. 2d 891 (Fla. 2002), the Court suspended an attorney from the practice of law for a period of 91 days for charging clearly excessive hourly fees. In one of the matters related to the complaint, the Referee found that Carlon charged a client $3,340.10 for looking up attorney names in a directory, sending two letters and answering two client inquiries. The other matter in the complaint dealt with Carlon charging a fee of $11,080.00 for a probate case where the statutory fee was $3,435.00.

Contingency fees are also addressed in detail under the Rule. A contingency fee is prohibited in certain matters outlined in the Rule, such as domestic relations and criminal cases. Additionally, contingency fee arrangements must be in writing and signed by the client. They are still subject to the reasonableness requirement. The rule also sets rebuttable presumptions as to the percentage of the contingency fee compared to the total recovery. For example, any contingency fee in excess of 33 1/3 % of any recovery under $1 million is presumed unreasonable.

In *The Florida Bar v. Kavanaugh*, 915 So. 2d 89 (Fla. 2005), the Court agreed with the recommendation of the Referee that Kavanaugh's 53% contingency fee was clearly excessive. Kavanaugh's contract with his client called for a 40% contingency fee or a Court awarded fee, whichever was greater. The matter was settled and Kavanaugh charged a 53% fee, rather than the 40% fee in the contract. He also failed to obtain court approval for the increased fee. The Court ordered restitution in the amount of the overcharged fee, plus interest, costs and a public reprimand. The Court referred the matter of revocation of his board certification to the Board of Governors of the Bar for consideration.

The Florida Bar v. Carlon, 820 So. 2d 891 (Fla. 2002)

We have for review a referee's report regarding an alleged ethical breach by respondent John T. Carlon, Jr., during his representation of Darlene Woodburn (Woodburn matter). We have jurisdiction. See art. V, § 15, Fla. Const. During the pendency of that review, Carlon requested review of a separate referee's report regarding another alleged ethical breach by Carlon committed during his representation of Bruce and Richard Whalley (Whalley matter). We have jurisdiction over that review pursuant to the same constitutional provision. We have consolidated our review of these cases.

WOODBURN MATTER

The Florida Bar filed a complaint against respondent John T. Carlon, Jr., alleging that Carlon charged a clearly excessive fee in connection with his representation of Darlene Woodburn. See R. Regulating Fla. Bar 4-1.5(a). The appointed referee found Carlon guilty of violating rule 4-1.5(a) and recommended that Carlon be: (1) suspended for ninety-one days; (2) ordered to pay restitution to Woodburn, within thirty days of the date of this Court's order, in the amount of $3,340.10 plus interest from December 18, 1997; and (3) ordered to pay the Bar's costs in the amount of $1,160.20.

The record indicates that Woodburn telephoned Carlon in December 1997 seeking assistance in securing an asset in Arizona improperly allocated to her ex-husband under an Arizona divorce decree. There was no prior attorney-client relationship. Carlon advised Woodburn that she would have to conform to both Florida and Arizona laws. On December 18, 1997, Woodburn and Carlon entered into a written retainer agreement. This agreement set forth Carlon's fee schedule and stated that Carlon's hourly rate was $250, that he required a $4000 retainer, and that he would charge a $500 administrative fee for opening the file. Woodburn paid Carlon the $4000 retainer.

Between December 18, 1997, and March 27, 1998, Carlon sent identical letters to twelve separate Arizona attorneys soliciting their interest in securing the asset. Carlon also sent identical letters to two separate Arizona attorneys soliciting their interest in a possible legal malpractice action against Woodburn's former attorney. The names of the Arizona attorneys were extracted by Carlon from a Martindale-Hubbell directory. After not hearing from Carlon, Woodburn independently hired an Arizona attorney on April 1, 1998. That attorney successfully obtained an amended Arizona divorce decree and consequently secured the asset for Woodburn. The Arizona attorney charged Woodburn $404. For his services Carlon charged Woodburn a total of $3,340.10 and refunded her $659.90 from the $4000 retainer. Carlon's total charge was the sum of $2825 in services, $15.10 in actual costs, and a $500 administrative fee for opening the file.

In her findings of fact, the referee found in pertinent part:

H. As evidenced by the two (2) bills rendered by respondent to Woodburn, the only services claimed to have been rendered by respondent to Woodburn consisted of an initial consultation, securing names from Martindale-Hubbell, drafting and mailing the two (2) above referenced form letters, and receiving and responding to his client's two correspondences regarding respondent's fees.

I. Respondent's task in securing names from Martindale-Hubbell for purposes of obtaining Arizona counsel for Woodburn did not present respondent with a novel, complex or difficult question requiring any skill other than the ability to extract names from a directory.

J. In undertaking representation of Woodburn there was no likelihood that the acceptance of such employment would preclude other client employment of respondent.

K. The significance of, amount and responsibility involved in the subject matter of Woodburn's representation was minimal.

L. Respondent obtained no results for Woodburn.

M. Woodburn imposed no time limitations upon respondent nor did any circumstances arise during the course of his representation of Woodburn which imposed any such time limitations.

N. Woodburn made no special time demands or requests of the respondent.

O. There was no prior attorney/client relationship between the respondent and Woodburn nor any unusual nature or length of the professional relationship.

P. Respondent's representation of Woodburn demonstrated no skill, expertise or efficiency of effort.

Q. Upon a review of the facts surrounding respondent's representation of Woodburn, a lawyer of ordinary prudence would be left with a definite and firm conviction that the fee (including a $500.00 administrative fee for opening Woodburn's file) exceeds a reasonable fee for services provided to such a degree as to constitute clear overreaching and/or an unconscionable demand by respondent.

R. Except for the $659.90 refund ... respondent has made no further refunds to Ms. Woodburn.

....

Following these findings, the referee determined that respondent violated rule 4-1.5(a). In considering her recommended sanctions, the referee found that Carlon had a dishonest motive and failed to acknowledge the wrongful nature of his conduct, and that Woodburn suffered actual and substantial harm as a result of respondent's misconduct. The referee also considered Carlon's previous disciplinary history:

In *Florida Bar v. Carlon*, 505 So.2d 1325 (Fla.1987), Carlon received a public reprimand for billing and suing a homeowner's *895 association, securing a default judgment and garnishing the association's bank account, all in violation of a fee

agreement.

In *Florida Bar v. Carlon*, October 15, 1996, Florida Bar File No. 95-51,391(17H), respondent received an admonishment for minor misconduct for running an advertisement considered to be misleading.

In *Florida Bar v. Carlon*, 727 So.2d 912 (Fla.1/28/99) respondent was placed on indefinite probation with conditions for failing to make restitution directed in connection with the admonishment he received in Florida Bar File No. 95-51,391(17H).

Woodburn Report at 9.

WHALLEY MATTER

The Florida Bar alleged that Carlon violated rule 4-1.5(a) by charging a clearly excessive fee in his representation of Bruce Whalley and Richard Whalley (the Whalleys) in connection with the administration of the estate of their mother, Stella A. Whalley, who died intestate on May 9, 1998. The appointed referee found Carlon guilty of violating rule 4-1.5(a) and recommended that Carlon be: (1) suspended for ninety-one days; (2) ordered to pay restitution to the Whalleys within thirty days of the date of this Court's order in the amount of $6580 plus interest from November 30, 1998 (the date of Carlon's final invoice); and (3) ordered to pay the Bar's costs in the amount of $1,155.25.

The record indicates that the Whalleys were referred to Carlon by a mutual friend of Carlon and the Whalleys. There was no previous relationship between Carlon and Bruce, Richard, or Stella Whalley. The estate consisted of a residence valued at $106,000, two bank accounts valued at approximately $8000, and miscellaneous personal property valued at $500. The estate had no creditors, and no claims were filed against the estate. The Whalleys were the sole beneficiaries and distributees of the estate.

The Whalleys agreed that Bruce would petition to be appointed personal representative. Carlon advised that there were two ways he could charge: either hourly or by a flat fee. The Whalleys requested that Carlon charge whichever way would be least expensive. The Whalleys and Carlon signed a written fee agreement on May 16, 1998, in which the Whalleys agreed to pay Carlon $200 per hour. Carlon charged and received $11,080 in fees for his representation of Bruce Whalley as personal representative. The amount included $120 which Carlon agrees was an overcharge due to a mathematical error on Carlon's part. Carlon was entitled to an approximate fee of $3435 under section 733.6171, Florida Statutes (2000).

The referee found that the administration of this estate was simple and presented no novel, complex, or difficult questions. The only unusual issue presented was a "wild mortgage" on the real property, which the purchaser's attorney resolved. The referee further found that there was no likelihood that Carlon's representation of the Whalleys would preclude other representation. The Whalleys made no special time demand. The estate was closed in ordinary fashion on waivers, without an accounting.

The referee found, consistent with the testimony of the Bar's expert, a board-certified wills, trusts, and estates attorney, that $3500 would have been a reasonable fee in this case, that $4500 would be excessive, and that any fee in excess of $6000 would be clearly excessive. The referee also found that Carlon charged for unnecessary research, unnecessary travel, secretarial functions, and other inappropriate activities, all at the $200 contract rate.

Based upon these findings, the referee found that Carlon violated rule 4-1.5(a). In developing her recommended sanctions, the referee found no mitigating factors. In aggravation, the referee found that Carlon had a selfish motive in charging a clearly excessive fee, that his client suffered actual harm, and that Carlon refused to acknowledge the wrongful nature of his conduct. The referee considered Carlon's prior disciplinary history, which was identical to that considered by the referee in the Woodburn matter.

Carlon raises four issues for our consideration in the Woodburn matter. He likewise raises four issues in the Whalley matter.

....

DISCIPLINE

This Court's review of a referee's recommended discipline is broader than the review afforded to a referee's factual findings because we have the ultimate responsibility and authority to determine appropriate sanctions. See *Vining*, 761 So.2d at 1048. Further, this Court views cumulative misconduct more seriously than an isolated instance of misconduct. See id. In respect to discipline, the Bar argues in both cases that *Florida Bar v. Richardson*, 574 So.2d 60 (Fla.1990), supports the imposition of a ninety-one-day suspension. In view of the same conduct being found in both of Carlon's cases when considered.

In *Richardson* there were several instances of excessive fees being charged to clients. See *Richardson*, 574 So.2d at 60. One instance in Richardson was a probate matter in which the disciplined lawyer charged nearly $11,000 in fees where the non- complex probate estate was valued at approximately $22,000. See *id*. There, the attorney charged his client a minimum of twenty minutes per phone call even if the recipient of the call did not answer, charged a minimum of forty-five dollars per page for document preparation, and charged a monthly cover charge. See *id*. This is similar to Carlon's conduct in inflating his statement for services rendered in both matters. Thus, a ninety-one-day suspension is appropriate. We now turn to the referees' other proposed sanctions. We accept the referees' findings that the Bar's costs are to be taxed against Carlon in both the Woodburn ($1,160.20) and Whalley ($1,155.25) matters. We also accept the proposed sanctions that Carlon must pay restitution to Woodburn with interest from December 18, 1997, and that Carlon must pay restitution to the Whalleys with interest from November 30, 1998. See R. Regulating Fla. Bar 3-5.1(i). We impose an additional requirement that Carlon must make the restitution payments to Woodburn and the Whalleys prior to his reinstatement to the practice of law. We disagree with the referee, however, with the amount of restitution found by the referees in both cases.

In the Woodburn matter, the referee recommended restitution in the amount of $3,340.10 plus interest from December 18, 1997, which is the entire amount charged by Carlon after the refund. In our original opinion, we did not agree that Carlon performed no services in researching Martindale-Hubbell and writing the letters; thus, we remanded the issue to the referee for a determination as to an amount considered clearly excessive given the services Carlon did perform. While the motion for rehearing was pending before this Court, the referee conducted further proceedings and determined $2,936.10 to be clearly excessive. See *Florida Bar v. Carlon*, No. SC95539, report of referee on remand at 5, (report filed Dec. 5, 2001). Neither Carlon nor The Florida Bar contest the referee's determination. Accordingly, we approve the referee's determination on remand. Carlon must pay to Woodburn $2,936.10 plus interest from December 18, 1997. Additionally, Carlon must pay Woodburn this amount before Carlon may be reinstated to the practice of law.

In the Whalley matter, we disagree with the amount due the Whalleys is $6580 plus interest from November 30, 1998. We agree with the Bar's argument before the referee that rule 4 1.5 proscribes only charging a clearly excessive fee. See R. Regulating Fla. Bar 3-5.1(i) ("[T]he amount of restitution ... shall not exceed the amount by which a fee is clearly excessive...."). Only restitution of the amount considered clearly excessive may be imposed as a condition for readmission or reinstatement. As the referee made separate determinations as to what was considered an excessive fee and what was considered a clearly excessive fee, the referee should have based her determination of the amount due the Whalleys on the clearly excessive figure. Thus, Carlon must pay the Whalleys $5080 plus interest from November 30, 1998. Carlon's failure to pay this restitution will bar any application by him for reinstatement to the practice of law.

In our original opinion, we imposed a ninety-one day suspension in each case with the suspensions to run concurrently. While the rehearing motion was pending, Carlon advised this Court that he began his suspension on November 3, 2001. Accordingly, we suspend John T. Carlon, Jr., from the practice of law for ninety-one days as discipline in each case with the suspensions to run concurrently, effective, nunc pro tunc, to November 3, 2001. Judgment is entered for The Florida Bar, 650 Apalachee Parkway, Tallahassee, Florida 32399, for recovery of costs from John T. Carlon, Jr., in the amount of $2,315.45, for which sum let execution issue.

It is so ordered.

Questions for Discussion

1.   What do you think a reasonable fee would have been in the Woodburn matter? What would you have charged?

2.   In the Whalley case, why do you think Carlon advised the hourly fee rather than a flat fee?

3.   What would you have charged for this "simple" probate case?

The Florida Bar v. Kavanaugh, 915 So. 2d 89 (Fla. 2005)

. . . .

Harry Pollak hired attorney Kenneth J. Kavanaugh to assist in his effort to cancel an automobile lease agreement and recover his trade-in automobile from Endicott Buick. When the initial effort failed, Pollak and Kavanaugh entered into a contingency fee agreement and Kavanaugh filed suit on Pollak's behalf against Endicott Buick for deceptive and unfair trade practices.

The contingency fee contract provided:

If there is a recovery, the fee for the professional services of the Attorney will be the greater of that amount awarded by the Court (to be paid by the Defendants) or that amount determined according to the following schedule:

....

(b) From the time of filing an Answer or the demand for appointment of arbitrators through the entry of judgment:

(1) 40% of any recovery up to $1 million....

The parties settled prior to trial for $44,868.06 entitling Kavanaugh to a fee of 40% of the recovery. However, Kavanaugh withheld a fee of 53% of the proceeds and had his client sign a copy of the closing statement which showed the retention of the 53% which amounted to some $23,780.07. When Pollak later realized the fee charged was in excess of the 40% agreed upon in the fee contract, he filed a complaint with The Florida Bar ("the Bar").

The matter proceeded to a hearing before a referee, and the referee made the following findings of fact:

B. On or about January of 1999, the Respondent was hired by Harry Pollak to represent him in a Deceptive and Unfair Trade Practices action against Endicott Buick.

C. Pollak and the Respondent agreed to a contingency fee contract which stated that Respondent would receive: "the greater of the amount awarded by the Court (to be paid by the defendants) or that amount determined according to the following schedule: ... 40% of any recovery up to $1 million...."

D. The case was eventually settled before trial in March of 2001 for $44,868.06.

E. After settlement of the case, Kavanaugh signed a final closing statement and presented it to Pollak on April 3, 2001. In the final closing statement, Kavanaugh's attorney's fee was $23,780.07, which amounted to 53% of the net proceeds.

F. Because Respondent charged an amount of fees above the limits set forth in the terms of the contingency agreement, respondent was required to get prior court approval for his increased fee.

G. Attorney Kavanaugh asserts in his defense that the amount of fees is appropriate and in conformity with the language set forth in the contract for representation. Kavanaugh claims that the contingency fee provision of the contract is not applicable in that Kavanaugh claims a greater amount of attorney's fees was awarded by the court. Kavanaugh argues the settlement reached in this matter is the equivalent to court ordered attorney's fees.

H. There is no evidence that any judge signed a settlement agreement. Nor was there a court order which delineated what portion of the $44,868.06 net proceeds was to be applied to attorney's fees.

I. It is unequivocal that at no time prior to the disbursement of funds was the matter of any award of attorney's fees submitted to the trial court. Rather, in September 2001, Kavanaugh motioned the court for its entry of an order approving fees charged. The trial court found that it lacked jurisdiction over the matter and denied Kavanaugh's motion as moot in that the proceeds of the lawsuit had already been disbursed.

J. Respondent failed to get prior court approval for his increased fee.

K. Respondent arbitrarily awarded himself 53% of the net proceeds.

Based on these findings, the referee recommended that Kananaugh be found guilty:

> I recommend that Respondent be found guilty of violating [Rule of Professional Conduct 4-1.5(a)], which provides that an attorney shall not enter into an agreement for, charge, or collect a clearly excessive fee.

The referee also made the recommendations as to disciplinary measures to be imposed:

> A. Public reprimand before the Supreme Court....

> B. Restitution to Pollak in the amount of $4,307.83, plus interest at the statutory rate from April 3, 2001 (the date of the final closing statement) to the present, to be payable within thirty (30) days of the entry of this order.

> C. Revocation of the Respondent's Florida Bar Board Certification in Civil Trial Law.

> D. Payment of the Bar's costs in these proceedings.

In recommending imposition of the above disciplinary measures, the referee took into account the following factors:

> A. Personal history of the Respondent:
>   Age: 61.
>
>   Date admitted to the Bar: June 1, 1976.
>
>   Board Certification: Civil Trial Law.

> B. Aggravating factors:
>
>   9.22(b) Dishonest or selfish motive.
>
>   9.22(g) Refusal to acknowledge wrongful nature of conduct.
>
>   9.22(h) Vulnerability of victim.
>
>   9.22(i) Substantial experience in the practice of law.

9.22(j) Indifference to making restitution.

C. Mitigating factors: None.

ANALYSIS

Kavanaugh has petitioned for review, arguing that he should be found not guilty of the alleged violation or, alternatively, that he should only be admonished and required to refund $4,307.83. The Bar has cross-petitioned, arguing that a thirty-day suspension, not a public reprimand, is the appropriate sanction.

The Court's standard of review for evaluating a referee's factual findings and recommendations as to guilt has been articulated in numerous decisions:

> This Court's review of such matters is limited, and if a referee's findings of fact and conclusions concerning guilt are supported by competent, substantial evidence in the record, this Court will not reweigh the evidence and substitute its judgment for that of the referee.

Fla. Bar v. Rose, 823 So.2d 727, 729 (Fla.2002). Implicit in this standard is the requirement that the referee's factual findings must be predicated upon evidence presented at the disciplinary hearing. Kavanaugh contends that the referee's recommendation that he be found guilty of collecting a clearly excessive fee is not supported by the evidence. We disagree.

The referee made findings that Kavanaugh and Pollak signed a contingency fee contract; the contract provided that Kavanaugh's fee would be the greater of either the amount awarded by the court or 40% of the recovery amount; the court did not award any fees; and Kavanaugh withheld 53% of the net recovery for his fees. A review of the record shows that each of these factual findings is supported by the testimony and uncontested documentary evidence. Kavanaugh's claim that the contractual fee provision was modified by an implied amendment to the agreement pursuant to his fee statement and his client's signature thereon is simply a re-argument of this fact-based claim before the referee. We approve the referee's rejection of this claim and the referee's factual findings, as well as the referee's recommendation that Kavanaugh be found guilty of collecting a clearly excessive fee in violation of rule 4-1.5(a).

The Court's standard of review for evaluating a referee's recommended discipline is as follows:

> In reviewing a referee's recommended discipline, this Court's scope of review is broader than that afforded to the referee's findings of fact because, ultimately, it is our responsibility to order the appropriate sanction. However, generally speaking, this Court will not second-guess the referee's recommended discipline as long as it has a reasonable basis in existing case law and the Florida Standards for Imposing Lawyer Sanctions.

Fla. Bar v. Springer, 873 So.2d 317, 321 (Fla.2004) (citations omitted). In the present case, we conclude the recommended discipline meets this standard with the exceptions noted herein.

Initially, we conclude the recommended sanction of a public reprimand has a reasonable basis in existing case law. See *Fla. Bar v. Hollander*, 594 So.2d 307 (Fla.1992) (imposing a public reprimand in an excessive fee case arising from a fee dispute involving a contingency fee agreement); *Fla. Bar v. Johnson*, 526 So.2d 53 (Fla.1988) (imposing a public reprimand in an excessive fee case arising from a fee dispute involving trust account violations). In contrast, the cases cited by the Bar to support suspension are distinguishable. See *Fla. Bar v. Forrester*, 656 So.2d 1273 (Fla.1995) (imposing a ninety-one day suspension where the attorney failed to return the unearned portion of his fees when he was discharged); *Fla. Bar v. McAtee*, 601 So.2d 1199 (Fla.1992) (imposing a ninety-one day suspension where the attorney deceived the client concerning both the nature of his representation and the fee amount); *Fla. Bar v. Richardson*, 574 So.2d 60 (Fla.1990) (imposing a ninety-one day suspension where the attorney overcharged his clients, encouraged the clients to obtain a home mortgage to pay for his excessive fees, and then charged one of the clients a finder's fee for helping the client in obtaining the loan to pay for his excessive fees).

Further, we conclude that in light of the aggravating and mitigating circumstances reflected in the record, the recommended sanction of a public reprimand has a reasonable basis in the Standards for Imposing Lawyer Sanctions ("Standards"). The Standards provide:

Standard 7.0 Violations of Other Duties Owed as a Professional

Absent aggravating or mitigating circumstances ... the following sanctions are generally appropriate in cases involving ... unreasonable or improper fees....

....

7.2 Suspension is appropriate when a lawyer knowingly engages in conduct that is a violation of a duty owed as a professional and causes injury or potential injury to a client, the public, or the legal system.

7.3 Public reprimand is appropriate when a lawyer negligently engages in conduct that is a violation of a duty owed as a professional and causes injury or potential injury to a client, the public, or the legal system.

Fla. Stds. Imposing Law. Sancs. 7.0, 7.2-7.3. Of course, a presumptive sanction under the Standards is subject to aggravating and mitigating circumstances. See Fla. Stds. Imposing Law. Sancs. 9.0.

In the present case, as noted above, the referee's report notes five aggravating circumstances but no mitigating circumstances. While we find no error in the determination of aggravating circumstances, we also agree that several mitigating circumstances are reflected on the face of the record. The Bar conceded at the hearing below that Kavanaugh has no prior disciplinary record. In addition, Kavanaugh contends that even after the higher fee was deducted from the settlement amount, Pollack still had an excellent result. At the hearing below, the referee stated: "Upon hearing the case, I can tell you this. I think Mr. Kavanaugh got an exceptional result for his client. There isn't any doubt about that.... I think that an excellent result was obtained by Mr. Kavanaugh." The Bar does not dispute this claim. Kavanaugh also asserts that the major reason Endicott Buick settled this case prior to trial was to avoid the threat of substantial statutory attorneys' fees; and a substantial portion of the settlement amount was paid to extinguish Endicott's liability for his fees, rather than to compensate Pollak for his liquidated damages. Again, the Bar does not dispute this claim. Kavanaugh claims that throughout his discussions with Pollak, Kavanaugh was forthright about his fee demands, and he cites Pollak's signature on the "Final Closing Statement," to support his claim.

Based on all these circumstances, including the aggravation and mitigation, we conclude the sanction of a public reprimand is appropriate. While we have declined the Bar's invitation to invoke a greater sanction, we nevertheless caution that lawyers who charge excessive fees are guilty of serious breaches that diminish public confidence in the legal profession.

. . . .

CONCLUSION

We find Kenneth J. Kavanaugh guilty of collecting a clearly excessive fee in violation of rule 4-1.5(a), and we order that he receive a public reprimand, which shall be administered by the Board of Governors of The Florida Bar upon proper notice to Kavanaugh to appear. Kavanaugh is also ordered to pay restitution forthwith to Harry Pollak in the amount of $4,307.83 with interest accruing at the statutory rate from April 3, 2001, to the present. Restitution is to be paid in full within thirty days after issuance of this opinion. Finally, judgment is hereby entered for The Florida Bar, 651 East Jefferson Street, Tallahassee, Florida 32399-2300, for recovery of costs from Kenneth J. Kavanaugh in the amount of $1,553.69, for which sum let execution issue.

It is so ordered.

Questions for Discussion

1.   What would have been a reasonable fee? Do you believe this was a complicated case that justified a higher fee?

2.   Why did Kavanaugh argue that the Court approved the fee when the Court ruled that it didn't have jurisdiction to approve or deny the fee?

Jason C. King

CHAPTER 6
CONFIDENTIALITY
RULE 4-1.6

Rule 4-1.6 provides that "A lawyer shall not reveal information relating to representation of a client..." The rule provides for two exceptions when the lawyer must reveal the information in order to prevent:

1. A client from committing a crime; and

2. Death or substantial bodily harm to another.

However, the lawyer may reveal such information when the lawyer reasonably believes it is necessary to do so to pursue the client's interest, unless the client instructs him not to. The lawyer may also reveal the information to establish a claim or defense in a dispute between the lawyer and client, defend a criminal charge against the lawyer stemming from the representation, respond to allegations in any proceeding concerning the lawyer's representation of the client and to comply with the Rules of

Professional Conduct.

In *The Florida Bar v. Knowles*, 99 So. 3d 918 (Fla. 2012), The Court imposed a one year rehabilitative suspension on an attorney that violated Rule 4-1.6 for making disparaging remarks about her client in two motions to withdraw, just a few days before a hearing, and calling the Assistant State Attorney to tell him she believed her client would lie to the immigration court.

Knowles was retained to represent her client in an immigration and civil matter. During a meeting, her client told her that she "would do anything, including lying in court, to avoid deportation." The Referee, and Court, agreed that this statement alone did not provide a sufficient basis for the lawyer betraying her client's trust and reporting it to the Assistant State Attorney. The Court also noted that the fundamental principle of confidentiality "contributes to the trust that is the hallmark of the client-lawyer relationship."

The Florida Bar v. Knowles, 99 So. 3d 918,(Fla. 2012)

. . . .

For the reasons more fully explained below, we approve the referee's findings of fact, as well as his recommendation that Respondent be found guilty of violating Rule Regulating the Florida Bar 4–8.4(d) (conduct prejudicial to the administration of justice). However, we disapprove the referee's recommendation that Respondent be found not guilty of violating rule 4– 1.6 (confidentiality of information), and his recommendation that

Respondent be suspended for ninety days. Considering Respondent's prior disciplinary history and the seriousness of the misconduct at issue here, we conclude that a one-year suspension is the appropriate sanction.

FACTS AND PROCEDURAL HISTORY

On June 3, 2010, The Florida Bar filed a complaint against Respondent Petia Dimitrova Knowles, alleging various instances of misconduct relating to her representation of a client in immigration and civil matters. Specifically, the Bar alleged that Respondent had violated Rules Regulating the Florida Bar 4–1.3 (diligence), 4–1.6 (confidentiality of information), 4–3.3 (candor toward the tribunal), 4–8.4(c) (conduct involving dishonesty, fraud, deceit, or misrepresentation), and 4–8.4(d) (conduct prejudicial to the administration of justice). A final hearing was held before a referee, and subsequently the referee filed his report in which he made the following findings of fact.

Respondent was admitted to The Florida Bar on April 22, 2005. In 2007, she represented a client in various immigration matters, including a request for political asylum. Respondent was diligent and ultimately successful in reopening her client's immigration case. However, on or about January 29, 2009, just four days before a hearing before the Immigration Court, Respondent filed a Motion to Withdraw as attorney of record. In that motion, Respondent asserted that her client had written her an insufficient funds check for $1,000 and implied that the uncollected funds pertained to an immigration matter, when they actually pertained to a prior automobile accident case in which Respondent had also represented her client. Respondent also stated in the motion that she regretted helping her client, who had been rightly convicted for grand theft, and that Respondent's office had received reports from the Romanian community that her client had robbed them. Respondent asserted in the motion that her client would not be prejudiced by her withdrawal as attorney.

Upon learning that her attorney was attempting to withdraw, the client met with Respondent, and Respondent indicated that she would continue the representation only if the client paid an additional $1,500. The client ultimately agreed to pay $3,000, and Respondent agreed to withdraw her Motion to Withdraw. Respondent filed a Notice of Cancellation of Motion to Withdraw Representation as Attorney, in which she stated that because of short notice, her client would, in fact, be prejudiced if Respondent withdrew representation.

In or about April 2009, the client decided to retain new counsel. Respondent filed a second Motion to Withdraw. However, rather than stating that she sought to withdraw because her client had retained new counsel, Respondent asserted in her motion that she had received more reports that her client had intentionally failed to honor her contractual promises and had refused to pay for fulfilled work assignments.

On or about May 11, 2009, the Assistant State Attorney assigned to the client's criminal case sent a letter to the Department of Homeland Security. In the letter, the Assistant State Attorney stated that Respondent had informed her that she had reason to believe her client would lie to the Immigration Court at an upcoming hearing. Further, the Assistant State Attorney advised that she had received confidential paperwork pertaining to Respondent's client's political asylum case. The paperwork had been sent via Priority Mail on May 7, 2009, from an unidentified source. The referee specifically noted that "[a]lthough the sender of the paperwork was unidentified, political asylum files are confidential in nature and not available to the public, and the only person known to be in possession of such paperwork was Respondent."

In addition to handling the immigration case, Respondent had also represented her client in an automobile accident case. Respondent failed to appear at mediation in that case after filing a Motion to Withdraw, and Respondent also failed to advise her client that a final judgment had been entered.

After making these factual findings, the referee recommended that Respondent be found not guilty of violating rule 4–3.3 (candor toward the tribunal), rule 4–8.4(c) (conduct involving dishonesty, fraud, deceit, or misrepresentation), rule 4–1.6 (confidentiality of information), and rule 4–1.3 (diligence).

However, the referee did find that the disparaging motions to withdraw filed by Respondent violated rule 4–8.4(d) (conduct prejudicial to the administration of justice). According to the referee, "regardless of intent, the very act of filing such a motion with such language is so prejudicial to the client so as to be actionable." The referee stated that it was inconceivable that anyone knowing the rules of ethics would think such statements would be appropriate. Accordingly, the referee recommended that Respondent be found guilty of violating rule 4–8.4(d).

Thus, in summary, the referee recommends that Respondent be found guilty of violating rule 4–8.4(d), but be found not guilty of any of the other alleged rule violations. As for discipline, the referee recommends that Respondent be suspended from the practice of law for ninety days and attend The Florida Bar's Ethics School and The Florida Bar's Professionalism Workshop. In recommending this sanction, the referee found and considered the following aggravating factors: (1) a pattern of misconduct; (2) multiple offenses; (3) vulnerability of victim; and (4) pending disciplinary case. The referee also found and considered one mitigating factor—absence of a prior disciplinary record. Costs were awarded to The Florida Bar as the prevailing party.

The Bar seeks review of the referee's recommendation that Respondent be found not guilty of violating rule 4–1.6 (confidentiality of information) and the referee's recommended discipline of a ninety-day suspension.

. . . .

DISCIPLINE

The Bar challenges the referee's recommended discipline of a ninety-day suspension and contends that a ninety-one-day suspension is warranted instead. In reviewing a referee's recommended discipline, this Court's scope of review is broader than that afforded to the referee's findings of fact because, ultimately, it is our responsibility to order the appropriate sanction. See *Fla. Bar v. Ratiner*, 46 So.3d 35, 39 (Fla.2010); art. V, § 15, Fla. Const. However, generally speaking, this Court will not second-guess the referee's recommended discipline as long as it has a reasonable basis in existing case law and the Florida Standards for Imposing Lawyer Sanctions. See *Fla. Bar v. Temmer*, 753 So.2d 555, 558 (Fla.1999).

The case law and the Florida Standards for Imposing Lawyer Sanctions support a suspension in this case. See, e.g., *Fla. Bar v. Lange*, 711 So.2d 518, 522 (Fla.1998) (imposing a one-year rehabilitative suspension where the respondent violated rule 4–1.6 by divulging confidential client communications in two motions filed with the court, among other violations); *Fla. Bar v. Morgan*, 938 So.2d 496, 499–500 (Fla.2006) (imposing a ninety-one-day rehabilitative suspension where the respondent violated rule 4–8.4(d) and rule 4–3.5(c) and had been disciplined for prior similar misconduct); *Fla. Bar v. Hagendorf*, 921 So.2d 611, 614 (Fla.2006) (stating that a violation of rule 4–8.4(d) "is a serious violation" and implying that such a violation may warrant suspension); *Fla. Bar v. Bloom*, 632 So.2d 1016, 1017 (Fla.1994) (imposing a ninety-one-day rehabilitative suspension where the respondent violated rule 4–8.4(d) and rule 4–3.4(d)); Florida Standard for Imposing Lawyer Sanctions 4.22 ("[s]uspension is appropriate when a lawyer knowingly reveals information relating to the representation of a client not otherwise lawfully permitted to be disclosed, and this disclosure causes injury or potential injury to a client"); Florida Standard for Imposing Lawyer Sanctions 7.2 ("[s]uspension is appropriate when a lawyer knowingly engages in conduct that is a violation of a duty owed as a professional and causes injury or potential injury to a client, the public, or the legal system"). Respondent's recent reprimand for conduct prejudicial to the administration of justice in Case Number SC09–403 further weighs in favor of a suspension. See *Fla. Bar v. Knowles*, 64 So.3d 1195 (Fla.2011); Florida Standard for Imposing Lawyer Sanctions 8.2 ("[s]uspension is appropriate when a lawyer has been publicly reprimanded for the same or similar conduct and engages in further similar acts of misconduct that cause injury or potential injury to a client, the public, the legal system, or the profession").

The Bar argues that a ninety-one-day rehabilitative suspension, rather than the referee's recommended ninety-day suspension, is warranted. We agree that a rehabilitative suspension is appropriate, but given the egregious nature of Respondent's conduct in this case, we believe that a one-year suspension is necessary. Respondent committed multiple improper acts relating to the representation of her client. Respondent filed two motions to withdraw in which she disparaged her client's character; she informed the Assistant State Attorney that she believed her client would lie in court; and she sent confidential client paperwork to the Assistant State Attorney. When lawyers desire to withdraw from representing a client, they are not entitled to act in such a manner. A lawyer who is upset with her client is not permitted to turn on her client and begin disparaging and betraying her.

Rather, the lawyer must maintain client confidences, even after withdrawing from representation. See *Lange*, 711 So.2d at 519– 20 (where lawyer revealed confidences of a former client in order to demonstrate the existence of a possible conflict, Court found that lawyer violated confidentiality rule).

We previously addressed misconduct of a nature similar to that of Respondent in the case of *Florida Bar v. Bailey*, 803 So.2d 683 (Fla.2001). There, the respondent had written an ex parte letter to the sentencing judge in his client's case. In that letter, the respondent had written, among other things, that his client had pled guilty because his client had no defense, not because his client was remorseful or cooperative. Further, the respondent had written that his client was a "multimillionaire druggie." *Id.* at 689. The Court ultimately disbarred the respondent for the combined violations of rule 4–8.4(d) (conduct prejudicial to the administration of justice), rule 4–1.6 (confidentiality of information), and many other rules. *Id.* at 685, 689, 693–95. The Court specifically stated its displeasure at the respondent's ex parte letter disparaging his client, stating that the respondent

> attempted to further his own interests by disparaging his client in an ex parte letter to the judge who would sentence his client. Bailey's self-dealing constitutes a complete abdication of his duty of loyalty to his client. His willingness to compromise his client for personal gain shows an open disregard for the relationship that must be maintained between attorney and client: one of trust, and one where both individuals work in the client's best interest. *Such misconduct strikes at the very center of the professional ethic of an attorney and cannot be tolerated.*

Id. at 694 (emphasis added). In disbarring the respondent, the Court indicated that many of the respondent's acts, standing alone, would merit disbarment. See *id.*

Like the respondent in *Bailey*, Respondent Knowles improperly turned on her client and breached her client's confidences, in violation of rule 4–8.4(d) and rule 4–1.6. See also *Lange*, 711 So.2d at 519, 524 (where the respondent, among other violations, had disclosed confidential communications made by a former client, the referee noted that the respondent should have advised the court of the necessary information in generalities and should have sought guidance from the court on how to proceed, and the Court imposed a one-year suspension).

Respondent's conduct in this matter is impermissible, but is even more egregious in light of the fact that the current bar discipline proceeding is not the first time Respondent has been sanctioned for misbehavior involving conduct prejudicial to the administration of justice. In April 2011, the Court determined that Respondent should receive a public reprimand administered by the Board of Governors of The Florida Bar. See *Knowles*, 64 So.3d at 1195. The referee in the instant case noted that the previous case involved "similar findings that Respondent engaged in conduct prejudicial to the administration of justice...." Given this prior similar misconduct, the seriousness of Respondent's misconduct in the instant proceeding, and the aggravating factors, we conclude that the ninety-day suspension recommended by the referee is not sufficient. Further, Respondent's apparent escalating pattern of misbehavior indicates that a more severe suspension than the ninety days recommended by the referee is appropriate. See *Fla. Bar v. Vining*, 761 So.2d 1044, 1048 (Fla.2000) ("[i]n determining the appropriate discipline, this Court considers prior misconduct and cumulative misconduct, and treats more severely cumulative misconduct than isolated misconduct"). Therefore, we disapprove the referee's recommended discipline and instead impose a one-year suspension.

CONCLUSION

We approve the referee's findings of fact, as well as his recommendation of guilt as to rule 4–8.4(d). However, we disapprove the referee's recommendation that Respondent be found not guilty of violating rule 4–1.6. We also disapprove the referee's recommended discipline of a ninety-day suspension. Accordingly, Petia Dimitrova Knowles is hereby suspended from the practice of law for one year. Because Knowles was suspended by order which issued January 17, 2012, it is unnecessary to provide her with thirty days to close out her practice to protect the interests of existing clients. As directed in the January 17, 2012 order, Knowles shall fully comply with Rule Regulating The Florida Bar 3–5.1(g) and shall accept no new business until she is reinstated. The suspension shall be effective, *nunc pro tunc*, February 16, 2012, the effective date of the suspension imposed by the January 17, 2012, order. Knowles is further directed to comply with the terms and conditions set out in the referee's report requiring her to attend The Florida Bar's Ethics School and The Florida Bar's Professionalism Workshop.

Judgment is entered for The Florida Bar, 651 East Jefferson Street, Tallahassee, Florida 32399–2300, for recovery of costs from Petia Dimitrova Knowles in the amount of $1,883.70, for which sum let execution issue.

It is so ordered.

Questions for Discussion

1. Was Knowles reasonable in her effort to withdraw? Why? Why not?

2. What should she have done if she felt she needed to withdraw from the case?

3. Is this case about confidentiality or privilege?

Jason C. King

CHAPTER 7
CONFLICTS OF INTEREST
RULE 4-1.7

Rule 4–1.7 provides that a lawyer shall not represent a client if the representation of one client will be directly adverse to another client. The rule also states that the lawyer shall not represent a client if "there is a substantial risk that the representation of one or more clients will be materially limited by the lawyer's responsibilities to another client, a former client or a third person or by a personal interest of the lawyer."

However, the rule provides for a few limited circumstances where the lawyer may obtain the clients informed consent and waiver of the conflict. In order to obtain the client's waiver of the conflict, the lawyer must reasonably believe that he will be able to provide competent and diligent representation to the affected client, the representation is not prohibited by law, and it must not involve the assertion of a position adverse to another client when the lawyer represents both of these clients in the same proceeding.

In *The Florida Bar v. Scott*, 39 So. 3d 309 (Fla. 2010), the Court determined that a three-year suspension was warranted where the attorney represented multiple clients who all had claims to the same limited funds in a frozen account in violation of the Rules regarding conflicts of interest. Scott represented numerous clients, including corporate entities, with adverse interests. Though Scott claimed that his retainer agreements waived any potential conflict, the Court noted that such a conflict was one that could not be waived.

Additionally rule 4–1.9 addresses conflicts of interest with former clients. The rule prohibits a lawyer from representing a client in a matter in which the client's interests are materially adverse to the interests of a former client unless the former client gives informed consent.

The Florida Bar v. Scott, 39 So. 3d 309 (Fla. 2010)

. . . .

FACTS

The referee found that The Florida Bar proved the following facts by clear and convincing evidence.

In 1995, Scott represented Richard Maseri's company, Private Research, Inc., in a suit for an injunction filed by the Commodity Futures Trading Commission (CFTC) in the United States District Court for the Southern

District of Florida-Commodity Futures Trading Commission v. Maseri, No. 95-6970-CIV-DAVIS, 1995 WL 17144922 (S.D. Fla. complaint filed Oct. 16, 1995). The CFTC complaint alleged that Maseri and Private Research defrauded customers, converted customer funds, and violated the registration provisions of the Commodity Exchange Act (the Act), 7 U.S.C. §§ 1-27f (1994), and CFTC Regulations, 17 C.F.R. §§ 1-199 (1995). The court issued preliminary injunctive orders and, in 1997, made them permanent. The orders prohibited Maseri and Private Research from contracting for the sale of any commodity; acting directly or indirectly as a commodities trading advisor (CTA) or commodities pooling operator (CPO) without being registered as such; and engaging in any fraudulent activities while acting as a CTA or CPO.

In the summer of 1998, Maseri advertised for investors for a commodities brokerage venture. Steven Frankel, who was unaware of Maseri's previous history, responded to the advertisement. In July 1998, Maseri hired Scott to represent him in negotiations with Frankel aimed at establishing a forex brokerage company. In August 1998, Maseri and Frankel created International Currency Exchange Corporation, a Nevada corporation, later renamed Intercontinental Currency Exchange Corporation (ICEC). They each owned a fifty-percent share of the company. They met, along with Scott, on August 4, 1998, to sign the stockholders' agreement. Before Maseri arrived for the meeting, Frankel questioned Scott about Maseri. Scott failed to tell Frankel about CFTC's suit against Maseri, the court order prohibiting Maseri from entering into certain business transactions, or Maseri's criminal history, even though this information was public and nonconfidential. During the course of their conversation, Scott made statements to the effect that Maseri was "an honest man."

During the August 4 meeting, Scott agreed to represent ICEC. At a minimum, Scott agreed to prepare new account form documents for ICEC. Frankel put up $5000 in equity for the venture and loaned ICEC $180,000.

In November 1998, the federal court entered a final order of judgment against Maseri in the Maseri case. Prudential Securities, Inc. (Prudential), as a holder of ICEC assets, filed an interpleader action against CFTC in the United States District Court for the Southern District of Florida and notified ICEC that its assets would be frozen until released by the court. Prudential Securities, Inc. v. Commodity Futures Trading Commission, No. 98-8891-CIV-MIDDLEBROOKS (S.D.Fla.). Maseri, as ICEC's president and chief operating officer, hired Scott to attempt to unfreeze ICEC's assets.

Frankel was unaware of these events until December 15, 1998. On that date, because he was unable to contact Maseri by telephone, he drove to the office and discovered that law enforcement officers had raided ICEC. At that point, Maseri told Frankel about his problems with the CFTC and referred him to Scott.

Frankel contacted Scott, who told him that he had been retained to represent ICEC and, since Frankel had loaned ICEC money, he would be representing Frankel in getting his funds released to him. On December 18, 1998, Frankel entered into a retainer agreement with Scott in which Scott agreed "to attempt to have the accounts which hold your funds at Prudential released." Three days later, Frankel signed an addendum to his retainer agreement with Scott in which "Frankel, not as a Director, but as a lender to ICEC," ratified, adopted, and approved his earlier hiring of Scott.

ICEC also maintained accounts at Donaldson, Luftkin & Jenrette (DLJ). These accounts were controlled by Dreyfus Service Corporation (Dreyfus). In 1999, Dreyfus, like Prudential, filed an interpleader action in the United States District Court for the Southern District of Florida. Dreyfus Service Corp. v. Intercont'l Currency Exch. Corp., No. 99-6151-CIV-DAVIS (S.D.Fla.). Scott, on behalf of ICEC investor Moresea, Ltd., filed a counterclaim against Dreyfus and a third-party complaint against DLJ, alleging that ICEC had conducted business in an illegal manner.

On January 6, 1999, Scott filed a petition for emergency relief on behalf of ICEC in the Prudential interpleader action. The petition included a cross-claim against Prudential on behalf of ICEC investors.

On January 15, 1999, the federal district court supplemented the final judgment in the Commodity Futures Trading Commission v. Maseri case to make ICEC subject to receivership. As a result, ICEC's assets went into receivership. The receiver notified Prudential that ICEC's assets were to be turned over to satisfy the judgment.

On February 9, 1999, on behalf of ICEC investor Investcan, Ltd., Scott filed an answer and a counterclaim against Prudential, alleging that Maseri and ICEC had operated in violation of Florida law. Prudential wrote to Scott on February 12 and 19, 1999, to object to his dual representation of ICEC and its investors on the basis of conflicts of interest. Despite Prudential's objection, Scott filed a counterclaim on February 24, 1999, on behalf of ICEC investors Roger Lennon and The Lennon Trust.

The court in Prudential dismissed the ICEC investors' cross-claim on

March 17, the Investcan cross-claim on April 13, and the Lennon counterclaim on April 19. Scott filed a first amended counterclaim against Prudential on behalf of ICEC investors on April 23; that counterclaim also asserted unlawful conduct by ICEC.

The court dismissed the Dreyfus case on June 14, 2000, and the Prudential case on January 4, 2001. Prudential released the ICEC funds to the receiver. Scott tried to reopen the Prudential case over a year later, on January 18, 2002, and to file a cross- claim against his former client Frankel on behalf of ICEC and its investors/depositors for breach of contract, legal malpractice, and fraud. The court denied his motion on February 4, 2002. That same day, Scott filed a motion on behalf of Investcan, seeking joinder to the cross-claim against Frankel. On February 13, Scott filed a motion to reconsider reopening the Prudential case on behalf of ICEC and all persons who opened an account with ICEC.

Meanwhile, on January 29, 2002, the federal district court in Commodity Futures Trading Commission v. Maseri issued an order discharging the receiver and granting the receiver's final report of distribution. On February 5, 2002, Scott filed a motion for reconsideration in that case on behalf of ICEC to contest the order of distribution. On February 19, Scott wrote to Frankel and Maseri, urging them to appeal the court's order of discharge and demanding a retainer for legal fees to represent ICEC in an appeal.

On February 20, 2002, Frankel demanded that Scott cease representing ICEC. Five days later, on February 25, 2002, Scott wrote to Frankel and Maseri, claiming that "no impasse of ICEC Nev[ada] management exists in regard to this case because both of you agreed for our firm to obtain recovery of the ICEC Nev [ada] deposits without regard to where they were located. We will keep you advised of developments."

On February 26, 2002, Frankel filed a motion to disqualify Scott on the basis of a conflict of interest. Scott wrote to Frankel on March 7, 2002, through Frankel's attorney, stating, "ICEC Nev[ada] depositors have a superior right to the proceeds taken from ICEC Nev[ada] to pay the fees and costs of the Receiver than does Mr. Frankel either as shareholder or lender to ICEC Nev[ada]," and affording Frankel the "opportunity to respond to the proposed appeal by ICEC Nev[ada] of the order that discharged the receiver."

On April 22, 2002, Scott filed suit against Frankel and Maseri, on behalf of ICEC investor Investcan, in the United States District Court for the Southern District of Florida, asserting Investcan's right to a return of its funds. Investcan Int'l, Ltd. v. Frankel, No. 02-60565-CIV-MIDDLEBROOKS (S.D. Fla. complaint filed Apr. 22, 2002).

The court denied Scott's motion for reconsideration in Prudential on May 24, 2002, noting

a serious question as to ICEC's putative counsel's ability to represent ICEC in this matter.... This raises conflict issues.... The fact appears to be that at this date, Mr. Scott has represented Mr. Frankel in his individual capacity, in an attempt to get back monies Mr. Scott apparently now seeks on behalf of another client.

Scott appealed the order. The Eleventh Circuit Court of Appeals affirmed. Moresea, Ltd. v. Prudential, No. 02-13523-JJ (11th Cir.).

On July 3, 2002, Scott amended the Investcan complaint to allege that Frankel and Maseri failed to ensure that ICEC operated legally and thus defrauded plaintiffs of their money. The court disqualified Scott on October 4, 2002, on the basis of a conflict of interest in violation of Rule Regulating the Florida Bar 4-1.9. That decision was affirmed by the Eleventh Circuit Court of Appeals on March 28, 2003. Investcan Int'l, Ltd. v. Frankel, 65 Fed.Appx. 715 (11th Cir. 2003).

Based on the factual findings, the referee recommends that Scott be found guilty of violating Rules Regulating the Florida Bar 4-4.1(a) (prohibiting lawyer from making false statement of material fact or law to third party in course of representing client)- one count; 4-1.7(a) (1993) (prohibiting lawyer from representing client if representation will be directly adverse to interests of another client unless lawyer reasonably believes representation will not adversely affect lawyer's responsibilities to and relationship with other client and each client consents after consultation)-five counts; 4-1.9(a) (1993) (prohibiting lawyer who formerly represented client from representing another person in same or substantially related matter in which that person's interests are materially adverse to interests of former client unless former client consents after consultation)-six counts; 4-1.16(a)(1) (1993) (prohibiting lawyer from representing client or requiring lawyer to withdraw where representation will result in violation of Rules of Professional Conduct or law)-seven counts; and 4-8.4(c) (prohibiting lawyer from engaging in conduct involving dishonesty, fraud, deceit, or misrepresentation)-one count.

The referee recommends that Scott be suspended for eighteen months and taxed with the Bar's costs. In recommending the eighteen-month suspension, the referee considered two mitigating factors-the absence of a prior disciplinary record and Scott's age (seventy). The referee found no aggravating factors. In recommending an eighteen-month suspension, the referee did not identify the particular Florida Standards for Imposing Lawyer Sanctions on which he relied. Neither did he cite to any previous cases involving similar fact patterns in which this Court imposed eighteen-month suspensions.

Scott petitioned for review of the referee's report. He argues that the Bar's complaint should have been dismissed as barred by the statute of limitations for Bar disciplinary proceedings; Scott was not obligated to tell Frankel about Maseri's criminal history or legal problems with the CFTC; the referee's finding that he misled Frankel was unsupported; the referee's finding that he represented Frankel was unsupported and Frankel had waived any real or potential conflict of interest; and Scott's duty to protect the public took precedence over his duty to maintain client confidentiality or to decline the representation of a client where a conflict of interest exists or is likely to arise. The Bar filed a cross-petition, seeking review of the sanction recommendation. The Bar argues that a three-year suspension is the appropriate sanction for the proven misconduct.

ANALYSIS

Scott previously raised the statute-of-limitations issue in a motion to dismiss filed in this Court. The Court rejected Scott's statute-of-limitations argument and denied the motion to dismiss. We will not now revisit this issue, which we have previously determined adversely to Scott.

Scott takes issue with the referee's finding that Scott misled Frankel by representing that Maseri was an honest man. Scott argues that he had no duty to advise Frankel of public, nonconfidential information about Maseri. The referee's finding in this regard is supported by competent, substantial evidence. Critically, if a referee's findings of fact are supported by competent, substantial evidence in the record, the Court will not reweigh the evidence and substitute its judgment for that of the referee. *Fla. Bar v. Frederick*, 756 So.2d 79, 86 (Fla.2000); see also *Fla. Bar v. Jordan*, 705 So.2d 1387, 1390 (Fla.1998).

In this instance, the referee found that Scott's action in telling Frankel that Maseri was an "honest man" triggered a duty on his part to also reveal to Frankel the negative information he had concerning Maseri that could have impacted Frankel's decision to go into business with Maseri. This finding is also supported by the record. Frankel, testifying about his conversation with

Scott at the August 4, 1998, meeting, stated: "I asked him what he knew of him, and he indicated to me that Mr. Maseri had never lied to him, that he was an honest man, that he had never lost any money with him, and generally he left me feeling very good about him." He further testified that Scott did not tell him anything negative about Maseri during their conversation and that if Scott had told him anything negative, specifically about the public nonconfidential information Scott had about Maseri, Frankel would have gotten up and left.

More importantly, Scott admitted that his intent was to convince Frankel that Maseri was an honest man so as to ensure that Frankel proceeded with the proposed business deal. Concerning his motivation in telling Frankel that Maseri had never lied to him, Scott testified:

> Q Isn't it true that in response to Mr. Frankel's questions, you told him that Maseri had never lied or cheated you because you wanted Frankel to infer that Maseri was an honest man?

> A I gave a deposition and acknowledged that. When he started asking his questions, my goal was to preserve the deal. I already knew that in the agreement there was no representation of past litigation or regulation history. I already knew and had discussions with Maseri about what had he disclosed to Frankel and what he had not.

> I felt that at a closing that had been going on and negotiations back and forth for seven or eight days, for those questions to come up, I felt blindsided and as though the guy was trying to make me personally responsible for his problems instead of serving as his own lawyer, which I told him at the outset he had to do, and I told him-I thought I gave him plenty of notice that there was something there for him to worry about when I told him he ought to go get his own lawyer. You know, you can only take a cripple so far.

> Q Do I understand you correctly to have just said that yes, you wanted him to infer that Maseri was an honest man because you didn't want the deal to get blown?

> A That is true.

Scott also admitted that if the deal had been "blown," he would not have been able to look forward to earning any fees from the ICEC venture.

The referee's finding that Scott represented Frankel is also supported by competent, substantial evidence in the record. The Bar introduced two retainer agreements, dated December 18 and 21, 1998, into evidence. The December 18 agreement states: "After my explanation to you of the existence of potential conflicts of interests among the depositors, you have requested that our firm represent you in the limited capacity to attempt to have the accounts which hold your funds at Prudential released." (Emphasis added.) In the December 21 "Addendum to Retainer Agreement," Frankel "consents, ratifies, and approves the employment of The Scott Law Firm, P.A. (the 'Firm') upon the terms outlined above."

In addition, both Scott and Frankel testified concerning Scott's representation. When discussing the December 18 and 21 retainer agreements, Scott stated: "I also believed that I needed to get [a] retainer from him, which I now prefer to characterize as a waiver." (Emphasis added.) The clear implication of this statement is that Scott himself viewed the documents as retainers at the time he sent them to Frankel.

We reject Scott's argument that it was permissible for him to represent the ICEC investors despite the conflicts presented by his representation under some kind of duty-to-the-public exception. No such exception exists. To the extent that ICEC investors wanted to pursue claims against Scott's past or present clients with interests adverse to theirs, Scott should have referred them to other counsel, someone without a disqualifying conflict.

We next address the referee's guilt recommendations. The Court has repeatedly stated that the referee's factual findings must be sufficient under the applicable rules to support the recommendations as to guilt. See *Fla. Bar v. Shoureas*, 913 So.2d 554, 557-58 (Fla.2005). Scott argues that the referee's guilt recommendations on the conflict-of-interest issue are unsupported by the factual findings. His argument fails.

An attorney engages in unethical conduct when he undertakes a representation when he either knows or should know of a conflict of interest prohibiting the representation. *Fla. Bar v. Cosnow*, 797 So.2d 1255, 1257 (Fla.2001). The referee recommends that Scott be found guilty of violating Rules Regulating the Florida Bar 4-1.7(a), 4-1.9(a), and 4-1.16(a)(1) for his conflict-of-interest conduct in this case.

Rule 4-1.7(a) provides that an attorney "shall not represent a client if the representation of that client will be directly adverse to the interests of another client" unless: (1) the lawyer reasonably believes the representation will not adversely affect the lawyer's responsibilities to and relationship with the other client; and (2) each client consents after consultation.

Rule 4-1.9(a) provides that a lawyer who formerly represented a client shall not "represent another person in the same or a substantially related matter in which that person's interests are materially adverse to the interests of the former client unless the former client consents after consultation."

Rule 4-1.16(a)(1) provides that a lawyer shall not represent a client or shall withdraw where "the representation will result in violation of the Rules of Professional Conduct or law."

Scott represented, either seriatim or in conjunction: Maseri's company, Private Research, in the Maseri case; Maseri in business negotiations with Frankel; ICEC (owned in equal parts by Maseri and Frankel) in the preparation of certain forms and in attempts to have ICEC's assets unfrozen; Frankel, individually, as the maker of a loan to ICEC, for the recovery of the money Frankel loaned to ICEC; and individual ICEC investors, for recovery of the money they invested with ICEC and in a lawsuit for fraud against Maseri and Frankel. All of the representations undertaken by Scott after the creation of ICEC involved claims for ICEC's assets in one way or another. The interests of ICEC, Maseri, Frankel, and the individual ICEC investors were all directly adverse to one another because all had claims to the same pool of money.

Furthermore, even if the documents Frankel signed on December 18 and 21, 1998, were waivers of conflict rather than retainer agreements, as Scott argues, Frankel's waiver would have been ineffective. Some kinds of conflicts of interest cannot be waived by a client. For example, in *Florida Bar v. Feige*, 596 So.2d 433, 434 (Fla.1992), Feige represented himself and his client in a suit by his client's ex-husband for the return of alimony payments made after Feige's client had remarried. Feige had not represented the client in the divorce proceedings, but was aware of the provision in the couple's marital settlement agreement requiring the ex-husband to pay alimony until the ex-wife, Feige's client, died or remarried. His client was aware of the conflict in Feige's representing himself and her and agreed to waive the conflict. This Court held that the conflict was the type that could not be waived and suspended him for two years.

The conflicts of interest in this case were as directly adverse as those in Feige and equally unwaivable. Even if the conflicts had been waivable, Frankel's waiver would have been, at best, void or voidable. At the time Frankel signed the retainer agreements, he was unaware of the severity of the conflict. Frankel testified that he believed that his and everyone else's money was intact, just frozen, when he retained Scott. He did not discover that most of the money was gone until much later.

Thus, the referee's findings more than amply support the referee's recommendations of guilt as to the conflict-of-interest claims, and accordingly, we approve these guilt recommendations.

Scott also argues that the recommendation that he be found guilty of a misrepresentation is unsupported by the factual findings. We reject this argument as well. The referee's findings adequately support his recommendation that Scott be found guilty of violating rules 4-4.1(a) (prohibiting lawyer from making false statement of material fact or law to third person in course of representing a client) and 4-8.4(c) (prohibiting lawyer from engaging in conduct involving dishonesty, fraud, deceit, or misrepresentation). The referee found that Scott made a misrepresentation to Frankel when he told Frankel that Maseri had never lied to him, indicating that Maseri was an honest man. The referee also found that Scott failed to tell Frankel about CFTC's suit against Maseri, the court order prohibiting Maseri from entering into certain business transactions, or Maseri's criminal history, even though this information was public and nonconfidential. The combination of the two circumstances constituted a misrepresentation. These factual findings are sufficient to support the referee's recommendations that Scott be found guilty of violating rules 4-4.1(a) and 4-8.4(c).

We next consider the appropriate sanction for Scott's misconduct. In reviewing a referee's recommended discipline, the Court's scope of review is broader than that afforded to the referee's findings of fact because ultimately it is the Court's responsibility to order the appropriate sanction. See *Fla. Bar v. Anderson*, 538 So.2d 852, 854 (Fla.1989); see also art. V, 15, Fla. Const. However, generally speaking, the Court will not second-guess the referee's recommended discipline as long as it has a reasonable basis in existing case law and the Florida Standards for Imposing Lawyer Sanctions. See *Fla. Bar v. Temmer*, 753 So.2d 555, 558 (Fla.1999). The referee in this case did not cite to any cases or standards in support of the sanction recommendations.

The Bar argues in its cross-petition that the referee's recommendation of an eighteen-month suspension is unsupported by the Florida Standards for Imposing Lawyer Sanctions and our caselaw and that the suspension should be for three years. We agree and instead impose a three-year suspension.

In support of its argument that a three-year suspension is the appropriate discipline, the Bar cites to standards 4.32 and 7.2, as well as *Florida Bar v.*

Dunagan, 731 So.2d 1237 (Fla.1999) (suspending attorney for ninety-one days for representing husband in dissolution proceeding after he had represented both husband and wife in connection with various business matters and business was marital asset); *Florida Bar v. Wilson,* 714 So.2d 381 (Fla.1998) (suspending attorney for one year for agreeing to represent wife in dissolution proceeding after previously representing couple in unrelated declaratory judgment action and for other misconduct); *Florida Bar v. Hmielewski,* 702 So.2d 218 (Fla.1997) (suspending attorney for three years for making deliberate misrepresentations in medical malpractice action despite significant mitigating factors); *Florida Bar v. Calvo,* 630 So.2d 548, 549 (Fla.1993) (disbarring attorney for his reckless misconduct with regard to securities offering, including failing to disclose to potential investors that one of principals involved had been indicted for mail fraud); *Florida Bar v. Mastrilli,* 614 So.2d 1081 (Fla.1993) (suspending attorney for six months for filing suit against one client on behalf of another client in matter for which attorney had been retained by both of them); and *Feige,* 596 So.2d 433 (suspending attorney for two years for representing himself and client when their interests were adverse, despite client's consent to dual representation).

Standard 4.32 provides that suspension is appropriate when a lawyer knows of a conflict of interest and does not fully disclose to a client the possible effect of that conflict, and causes injury or potential injury to a client. Standard 7.2 provides that suspension is appropriate when a lawyer knowingly engages in conduct that is a violation of a duty owed as a professional and causes injury or potential injury to a client, the public, or the legal system. Of course, the standards do not distinguish between suspensions of different lengths. These standards support the referee's recommendation to the same extent that they support the Bar's position.

However, if the egregiousness of the conduct is viewed as falling along a continuum, the closer the conduct falls on the continuum to the dividing line between suspension and disbarment, the longer the suspension that such conduct would warrant. In looking at the corresponding standards for disbarment in these same categories, it appears that Scott's conduct comes close to that dividing line in both cases. Standard 4.31 provides, in pertinent part, that disbarment is appropriate when a lawyer, without the informed consent of the client, simultaneously represents clients that the lawyer knows have adverse interests with the intent to benefit the lawyer or another, and causes serious or potentially serious injury to a client, or represents a client in a matter substantially related to a matter in which the interests of a present or former client are materially adverse, and knowingly uses information relating to the representation of a client with the intent to benefit the lawyer or another, and causes serious or potentially serious injury to a client.

Standard 7.1 provides that disbarment is appropriate when a lawyer intentionally engages in conduct that is a violation of a duty owed as a professional with the intent to obtain a benefit for the lawyer or another, and causes serious or potentially serious injury to a client, the public, or the legal system.

In the case of both standards, it appears that Scott's conduct falls close to the dividing line on the continuum between disbarment and suspension. This supports the imposition of a suspension close to the dividing line between suspension and disbarment. The maximum length of a definite-term suspension under the Rules Regulating the Florida Bar is three years. R. Regulating Fla. Bar 3-5.1(e).

Feige is particularly helpful in gauging an appropriate sanction in this case. *Feige* involved a lawyer who engaged in an unwaivable conflict of interest and who failed to inform a third party of nonconfidential information under circumstances that allowed his client to perpetrate a fraud on her ex-husband, the third party. Scott engaged in precisely the same kinds of misconduct in this case but to a more egregious extent. This Court suspended Feige for two years. Because Scott's misconduct was more egregious, it warrants a longer suspension than that imposed in Feige.

The more recent cases of *Florida Bar v. Head*, 27 So.3d 1 (Fla.2010), and Florida Bar v. Herman, 8 So.3d 1100 (Fla.2009), also involved similar but less egregious misconduct. In Head we suspended a lawyer for one year after he created a conflict of interest between himself and his clients by convincing them to pay him $10,000 from the proceeds of a mortgage refinancing when his clients' primary objective in arranging the mortgage refinancing had been to pay off their biggest creditor and paying the lawyer $10,000 frustrated that objective. Head, 27 So.3d at 9. In addition, the lawyer was not forthcoming in advising the bankruptcy court in his clients' case that he had received $10,000 in fees. He also filed a "Suggestion of Bankruptcy" for his firm in his clients' bankruptcy case when he had not filed a petition for bankruptcy for the firm. Id. at 5.

In *Herman* we suspended a lawyer for eighteen months for going into direct business competition with a client of his firm and representing both companies without advising the first client of the conflict or obtaining a waiver. *Herman*, 8 So.3d at 1103. We found his failure to inform his first client about his own company was "dishonest and deceitful" and motivated by "monetary concerns." Id.

CONCLUSION

Accordingly, William Sumner Scott is hereby suspended from the practice of law for three years and ordered to reimburse the Bar for its costs. The suspension will be effective thirty days from the filing of this opinion so that Scott can close out his practice and protect the interests of existing clients. If Scott notifies this Court in writing that he is no longer practicing and does not need the thirty days to protect existing clients, this Court will enter an order making the suspension effective immediately. Scott shall accept no new business from the date this opinion is filed until he is reinstated by this Court.

Judgment is entered for The Florida Bar, 651 East Jefferson Street, Tallahassee, Florida 32399-2300, for recovery of costs from William Sumner Scott in the amount of $5,637.71, for which sum let execution issue.

It is so ordered.

Questions for Discussion

1.   What should Scott have done when asked by Frankel about Maseri?

2.   Who did Scott represent? Who should he have represented?

3.   What is the significance of Scott knowing about Maseri's prior problems?

CHAPTER 8
TRUST ACCOUNTS
RULE 5-1.1

One of the most important aspects of being a lawyer deals with handling of the client's property. Chapter 5 of the Rules Regulating the Florida Bar deals with client property and outlines several duties an attorney has in handling same. Rule 5-1.1 titled "Trust Accounts" provides several rules and regulations of attorney trust accounts. This Rule applies not only to trust accounts, but to physical property being held by the attorney. Some important parts of the Rule follow:

> (a) Nature of Money or Property Entrusted to Attorney.
>
> > (1) *Trust Account Required; Commingling Prohibited.* A lawyer shall hold in trust, separate from the lawyer's own property, funds and property of clients or third persons that are in a lawyer's possession in connection with a

representation. All funds, including advances for fees, costs, and expenses, shall be kept in a separate bank or savings and loan association account maintained in the state where the lawyer's office is situated or elsewhere with the consent of the client or third person and clearly labeled and designated as a trust account. A lawyer may maintain funds belonging to the lawyer in the trust account in an amount no more than is reasonably sufficient to pay bank charges relating to the trust account.

(2) *Compliance With Client Directives.* Trust funds may be separately held and maintained other than in a bank or savings and loan association account if the lawyer receives written permission from the client to do so and provided that written permission is received before maintaining the funds other than in a separate account.

(3) *Safe Deposit Boxes.* If a member of the bar uses a safe deposit box to store trust funds or property, the member shall advise the institution in which the deposit box is located that it may include property of clients or third persons.

(b) *Application of Trust Funds or Property to Specific Purpose.* Money or other property entrusted to an attorney for a specific purpose, including advances for fees, costs, and expenses, is held in trust and must be applied only to that purpose.

> Money and other property of clients
> coming into the hands of an attorney are
> not subject to counterclaim or setoff for
> attorney's fees, and a refusal to account
> for and deliver over such property upon
> demand shall be deemed a conversion.

Several reported cases can be found involving violations of this Rule. In fact, disbarment is presumed an appropriate sanction for a lawyer that "engages in misconduct involving the misuse or misappropriation of client funds." See *The Florida Bar v. Mirk*, 64 So. 3d 1180 (Fla. 2011).

In *Mirk*, the Florida Supreme Court held that disbarment was the appropriate sanction for attorney misconduct dealing with misappropriating funds from the client trust account. Mirk was retained by a client and paid an advance fee of $750.00. Rather than placing the unearned portion of the fee in his trust account, Mirk deposited the monies in his operating account in violation of the Rule. Mirk's more egregious offense involves taking client proceeds, in the amount of $31,487,50, held in his trust account and applying them to an alleged attorney fee in the amount of $40,000 Mirk claimed he was owed based on an oral agreement with the client.

The client hired an attorney to resolve the dispute. Mirk failed to produce any agreement or invoices with regard to the alleged fee. Mirk never returned the proceeds to the client and a Bar complaint ensued. The Referee found him guilty of violating Rule 5-1.1 and also found several aggravating factors including: dishonest or selfish motive, bad faith obstruction of the disciplinary proceeding in failing to comply with rules or orders of the disciplinary agency, substantial experience in the practice of law, and indifference towards making restitution. The Referee recommended disbarment and the Supreme Court agreed stating that "an attorney is never permitted to withdraw or otherwise use client funds held in trust except as specifically authorized under the Bar Rules. To engage in such conduct, a lawyer risks full disciplinary sanctions under the Rules Regulating the Florida Bar, including disbarment." *Id* at 1186.

In *The Florida Bar v. Martinez-Genova*, 959 So. 2d 241 (Fla. 2007), the Supreme Court overruled the Referee's recommendation of a three year suspension and ordered disbarment. Martinez-Genova was found to have misappropriated nearly $60,000 of client's funds. While Martinez-Genova admitted to a cocaine addiction and entered into a three year contract with Florida Lawyers Assistance Program, presented good character evidence, submitted to rehabilitation and periodic drug testing, the Court stated that she did not overcome the presumption for disbarment.

In its decision, the Court cited several cases resulting in disbarment of attorneys who misappropriated client funds even though they were suffering from mental problems, drug use, or alcoholism. See *Florida Bar v. Shuminer*, 567 So.2d 430 (Fla.1990) and *Florida Bar v. Clement*, 662 So.2d 690

(Fla.1995). It is very clear that no excuse can and should be made to misappropriate a client's property, including funds held in an attorney's trust account.

The Florida Bar v. Mirk, 64 So. 3d 1180 (Fla. 2011)

....

BACKGROUND

The Bar filed a two-count complaint against Mirk, alleging that he violated several of the Rules Regulating the Florida Bar (Bar Rules). A referee was appointed. After holding a hearing, the referee has submitted his report for the Court's *1182 review, in which he makes the following findings and recommendations.

Count I

Lorne Lyles retained Patrick Mirk to represent him in a dispute with a contractor concerning a residential construction project. Lyles agreed to pay Mirk $250 per hour for his work on the case. He also made an initial payment to Mirk, totaling$750. Mirk did not inform Lyles that the $750 payment would be treated as a "non-refundable retainer." Nonetheless, Mirk deposited Lyles' $750 check into his operating account, rather than in his trust account as is required under the Bar Rules.

Given these facts, the referee found clear and convincing evidence that Lyles' $750 payment was an advance payment for legal fees, and was not a non-refundable retainer. Absent an agreement that the $750 would be treated as a non-refundable retainer, Mirk was obligated to hold the advance fee payment in trust until earned. The referee found that by failing to deposit Lyles' advance payment into his trust account, Mirk failed to apply trust funds for the intended purpose. For this misconduct, the referee recommended that Mirk be found guilty of violating the following Bar Rules: 5–1.1(a) (a lawyer shall hold in trust, separate from the lawyer's own property, any property of clients or third persons that are in a lawyer's possession in connection with a representation); and 5–1.1(b) (money or other property entrusted to an attorney for a specific purpose, including advances for fees, costs, and expenses, is held in trust and must be applied only to that purpose). The referee has also recommended that Mirk be found guilty of violating 4–8.4(g) (a lawyer shall not fail to respond to an official inquiry made by bar counsel or a disciplinary agency).

Count II

During the course of his practice, Mirk developed a professional relationship with Frank Bragano. Mirk represented Bragano and the business entities with which Bragano was involved in various projects over a number of years. Two such projects are at issue in this case.

First, Bragano hired Mirk to help resolve a dispute with Bragano's former attorney concerning an investment deal known as the "Meridian Project." Mirk was successful in negotiating a resolution to the dispute. As a result of the settlement, Mirk received a check for $100,462.50, to be distributed equally to each of the investors in the Meridian Project. Mirk deposited the check into his trust account. On June 30, 2004, Mirk wrote a check to Bragano for $31,487.50, representing his share of the settlement. At that time, Bragano placed the check in a desk drawer and it was not cashed.

As to the second project, in June 2004 Mirk began discussions with Bragano and others about plans to establish a large multi- million dollar "investment platform." Mirk would serve as corporate counsel for the venture. The project was intended to include four separate limited liability corporations; the first of these corporations to be established was called Montpelier, LLC.

The primary dispute in this case concerns Mirk's compensation for his work on the Montpelier venture. Mirk testified that he and Bragano had an oral agreement that Mirk would be paid a $40,000 flat fee for each company he established and $100,000 per year to act as corporate counsel. In contrast, Bragano testified before the referee that he did not agree to any type of flat fee arrangement. Instead, Bragano maintained that Mirk agreed to be paid a portion of the future profits from the investment venture in the event it was ultimately successful. On this central point, the referee found Bragano's testimony to be credible and that Mirk's testimony was not credible. Indeed, based on the evidence, the referee found that Mirk did not have an agreement to be paid a $40,000 flat fee for his work on the Montpelier project.

In October 2004, Bragano informed Mirk for the first time that he had not cashed the Meridian Project check for $31,487.50. Within a short time thereafter, Mirk executed a stop payment on that check without advising Bragano; bank records submitted into evidence show the stop payment was issued October 25, 2004. At this point, Mirk began a series of transactions disbursing the Meridian Project funds represented in the check for which Mirk had issued the stop payment order to himself. First, on October 25, 2004, the date the stop payment was entered, Mirk wrote a check to himself for $10,000. Next, Mirk issued three checks, each for $2,000, on November 10, November 12, and November 15, 2004, payable to himself. On November 22, 2004, Mirk wrote a check payable to the United States Treasury in the amount of $7,068.14. On November 24, 2004, he wrote a check to himself for $1,931.86, and on December 13, 2004, he wrote another check for $4500. Mirk later disbursed the remainder of the Meridian Project funds to himself on April 11, 2005. The referee found that Bragano had no knowledge of these disbursements and did not authorize them. In fact, the referee found that Mirk intentionally concealed these distributions from his client.

In December 2004, Bragano called Mirk to inform him that he was planning to cash the Meridian Project check to loan the money to a friend. The following day, December 20, 2004, Mirk sent Bragano a letter informing him for the first time that he had stopped payment on the check. In the letter, Mirk explained that he distributed and applied the Meridian Project funds, among other things, toward the $40,000 claim he asserted he was owed for his work on the Montpelier project and the other limited liability corporations involved in the investment platform, as well as toward the $100,000 he argued he was owed as corporate counsel.

Upon receiving the letter of December 20, Bragano was furious with Mirk. However, his business partners urged Bragano to take no action at the time to protect their investment venture. In June 2005, the Montpelier project came to an unsuccessful end. At that time, Bragano hired a new attorney to secure the return of the Meridian Project funds. On August 11, 2005, new counsel held a meeting with Mirk to discuss the matter. Notably, the referee found that Mirk did not produce any invoices or billing statements at this meeting to support his claim that he was owed $40,000 for his work on Montpelier. Thus, the referee found that the parties did not resolve their dispute at the August 2005 meeting. Ultimately, Mirk never returned the $31,487.50 he had withdrawn from Bragano's trust funds, and in June 2006 Bragano filed a complaint with the Bar.

Given the conduct described, the referee found:

> The clear and convincing evidence shows that Respondent did not have an agreement to be paid a $40,000 flat fee for work done in relation to

Montpelier. Although it is not necessary to have a written fee agreement in this instance, the clear and convincing evidence is that Respondent did not have a written fee agreementoraverbalfeeagreementfora$40,000 flat fee for work performed on Montpelier.

The evidence cited by Respondent to support the alleged flat fee agreement is not persuasive and is directly contradicted by the record. Respondent's claim of an agreement for a $40,000 flat fee is flatly contradicted by Bragano and further undermined by the testimony of Bragano's partner Lynch, and attorney Ricardo Roig. Respondent's evidence consists of his own testimony, handwritten notes he claims to have made contemporaneously, or letters he wrote after the fact.

The referee recommended that Mirk be found guilty of violating Bar Rules 5–1.1(a) (a lawyer shall hold in trust, separate from the lawyer's own property, property of clients or third persons that are in a lawyer's possession in connection with a representation); 5–1.1(b) (money or other property entrusted to an attorney for a specific purpose, including advances for fees, costs, and expenses, is held in trust and must be applied only to that purpose); 5–1.1(e) (upon receiving funds or other property in which a client or third person has an interest, a lawyer shall promptly notify the client or third person); and 5–1.2(g) (failure of a member to timely produce trust accounting records shall be considered as a matter of contempt).

The referee found several aggravating factors: (1) prior disciplinary offenses; (2) dishonest or selfish motive; (3) bad faith obstruction of the disciplinary proceeding by intentionally failing to comply with rules or orders of the disciplinary agency; (4) substantial experience in the practice of law; and (5) indifference toward making restitution. The referee also found one mitigating factor: (1) favorable reputation for character and professional skill.

As to the disciplinary sanction, the referee considered the Florida Standards for Imposing Lawyer Sanctions and case law, together with the aggravating and mitigating factors, and has recommended that Mirk be disbarred from the practice of law in Florida. The referee also awarded costs to the Bar in the amount of $11,504.95.

Mirk has filed a petition for review in this case, raising a number of challenges to the referee's report. We approve the referee's findings of fact and his recommendations of guilt without further discussion. The findings are supported by competent evidence and those findings support the recommended finding of guilt. Mirk also challenges the referee's recommended discipline. He urges the Court to disapprove the referee's recommendation for disbarment. However, as discussed below, we conclude that the referee's recommended sanction based on the findings is supported in the Standards and case law.

ANALYSIS

In reviewing a referee's recommended discipline, this Court's scope of review is broader than that afforded to the referee's findings of fact because, ultimately, it is our responsibility to order the appropriate sanction. See *Fla. Bar v. Anderson*, 538 So.2d 852, 854 (Fla.1989); see also art. V, § 15, Fla. Const. However, generally speaking this Court will not second-guess the referee's recommended discipline as long as it has a reasonable basis in existing case law and the Florida Standards for Imposing Lawyer Sanctions. See *Fla. Bar v. Temmer*, 753 So.2d 555, 558 (Fla.1999).

The referee's findings of fact demonstrate that Mirk misappropriated $31,487.50 in client funds held in his trust account. This Court has long held that attorney misconduct involving the misuse or misappropriation of client funds is unquestionably one of the most serious offenses a lawyer can commit. See *Fla. Bar. v. Martinez–Genova*, 959 So.2d 241, 246 (Fla.2007). Indeed, disbarment is presumed the appropriate discipline when an attorney engages in this type of misconduct. Id.; see also *Fla. Bar v. Valentine–Miller*, 974 So.2d 333, 338 (Fla.2008) (holding that disbarment is the presumptively appropriate sanction, under both the Florida Standards for Imposing Lawyer Sanctions and case law, when a lawyer misappropriates trust funds). We have also emphasized that the presumption of disbarment is exceptionally weighty when the attorney's misuse is intentional rather than a result of neglect or inadvertence. See *Fla. Bar v. Travis*, 765 So.2d 689, 691 (Fla.2000).

In defense of his actions in this case, Mirk asserts that he was owed a $40,000 flat fee for his work on Montpelier and each of the other limited liability corporations he planned to establish for the investment platform. Thus, he contends that he was entitled to retain the Meridian Project funds held in trust as payment toward Bragano's debt. We disagree. At the outset, we note that Mirk's compensation arrangement was never reduced to writing. When a lawyer fails to place an agreement for representation in writing, he or she is always at risk of becoming involved in a fee dispute with the client. In situations such as the instant case, absent a written agreement, the referee is required to consider all evidence and weigh the parties' testimony at the disciplinary hearing and evaluate credibility. We have long held that because the referee is in the best position to judge the credibility of the witnesses, we defer to the referee's assessment and his resolution of the conflicting testimony. See *Fla. Bar v. Batista*, 846 So.2d 479, 483 (Fla.2003).

Moreover, the facts here demonstrate that Mirk made a number of secret withdrawals from his client trust account without his client's knowledge or permission. When lawyers do face disputes over fees with their clients, the Bar Rules certainly do not permit attorneys to resolve such disputes in this manner. There is never a valid reason for misappropriating client funds held in trust. See *Fla. Bar v. Valentine–Miller*, 974 So.2d at 338. Once again, we emphasize to the members of the Bar that an attorney is never permitted to withdraw or otherwise use client funds held in trust except as specifically authorized under the Bar Rules. To engage in such conduct, a lawyer risks full disciplinary sanctions under the Rules Regulating the Florida Bar, including disbarment.

As we have stated, disbarment is presumed the appropriate discipline when an attorney misappropriates client money held in trust and Mirk simply has not presented any arguments to rebut the presumption in this case. The Florida Standards for Imposing Lawyer Sanctions applicable to Mirk's misconduct state that disbarment is the appropriate sanction. See Fla. Stds. Imposing Law. Sancs. 4.11 ("Disbarment is appropriate when a lawyer intentionally or knowingly converts client property regardless of injury or potential injury."); Fla. Stds. Imposing Law. Sancs. 4.61 ("Disbarment is appropriate when a lawyer knowingly or intentionally deceives a client with the intent to benefit the lawyer or another regardless of injury or potential injury to the client.").

Additionally, this Court has previously imposed disbarment for violations of the ethical rules similar to those found in this case. See *Fla. Bar v. Brownstein*, 953 So.2d 502 (Fla.2007) (disbarring respondent who misappropriated $20,000 in client funds held in trust, a portion of the total amount entrusted to the respondent by the client for the purpose of paying a bankruptcy settlement); see also *Fla. Bar v. Barley*, 831 So.2d 163 (Fla.2002) (disbarring respondent who misappropriated $76,760.68 in client funds held in trust, making a series of withdrawals from the funds over a period of three months, and ultimately depleting the entire amount).

In sum, after considering the referee's factual findings, the rules violated, the Standards, and the case law, we approve the referee's recommendation of disbarment as the appropriate sanction.

CONCLUSION

Accordingly, we approve the referee's findings of fact, recommendations of guilt, recommended sanction, and award of costs. R. Patrick Mirk is hereby disbarred. The disbarment will be effective thirty days from the filing of this opinion so that Mirk can close out his practice and protect the interests of existing clients. If Mirk notifies this Court in writing that he is no longer practicing and does not need the thirty days to protect existing clients, this Court will enter an order making the disbarment effective immediately. Mirk shall fully comply with Rule Regulating the Florida Bar 3–5.1(g). Further, Mirk shall accept no new business from the date this opinion.

Judgment is entered for The Florida Bar, 651 East Jefferson Street, Tallahassee, Florida 32399–2300, for recovery of costs from R. Patrick Mirk in the amount of $11,504.95, for which sum let execution issue.

It is so ordered.

Questions for Discussion

1.   What should Mirk have done with the initial retainer from Lyles? What should he have done if it were in fact a non-refundable retainer?

2.   What should Mirk have done in the beginning of the representation on the Meridian Project?

3.   What would make Mirk think he could cancel a trust account check to his client and write new checks to himself?

The Florida Bar v. Martinez-Genova, 959 So. 2d 241 (Fla. 2007)

....

FACTS

On December 16, 2004, The Florida Bar filed a two-count complaint against respondent Elizabeth Martinez-Genova. In count one, the Bar alleged that Martinez-Genova intentionally misappropriated third-party funds and failed to maintain proper trust accounting procedures. In count two, the Bar alleged that Martinez-Genova's arrests for cocaine use and possession were a violation of rule 4-8.4(b) (a lawyer shall not commit a criminal act that reflects adversely on the lawyer's honesty, trustworthiness, or fitness as a lawyer in other respects) of the Rules Regulating the Florida Bar. After conducting a hearing, the referee issued a report in which she made the following findings and recommendations.

Count I

Martinez-Genova represented her client Gary Wyckle, President of Charter One Group, Inc. (Charter One), in a series of transactions with Juan Aramendia and Eduardo Solares of Nikita Investment Corporation (Nikita). Charter One and Nikita entered into a conditional loan commitment agreement under which Charter One was to assist Nikita in obtaining a loan for $35 million to fund the acquisition of a pulp plant and saw mill in Guatemala. This conditional loan commitment was signed by Solares and Wyckle. The commitment stated that the borrowers would deliver $60,000 to Charter One's attorney, to be held in trust and credited to loan fees at closing. Martinez-Genova testified that she believed that Wyckle asked her, as his attorney, to hold the funds because doing so would make Wyckle appear "more credible" to his business partners.

Martinez-Genova did not sign the conditional loan commitment. However, Martinez-Genova did approve sending, on her letterhead stationery stating that she was an attorney, two letters, dated February 11, 2004, and February 19, 2004, directing Aramendia and Solares to wire transfer their deposits to her bank account. Both letters stated that the wire transfer funds would be credited to the loan commitment fee stipulated in the loan commitment. On February 12, 2004, Solares wired $8000 to Martinez-Genova's account. On February 19, 2004, Aramendia wired an additional $52,000 to Martinez-Genova's account. Ultimately, Charter One did not obtain financing on behalf of Nikita. Charter One also failed to refund any of the $60,000 deposit.

In response, Nikita retained Richard Brenner, who filed a complaint with The Florida Bar on August 28, 2004, regarding Martinez-Genova's involvement in the failed loan transaction. A Bar staff auditor examined Martinez-Genova's sole bank account for the period of June 21, 2003, to August 23, 2004. The auditor discovered that as of February 12, 2004, Martinez- Genova had a balance of $11.04. Then, on February 13, 2004, Martinez-Genova received a wire transfer in the amount of $8000 from Solares, acting under the name Helicopteros Del Norte. In the following days, Martinez-Genova made a $7700 over-the-counter cash withdrawal and several ATM withdrawals of smaller amounts. As of February 17, 2004, only $18.82 remained in Martinez-Genova's account.

On February 20, 2004, Martinez-Genova received a wire transfer in the amount of $52,000 from Aramendia. During the following week, Martinez-Genova made four over-the-counter cash withdrawals from her account totaling $25,150. Martinez- Genova also authorized three wire transfers to Charter One and its designees totaling $26,103. Finally, Martinez-Genova made a number of debit card purchases and ATM withdraws from her account during that same week. On February 27, 2004, the balance in Martinez-Genova's operating account was $327.50. By March 8, 2004, Martinez-Genova had a balance of negative $26.96.

Martinez-Genova testified that she agreed to act as Wyckle's agent in the Nikita transaction in exchange for a fee of three percent of the $60,000 deposit. She claims to have only retained or spent her $1800 fee and to have given the balance of the cash she withdrew to Wyckle. However, Martinez-Genova did not keep any records of the above transactions or document her fee.

Martinez-Genova's pattern of receiving third-party funds and disbursing them to herself or Wyckle resumed on May 13, 2004. Beginning with a balance of $1, Martinez-Genova received wire transfers totaling $59,800 over a three-month period. From these funds, Martinez-Genova transferred $53,850 to American Escrow Company, LLC, which was owned by Gary Wyckle, withdrew $5811 in cash and used $139 to pay bank charges.

After a hearing, the referee found Martinez-Genova guilty of violating Rule of Professional Conduct 4-8.4(c) (a lawyer shall not engage in conduct involving dishonesty, fraud, deceit, or misrepresentation) and Rules Regulating Trust Accounts 5-1.1(a) (Nature of Money or Property

Entrusted to Attorney), 5-1.1(b) (Application of Trust Funds or Property to Specific Purpose), 5-1.1(e) (Notice of Receipt of Trust Funds; Delivery; Accounting), 5-1.1(f) (Disputed Ownership of Trust Funds), 5-1.2(b) (Minimum Trust Accounting Records), 5-1.2(c) (Minimum Trust Accounting Procedures), and 5-1.2(d) (Record Retention).

Specifically, the referee found that the deposit sent to Martinez-Genova by Nikita was to be held in trust according to the loan commitment and that despite this expectation of trust, Martinez-Genova "had a pattern of receiving third-party funds and simultaneously withdrawing and disbursing from those funds." The referee found that "third-party funds were not being used for their intended purpose" and that Martinez-Genova "willfully ignored her responsibilities as an attorney during the period in which she misappropriated money from third-parties." Finally, the referee found that Martinez-Genova "knew that what she was doing was wrong" and noted that neither Martinez-Genova nor Wyckle had made restitution.

Count II

The Bar's complaint also addressed Martinez-Genova's history of drug use and repeated arrests for drug possession. Martinez-Genova was arrested three times for possession of cocaine between June 20, 2002, and June 4, 2004. After the last arrest, Martinez-Genova was incarcerated and remained in custody until she was transferred to St. Luke's Addiction Recovery Center, an in-patient drug treatment facility, in July 2004. She remained in St. Luke's until she was successfully discharged in September 2004. The referee found that Martinez-Genova's drug use and possession violated Rule of Professional Conduct 4-8.4(b) (A lawyer shall not commit a criminal act that reflects adversely on the lawyer's honesty, trustworthiness, or fitness as a lawyer in other respects).

Applying the Florida Standards for Imposing Lawyer Sanctions, the referee found four aggravating factors: (1) Martinez- Genova acted from a selfish motive-the support of her drug habit; (2) she displayed a pattern of misconduct over a substantial period of time; (3) she was involved in a series of improper transactions, amounting to multiple offenses; and (4) she caused actual harm to third parties without payment of restitution to them.

The referee found nine mitigating factors: (1) Martinez-Genova had personal and emotional problems including a cocaine addiction and clinical depression; (2) she cooperated with the Bar during its investigation; (3) she was inexperienced in the practice of law; (4) she made a good-faith effort to rectify the misconduct set out in Count II by voluntarily entering into a three-year contract with Florida Lawyers Assistance, Inc. (FLA); (5) she presented evidence of good character; (6) she had a mental disability (cocaine addiction, clinical depression); (7) she expressed remorse for her misconduct; (8) she entered into interim rehabilitation programs (three-year contract with FLA, outpatient therapy, Narcotics Anonymous); and (9) she had imposed upon her other penalties or sanctions (Martinez-Genova must attend Miami Behavioral meetings, submit to semiweekly drug tests, and attend Alcoholics Anonymous and Narcotics Anonymous meetings for a period of one year by court order; Martinez-Genova suffered negative publicity in The Miami Herald; Martinez-Genova lost visitation with her son in part due to her drug use).

Based on these factors and Florida case law, the referee recommended that Martinez-Genova be sanctioned by a three-year suspension, retroactive to the date of her emergency suspension, followed by a two-year period of probation if reinstated. During this probationary period, Martinez-Genova would be required to participate in FLA, submit to mandatory semimonthly urine tests, participate in outpatient therapy, and enroll in the Law Office Management Assistance Service (LOMAS) program regarding the operation of trust accounts. Martinez-Genova's trust transactions would be monitored by a suitable mentor during the probationary period. The referee also recommended that the Bar's costs be imposed against Martinez-Genova.

The Bar filed a petition for review with this Court, seeking disbarment rather than the recommended discipline. Martinez- Genova argues that suspension is appropriate given the referee's findings of mitigating factors.

ANALYSIS

Neither party challenges the findings of fact or recommendations as to guilt. Accordingly, we approve without further discussion the referee's recommendation that Martinez-Genova be found guilty of violating the above rules. As to the recommended discipline, the Bar argues that case law requires this Court to reject the referee's recommendation of discipline. We agree.

In reviewing a referee's recommended discipline, this Court's scope of review is broader than that afforded to the referee's findings of fact because ultimately it is the Court's responsibility to order the appropriate sanction. See *Fla. Bar v. Lawless*, 640 So.2d 1098, 1100 (Fla.1994); see also art. V, § 15, Fla. Const. However, generally speaking, this Court will not second-guess the referee's recommended discipline as long as it has a reasonable basis in existing case law and the Florida Standards for Imposing Lawyer Sanctions.

Fla. Bar v. McFall, 863 So.2d 303, 307 (Fla.2003).

In this case, existing law indicates that the referee's recommendation of suspension is not sufficient discipline in accord with our case law in respect to a lawyer's misuse of client funds. Disbarment is the presumptive discipline for misuse of client funds because it is unquestionably one of the most serious offenses a lawyer can commit. *Fla. Bar v. Gross*, 896 So.2d 742 (Fla.2005); *Fla. Bar v. Barley*, 831 So.2d 163 (Fla.2002); *Fla. Bar v. Tillman*, 682 So.2d 542 (Fla.1996); *Fla. Bar v. Weinstein*, 635 So.2d 21 (Fla.1994); *Fla. Bar v. Shanzer*, 572 So.2d 1382 (Fla.1991). This presumption of disbarment is "exceptionally weighty when the attorney's misuse is intentional rather than a result of neglect or inadvertence." *Barley*, 831 So.2d at 171.

Martinez-Genova's misuse of third-party funds was intentional. Martinez-Genova's letters to Aramendia and Solares indicated that the wire-transferred funds, totaling $60,000, would be credited to the loan commitment fee. Aramendia and Solares had a right to rely upon her not misusing the funds since the funds were sent to Martinez-Genova, who had sent them letters as an attorney. The referee found the commitment fee was to be held in trust. Yet, bank records indicate that on February 23, 2004, Martinez-Genova completed a withdrawal ticket for a $4500 cashier's check and another for $8000 in cash. A few days later, on February 27, 2004, Martinez-Genova again completed two withdrawal tickets, one for a $6600 cashier's check and another for $6050 in cash. During this period, Martinez-Genova also initiated three separate wire transfers, totaling $26,103, to Charter One and its creditors. Martinez-Genova could not have inadvertently walked into her bank branch and unintentionally made these withdrawals from her account.

This Court agrees with the referee's finding that Martinez-Genova "willfully ignored her responsibilities as an attorney during the period in which she misappropriated money from third-parties." As a result, Martinez-Genova's misconduct is not analogous to negligent misappropriation cases such as *Florida Bar v. Mason*, 826 So.2d 985 (Fla.2002), and Florida Bar v. Wolf, 930 So.2d 574 (Fla.2006), where this Court has found suspension to be an adequate sanction.

In both *Mason* and *Wolf* the Court found that the attorneys' misappropriations were due to mistakes in accounting practices and that there was no evidence that any clients ultimately sustained losses. *Mason*, 826 So.2d at 988; *Wolf*, 930 So.2d at 578. In contrast, Martinez-Genova kept no bank account records at all and intentionally withdrew funds that were to be held in trust. Moreover, Martinez-Genova has not made restitution to any of the injured parties.

The Florida Standards for Imposing Lawyer Sanctions confirms that disbarment is the appropriate sanction in the present disciplinary action. Section 7.1 states:

Disbarment is appropriate when a lawyer intentionally engages in conduct that is a violation of a duty owed as a professional with the intent to obtain a benefit for the lawyer or another, and causes serious or potentially serious injury to a client, the public, or the legal system.

The referee found that Martinez-Genova knowingly caused injury to members of the public for the benefit of herself and her client Wyckle. Thus, disbarment is appropriate under the Florida Standards for Imposing Lawyer Sanctions.

Martinez-Genova argues that the circumstances surrounding her misappropriation mitigate against disbarment. This Court has considered whether an attorney's personal and emotional problems, such as drug addiction, outweigh the seriousness of the attorney's misconduct when determining what discipline to impose. However, the Court finds mitigating factors to overcome the presumption of disbarment for misappropriation only in exceptional and unusual circumstances because this Court refuses to "excuse an attorney for dipping into his trust funds as a means of solving personal problems." *Fla. Bar v. Shanzer*, 572 So.2d at 1384.

For example, in *Florida Bar v. Shuminer*, 567 So.2d 430 (Fla.1990), the Court disbarred an attorney who misappropriated client funds despite finding the mitigating factors present in the current action, personal and emotional problems, cooperation with the Bar, inexperience in the practice of law, good reputation, mental impairment due to addiction, successful rehabilitation efforts, and remorse, plus the additional factors that Shuminer had no prior disciplinary history and he had made a good-faith effort at restitution. Notwithstanding this long list of mitigating factors, the Court found that Shuminer "failed to establish that his addictions rose to a sufficient level of impairment to outweigh the seriousness of his offenses." Id. at 432.

Similarly, in *Florida Bar v. Clement*, 662 So.2d 690 (Fla.1995), the Court disbarred an attorney for intentional misappropriation where the attorney was diagnosed with bipolar disorder. The Court held that Clement's psychological disorder did not outweigh the seriousness of his misconduct because the referee found that Clement could distinguish right from wrong at the time of his misconduct. Id. at 699.

Martinez-Genova makes no more showing of impairment than Shuminer or Clement. Just as Shuminer "continued to work effectively" during his struggle with alcoholism, the referee found that Martinez-Genova passed the Florida Bar Examination and handled a complex litigation case despite daily cocaine use. *Shuminer*, 567 So.2d at 432. And the referee found that, like Clement, Martinez-Genova was able to distinguish right from wrong at the time of the misappropriation despite the effects of her drug addiction and depression.

Furthermore, Martinez-Genova's situation is distinguishable from a case where this Court found an attorney's personal problems to outweigh the seriousness of her misconduct. In *Florida Bar v. Tauler*, 775 So.2d 944, 947 (Fla.2000), the Court approved the referee's recommendation of suspension and distinguished *Shuminer* and *Shanzer* after the referee found that Tauler was "less culpable" because her misconduct was the product of personal and emotional distress. Specifically, the referee found that Tauler's husband was the "prime mover" behind her wrongdoings. *Id.* Yet, in Tauler, we expressly cautioned that "without the unique mitigating circumstances presented in the instant case and Tauler's clear commitment to providing legal assistance to those in need, we would not hesitate to disbar Tauler." *Id.* at 949.

Martinez-Genova's case does not present the same unique mitigating circumstances as Tauler. Most notably, while Martinez- Genova has made no attempt at restitution, Tauler made timely and good-faith restitution. Also, while Martinez-Genova has provided some pro bono assistance, Tauler dedicated hundreds of hours to assisting the poor prior to her suspension. Finally, Martinez-Genova has some history of misconduct, whereas the Court did not note any previous discipline in Tauler.

Martinez-Genova's struggle with drug addiction and clinical depression and her admirable progress towards rehabilitation are relevant to this Court's determination of discipline. However, this is not a case where an attorney's substance abuse and personal turmoil cast doubt on the knowing, intentional nature of his or her misconduct. Upon review of all of the facts, prior case law, and the Florida Standards for Imposing Lawyer Sanctions, we find disbarment to be the appropriate level of discipline.

Finally, the referee recommended that costs in the amount of $8,235.52 be charged to Martinez-Genova. The Bar has requested that the costs incurred in seeking appellate review of the referee's erroneous recommendation of discipline also be charged to the respondent. This Court has final discretionary authority to award costs. Fla. Bar v. Lechtner, 666 So.2d 892 (Fla.1996); Fla. Bar v. Bosse, 609 So.2d 1320 (Fla.1992). In Lechtner, this Court explained:

> [G]enerally, when there is a finding that an attorney has been found guilty of violating a Rule Regulating the Florida Bar, the Bar should be awarded its costs. Assessment of costs against a respondent who has violated the Rules of Discipline is a policy decision. The choice is between imposing the costs of discipline on those who have violated our Rules of Professional Conduct or on the membership of the Bar who have not. In these situations, it is only fair to tax those costs against the member who has violated the rules.

666 So.2d at 894 (citations omitted). In the instant case, we agree that the Bar's appellate costs were reasonable and necessary to correct the referee's erroneous recommendation of discipline for such serious misconduct. We further agree that these costs should be borne by the respondent as a matter of policy.

CONCLUSION

Based on the above, we approve the referee's findings of fact and recommendations as to guilt but reject the recommended discipline and instead order disbarment. Accordingly, Elizabeth Martinez-Genova is hereby disbarred for a period of five years, effective nunc pro tunc, October 20, 2004, the effective date of the emergency suspension in Florida Bar v. Martinez- Genova, 888 So.2d 19 (Fla.2004) (table). Martinez-Genova may petition the Florida Board of Bar Examiners for readmission five years from the date of the suspension. Judgment is entered for The Florida Bar, 651 East Jefferson Street, Tallahassee, Florida 32399-2300, for recovery of costs from Elizabeth Martinez-Genova in the amount of $12,651.61, for which sum let execution issue.

It is so ordered.

Questions for Discussion

1. Why do you think she withdrew the money?

2. Is there any conceivable scenario where you would trust Martinez-Genova to hire her as your lawyer in the future? What would she need to do to prove rehabilitation? Can she?

CHAPTER 9
TRUTHFULNESS IN STATEMENTS TO OTHERS
RULE 4-4.1

A Lawyer is under an ethical obligation to be truthful when dealing with others on behalf of his client. Rule 4-4.1 provides the framework for this responsibility. The Rule states that "[i]n the course of representing a client a lawyer shall not knowingly:

> (a) Make a false statement of material fact or law to a third person; or
>
> (b) Fail to disclose a material fact to a third person when disclosure is necessary to avoid assisting a criminal or fraudulent act by a client, unless disclosure is prohibited by rule 4-1.6

In *The Florida Bar v. Letwin*, 70 So. 3d 578 (Fla. 2011) the Court imposed a one year rehabilitative suspension from the practice of law and three year probationary period upon readmission on a lawyer found to have violated Rule 4-4.1. Letwin sent over 900 letters to potential clients that contained inaccurate statements of fact. The Court reiterated that it has imposed a wide variety of disciplinary measures involving unethical solicitation of clients and that suspension is an appropriate sanction "when respondent's actions are knowing, intentional and potentially injurious to a client, the public or the legal system as a whole." *Id* at 583 citing *The Florida Bar v. Barrett*, 897 So. 2d 1269 (Fla. 2005).

The Florida Bar v. Letwin, 70 So. 3d 578 (Fla. 2011)

FACTS

On December 23, 2009, the Bar filed a complaint against Respondent Letwin alleging that in August 2008, she sent an improper solicitation letter to numerous current and former part-time adult education teachers in Broward County, Florida. After a hearing, the assigned referee made the following findings of fact:

1. In or about August 2008, respondent sent a letter to numerous current and former part time adult education teachers in Broward County, Florida. The number of letters sent, according to the respondent's own testimony, was over 900 letters to these individuals.

2. Each letter improperly solicited these part time teachers to join a purported class action suit against the Broward County School Board. A copy of respondent's August 28, 2008, correspondence to the over 900 prospective clients with attachment was attached to the complaint as Composite Exhibit B.

3. The letter contained inaccuracies and statements of fact that induced approximately 50 clients to retain respondent's legal services.

4. First, the case referenced by respondent in the letter had not been certified as a class action by the trial court.

5. Respondent's letter further did not identify it as an advertisement, as required by The Rules Regulating The Florida Bar.

6. Further, the contract that respondent enclosed with the letter was not marked as a sample, as required by The Rules Regulating The Florida Bar.

7. The letter also stated that "I need to have your express acceptance of my legal representation or the COURT will not recognize your claim."

8. Such statement was improper and not an accurate statement of law or fact.

9. Respondent failed to explain that the recipients of the letter were free to choose and hire any attorney to represent them in a lawsuit.

10. Statements contained within her solicitation letter were both inaccurate and erroneous, and meant to induce prospective clients to hire her.

11. Finally, respondent's actions were clearly prejudicial to the proper administration of justice.

Based on these findings of fact, the referee recommended that Respondent be found guilty of violating rules 3–4.2 (violation of the rules of professional conduct is a cause for discipline), 4–7.4(a) (solicitation), and 4–8.4(d) (lawyer shall not engage in conduct in connection with practice of law that is prejudicial to administration of justice), but not guilty of violating rules 4–4.1 (in course of representing client, lawyer shall not make false statement of material fact to third person), 4–8.4(a) (lawyer shall not violate or attempt to violate rules of professional conduct), and 4–8.4(c) (lawyer shall not engage in conduct involving dishonesty, fraud, deceit or misrepresentation).

The referee recommended that Respondent be suspended for ninety days and attend an "education workshop dealing with Solicitations/Advertisements, if available or obtain written materials on the topic." In recommending this sanction, the referee noted the following aggravating factors: (1) prior disciplinary offenses, (2) pattern of misconduct, and (3) multiple offenses. The referee also found and considered three mitigating factors: (1) personal or emotional problems (illness and subsequent death of Respondent's spouse); (2) absence of selfish or dishonest motive; and (3) interim rehabilitation.

The Bar seeks review of the referee's recommendation that Respondent be found not guilty of violating rules 4–4.1 (in course of representing client, lawyer shall not make false statement of material fact to third person), 4–8.4(a) (lawyer shall not violate or attempt to violate rules of professional conduct), and 4–8.4(c) (lawyer shall not engage in conduct involving dishonesty, fraud, deceit or misrepresentation) and the referee's recommendation of a ninety-day suspension. Respondent has filed a cross-petition for review challenging the referee's recommendations as to guilt and discipline.

ANALYSIS

Both parties challenge the referee's recommendations as to guilt. First, the Bar challenges the referee's recommendation that Respondent be found not guilty of violating rules 4–4.1, 4–8.4(a), and 4–8.4(c) as charged in the complaint.

The Bar's arguments in this regard are well taken. Rule 4–4.1 states, in pertinent part, that "[i]n the course of representing a client a lawyer shall not knowingly make a false statement of material fact or law to a third person." Rule 4–8.4(c) states, in pertinent part, that a lawyer shall not "engage in conduct involving dishonesty, fraud, deceit, or misrepresentation." The referee found that the letter Respondent sent "contained inaccuracies and statements of fact that induced approximately 50 clients to retain respondent's legal services," and that statements contained in the letter were "both inaccurate and erroneous, and meant to induce prospective clients to hire her." Specifically, the referee found that the case referenced by Respondent as a "class action" had not yet been certified as a class action in the trial court, and that her statement in the letter that "I need to have your express acceptance of my legal representation or the COURT will not recognize your claim" was "improper and not an accurate statement of law or fact." These factual findings are in direct contravention to the recommendations that Respondent be found not guilty of violating rules 4–4.1 and 4–8.4(c). Accordingly, the referee's recommendation in this regard is disapproved, and we conclude that Respondent is guilty of violating rules 4–1.4 and 4–8.4(c).

We also disapprove the referee's recommendation that Respondent be found not guilty of violating rule 4–8.4(a). That rule states that a lawyer shall not "violate or attempt to violate the Rules of Professional Conduct, knowingly assist or induce another to do so, or do so through the acts of another." Thus, by its plain language, that rule is necessarily violated whenever any other rule of professional conduct is violated. Because the referee recommended that Respondent be found guilty of violating other rules, she should have recommended Respondent be found guilty of violating rule 4–8.4(a).

Respondent challenges the referee's recommendation that she be found guilty of violating rule 4–7.4(a) (solicitation). In pertinent part, this rule provides that, except as set forth in subdivision (b) of the rule (setting out the parameters of permissible written communications with prospective clients), "a lawyer shall not solicit professional employment from a prospective client with whom the lawyer has no family or prior professional relationship, in person or otherwise, when a significant motive for the lawyer's doing so is the lawyer's pecuniary gain." The rule also provides that a lawyer "shall not enter into an agreement for, charge, or collect a fee for professional employment obtained in violation of this rule," and that the term "solicit" includes "any written form of communication directed to a specific recipient and not meeting the requirements of subdivision (b) of this rule." R. Regulating Fla. Bar 4–7.4(a). Subdivision (b) prohibits unsolicited written communications with prospective clients if, among other things, the communication "contains a false, fraudulent, misleading, or deceptive statement or claim." Subdivision (b) also sets forth certain requirements for such written communications, such as they must be marked in red ink as "advertisements," they must be sent only by regular U.S. mail, they must be accompanied by a written statement of the lawyer's background, training, and experience, and if a contract for representation is included, the contract must be marked as a "sample" and the words "do not sign" must appear on the client signature line. R. Regulating Fla. Bar 4–7.4(b). Here, the referee found, and Respondent does not dispute, that she sent a written communication to prospective clients for the purpose of obtaining professional employment that did not meet the requirements of rule 4–7.4. Although Respondent contends that she already viewed the recipients of the letter as her "clients" and that because of the multiple lawsuits she had filed, there was a "budding attorney-client relationship" between her and the putative class members, nothing in the record showed that a true attorney-client relationship had been established. Accordingly, we approve the referee's recommendation that Respondent be found guilty of violating rule 4–7.4(a).

Next, both parties have challenged the referee's recommended discipline of a ninety-day suspension. The Bar contends that at least a ninety-one-day suspension is warranted, mainly due to Respondent's prior misconduct and prior discipline. Respondent argues that only a public reprimand is warranted.

In reviewing a referee's recommended discipline, this Court's scope of review is broader than that afforded to the referee's findings of fact because, ultimately, it is our responsibility to order the appropriate sanction. See *Fla. Bar v. Anderson*, 538 So.2d 852, 854 (Fla.1989); see also art. V, § 15, Fla. Const. However, generally speaking this Court will not second-guess the referee's recommended discipline as long as it has a reasonable basis in existing case law and the Florida Standards for Imposing Lawyer Sanctions. See *Fla. Bar v. Temmer*, 753 So.2d 555, 558 (Fla.1999).

In cases involving unethical solicitation of clients, we have imposed a wide variety of disciplinary measures. See *Fla. Bar v. Barrett*, 897 So.2d 1269 (Fla.2005) (noting wide variety of discipline depending on the specific facts of each case; citing cases ranging from public reprimand to disbarment). Citing our decision in Barrett, the referee in this case correctly concluded that a suspension is appropriate in such cases "when respondent's actions are knowing, intentional and potentially injurious to a client, the public or the legal system as a whole." Further, the referee correctly noted that a suspension in this case is supported by standards 7.2 (suspension is appropriate when lawyer knowingly engages in conduct in violation of duty owed as a professional and causes injury or potential injury to client, public, or legal system) and 8.0 (suspension is appropriate when lawyer has been publicly reprimanded for same or similar conduct and engages in further similar misconduct that causes injury or potential injury to client, public, legal system, or profession).

Although we agree with the referee that a suspension is warranted in this case, we disagree that a ninety-day suspension is sufficient, given Respondent's disciplinary history and continuing pattern of misconduct.

In 2009, Respondent was found guilty of four separate counts of serious and intentional misconduct. In count I, she was found guilty of failing to respond to a request for production and interrogatories propounded to her client, intentionally failing to appear at a hearing on attorneys' fees that had been awarded against her client, failing to answer calls from the court inquiring into her whereabouts during the hearing, and knowingly failing to comply with terms of a six-month probation sentence (and order that she pay the entire amount of attorneys' fees awarded to the opposing party) imposed upon her as a result of being held in indirect criminal contempt of court. In count II, she was found guilty of refusing to produce her client for a deposition, resulting in an order for sanctions against her and her client (and ordering her to pay $3100) for her intentional interference with the opposing parties' discovery attempts. In count III, she was found guilty of failing to execute on a default judgment that had been entered in favor of her client, resulting in dismissal of the case for failure to prosecute and failing to properly communicate with and inform her client with regard to the case. Finally, as found in count IV, a federal judge ordered that she pay $5,802.25 in attorneys' fees as a sanction. She failed to make any payment on such sanction, was held in contempt and again ordered to pay the sanction, improperly appealed the sanction to the U.S. Court of Appeals for the Eleventh Circuit, again failed to pay the sanction, and was again held in contempt. The federal magistrate in that case found that Respondent "contemptuously defied" the court's order and further stated that Respondent practiced law "in a manner that unreasonably burdens the judiciary and harms other parties by causing them to needlessly expend time and effort and incur legal fees. Her repeated poor judgment and unprofessional conduct puts at risk the legitimate interests of her clients." *Aldavero v. St. Louis*, No. 05–22098 (S.D. Fla. filed Mar. 19, 2007) (Report and Recommendation of United States Magistrate Judge). The magistrate also recommended that Respondent's actions be referred to The Florida Bar as well as the Southern District Ad Hoc Committee on Attorney Admissions, Peer Review, and Attorney Grievance. Id.

As a result of these instances of misconduct, the referee in the prior disciplinary case recommended that Respondent be found guilty of violating multiple rules and be suspended for ninety days followed by a three-year period of probation with a supervising attorney providing "continuous monitoring" of her clients' case files and providing quarterly reports to the Bar. The referee also recommended that she be required to pay $1600 in restitution to one of the injured clients. In making this disciplinary recommendation, the referee noted, in mitigation, that during the period in which the misconduct took place, Respondent's husband became very ill and subsequently died. The referee's uncontested report and recommendation was approved by the Court on July 9, 2009. *Fla. Bar v. Letwin*, 14 So.3d 243 (Fla.2009).

Given the seriousness of this prior misconduct and Respondent's continuing pattern of misconduct as proven here, we conclude that a one-year suspension is warranted in this case. We have previously imposed rehabilitative suspensions in unethical solicitation cases. See *Fla. Bar v. Wolfe*, 759 So.2d 639 (Fla.2000) (imposing one-year suspension followed by three years' probation where attorney engaged in in-person solicitation of clients in areas damaged by tornado, offering legal services and presenting individuals with pamphlets and prepared contingency fee contracts that did not comply with rules); *Fla. Bar v. Stafford*, 542 So.2d 1321 (Fla.1989) (imposing six-month suspension where attorney engaged in arrangement for solicitation of clients with police officer); *Fla. Bar v. Curry*, 211 So.2d 169 (Fla.1968) (imposing six-month suspension where attorney, who was also an accountant, mailed out approximately 800 letters to individuals for whom he had previously prepared income tax returns soliciting those individuals as legal clients). The over 900 letters sent by Respondent clearly fell under the restrictions of rule 4–7.4 and clearly violated that rule. Although the illness and subsequent death of Respondent's spouse shortly before the letter was sent does constitute significant mitigation, given the clear violation and the seriousness of Respondent's prior misconduct, we conclude that under the specific circumstances of this case, the referee's recommendation is inadequate, and a one-year rehabilitative suspension, followed by three years of probation and attendance at The Florida Bar's Advertising Workshop, is required.

Accordingly, Respondent, Jane Marie Letwin, is hereby suspended from the practice of law for one year. The suspension will be effective thirty days from the filing of this opinion so that Respondent can close out her practice and protect the interests of existing clients. If Respondent notifies this Court in writing that she is no longer practicing and does not need the thirty days to protect existing clients, this Court will enter an order making the suspension effective immediately. Respondent shall fully comply with Rule Regulating the Florida Bar 3–5.1(g). Further, Respondent shall accept no new business from the date this opinion is filed until she is reinstated. As a condition of reinstatement, Respondent shall be required to attend The Florida Bar's Advertising Workshop. Upon reinstatement, Respondent shall be further placed on probation for three years.

Judgment is entered for The Florida Bar, 651 East Jefferson Street, Tallahassee, Florida 32399–2300, for recovery of costs from Jane Marie Letwin in the amount of $2,026.75, for which sum let execution issue.

It is so ordered.

Questions for Discussion

1.   What items did the Court find wrong with the letter? Could she have sent the prospective clients a different letter?

2.   Before you send a letter to a potential client, what should you do?

Jason C. King

CHAPTER 10
MISCONDUCT
RULE 4-8.4

The Rules regarding misconduct, delineated in Rule 4-8.4, are expansive and are birthed from the core of the duties of a lawyer. A lawyer must be honest and trustworthy. Acts committed by the lawyer, even in his or her private life, can raise questions and concerns of that individual's ability to practice law in an honest and trustworthy manner. Many types of illegal conduct reflect adversely on an individual's fitness to practice law. These include crimes involving morality or moral turpitude such as theft, fraud, conspiracy, spousal and child abuse, kidnapping, robbery, rape, and murder. The Rule states as follows:

> A lawyer shall not:
>
> (a) violate or attempt to violate the Rules of Professional Conduct, knowingly assist or induce another to do so, or do so through the acts of another;

(b) commit a criminal act that reflects adversely on the lawyer's honesty, trustworthiness, or fitness as a lawyer in other respects;

(c) engage in conduct involving dishonesty, fraud, deceit, or misrepresentation, except that it shall not be professional misconduct for a lawyer for a criminal law enforcement agency or regulatory agency to advise others about or to supervise another in an undercover investigation, unless prohibited by law or rule, and it shall not be professional misconduct for a lawyer employed in a capacity other than as a lawyer by a criminal law enforcement agency or regulatory agency to participate in an undercover investigation, unless prohibited by law or rule;

(d) engage in conduct in connection with the practice of law that is prejudicial to the administration of justice, including to knowingly, or through callous indifference, disparage, humiliate, or discriminate against litigants, jurors, witnesses, court personnel, or other lawyers on any basis, including, but not limited to, on account of race, ethnicity, gender, religion, national origin, disability, marital status, sexual orientation, age, socioeconomic status, employment, or physical characteristic;

(e) state or imply an ability to influence improperly a government agency or official or to achieve results by means that violate the Rules of Professional Conduct or other law;

(f) knowingly assist a judge or judicial officer in conduct that is a violation of applicable rules of judicial conduct or other law;

(g) fail to respond, in writing, to any official inquiry by bar counsel or a disciplinary agency, as defined elsewhere in these rules, when bar counsel or the agency is conducting an investigation into the lawyer's conduct. A written response shall be made:

(1) within 15 days of the date of the initial written investigative inquiry by bar counsel, grievance committee, or board of governors;

(2) within 10 days of the date of any follow-up written investigative inquiries by bar counsel, grievance committee, or board of governors;

(3) within the time stated in any subpoena issued under these Rules Regulating The Florida Bar (without additional time allowed for mailing);

(4) as provided in the Florida Rules of Civil Procedure or order of the referee in matters assigned to a referee; and

(5) as provided in the Florida Rules of Appellate Procedure or order of the Supreme Court of Florida for matters pending action by that court.

Except as stated otherwise herein or in the applicable rules, all times for response shall be calculated as provided elsewhere in these Rules Regulating The Florida Bar and may be extended or shortened by bar counsel or the disciplinary agency making the official inquiry upon good cause shown.

Failure to respond to an official inquiry with no good cause shown may be a matter of contempt and processed in accordance with rule 3-7.11(f) of these Rules Regulating The Florida Bar.

(h) willfully refuse, as determined by a court of competent jurisdiction, to timely pay a child support obligation; or

(i) engage in sexual conduct with a client or a representative of a client that exploits or adversely affects the interests of the client or the lawyer-client relationship.

If the sexual conduct commenced after the lawyer-client relationship was formed it shall be presumed that the sexual conduct exploits or adversely affects the interests of the client or the lawyer-client relationship.

A lawyer may rebut this presumption by proving by a preponderance of the evidence that the sexual conduct did not exploit or adversely affect the interests of the client or the lawyer-client relationship.

The prohibition and presumption stated in this rule do not apply to a lawyer in the same firm as another lawyer representing the client if the lawyer involved in the sexual conduct does not personally provide legal services to the client and is screened from access to the file concerning the legal representation.

In the consolidated case of *The Florida Bar v. Winters*, 104 So. 3d 299 (Fla. 2012) the Court suspended the partners of Winters & Yonker, P.A., William Winters and Marc Yonker, for their conduct in their secret plans of leaving their former employer, the Law Firm of Mulholland & Associates, to start their own law firm. The Referee found that, among other things, the two had lied to Mulholland, taken files from Mulholland's office, contacted current clients of Mulholland, and had a paralegal in Mulholland's office assist them in the deception. The Referee recommended an admonishment. The Court disagreed and suspended Winters for 91 days and Yonker for 60 days. The Court opined that "Winters' and Yonker's conduct in appropriating client files from their employer for their own personal use constitutes theft" and that "theft inherently reflects adversely on a lawyer's honesty, trustworthiness, or fitness as a lawyer" *Id* at 301.

In *The Florida Bar v. Berthiaume*, 78 So. 3d 503 (Fla. 2011), the Court suspended a lawyer for 91 days for violating Rule 4-8.4 when she signed and served by United States mail a document entitled "Subpoena Duces Tecum" on a bank attempting to secure bank records of her client who had written her bad checks. The Court recognized the deceptive activity of issuing an invalid Subpoena and held that it did rise to the level of intentional misrepresentation and a violation of the Rule.

The Court went on to state that "basic, fundamental dishonesty ... is a serious flaw, which cannot be tolerated [because] '[d]ishonesty and a lack of candor cannot be tolerated by a profession that relies on the truthfulness of its members." *Id* at 510, citing *The Florida Bar v. Rotstein*, 835 So.2d 241, 246 (Fla.2002) (quoting *The Florida Bar v. Korones*, 752 So.2d 586, 591 (Fla.2000)); see also *The Florida Bar v. Head*, 27 So.3d 1 (Fla.2010). The Court further stated that Berthiaume "engaged in serious misconduct—she abused the subpoena power, which is a power of the court, for her personal investigation. Such dishonest conduct demonstrates the utmost disrespect for the court and is destructive to the legal system as a whole." *Berthiaume* at 510.

The Florida Bar v. Winters, 104 So. 3d 299 (Fla. 2012)

....

FACTS

On July 9, 2010, The Florida Bar filed separate complaints against William Henry Winters and Marc Edward Yonker. The complaints alleged various instances of misconduct by Winters and Yonker in relation to their departure as employees from the Law Firm of Richard Mulholland and Associates ("Mulholland Firm"). Essentially, the complaints alleged that in 2001, Winters and Yonker made secret plans to leave the Mulholland Firm and begin practicing together, and that in the process, Winters and Yonker: (1) themselves and through a former paralegal for the Mulholland Firm, solicited Mulholland Firm clients to terminate representation by the Mulholland Firm and be represented by Winters' and Yonker's new firm;

(2) made misrepresentations to the Mulholland Firm and to Mulholland Firm clients; (3) made copies of and took possession of Mulholland Firm client files without authorization; and (4) improperly used a third attorney's name, who never actually joined the new firm, in their new firm name on documents. The complaints alleged that through this conduct, Respondents violated numerous Rules Regulating the Florida Bar.

The two cases were consolidated at the referee level, and on July 20, 2011, the referee filed his report and recommendation. The referee found that during the time that Winters and Yonker were considering their exit from the Mulholland Firm, Winters had discussions with a third attorney about forming a new firm. Based on the ongoing discussions, letterhead was generated that included the third attorney's name. When the attorney realized his name had been included, he promptly notified Winters that he was not interested in becoming part of the law firm and that the letterhead should no longer be used. However, the letterhead was used for a short period of time thereafter.

The referee further found that when Winters and Yonker decided to leave the Mulholland Firm they "began contacting clients who they had represented during the course of their employment with the Mulholland law firm." He further found that Respondent Yonker took client files from the Mulholland Firm over a lunch period and had information from those files copied for his own personal use, and that such "was not within the scope of his employment and was not done for advancing the good of the law firm," and that Respondent Winters "maintained control over less than ten files" after leaving the law firm, and that those files were recovered within a few days by the law firm. The referee recommended that Winters and Yonker be found guilty of violating rule 4–7.10(f) (lawyers may state or imply that they practice in a partnership or authorized business entity only when that is the fact), due to the improper inclusion of the third attorney's name on the new firm letterhead for a short period of time, and rule 3–4.3 (misconduct and minor misconduct—conduct not otherwise enumerated), due to their personal use of the files of the Mulholland Firm. The referee recommended that Respondents be found not guilty of all other charged rule violations.

The Bar filed a petition seeking review of the referee's recommendations that Winters and Yonker be found not guilty of violating rules 4–8.4(b) (commission of a criminal act reflecting adversely on lawyer's honesty, trustworthiness, or fitness as a lawyer in other respects), 4–8.4(c) (conduct involving dishonesty, fraud, deceit, or misrepresentation); and 4–8.4(d) (conduct prejudicial to administration of justice), and the referee's recommended discipline.

ANALYSIS

I. RECOMMENDATIONS OF GUILT

The standard of review for a referee's recommendations as to guilt is whether the referee's factual findings are sufficient under the applicable rules to support the recommendations as to guilt. See *Fla. Bar v. D'Ambrosio*, 25 So.3d 1209, 1216 (Fla.2009); *Fla. Bar v. Shoureas*, 913 So.2d 554, 557–58 (Fla.2005). Here, the Bar first argues that the referee erred in recommending that Winters and Yonker be found not guilty of violating rule 4–8.4(b). The Bar argues that Winters' and Yonker's "personal use" of the Mulholland Firm's client files constituted acts of criminal theft under section 812.014, Florida Statutes (2001), and that theft inherently reflects adversely on a lawyer's honesty, trustworthiness, or fitness as a lawyer. We agree. At the time of the misconduct here, as now, criminal theft was defined as knowingly obtaining or using the property of another with intent to temporarily or permanently: (a) deprive the other person of a right to or benefit from the property; (b) appropriate the property to one's own use or the use of another person not entitled to use the property. § 812.014(1), Fla. Stat. (2001). Winters' and Yonker's conduct in appropriating client files from their employer for their own personal use constitutes theft. The referee's factual findings do not support the recommendation that Respondents be found not guilty of violating rule 4–8.4(b). Accordingly, this recommendation is disapproved.

The Bar next argues that Winters' and Yonker's conduct with regard to the client files constituted conduct involving dishonesty, fraud, deceit, or misrepresentation in violation of rule 4–8.4(c). In support of its argument, the Bar cites to the Court's decision in Florida Bar v. Shankman, 908 So.2d 379 (Fla.2005). In Shankman, the respondent, a partner in a firm, was found guilty of, among many other rule violations, violating rule 4–8.4(c) for (1) failing to disclose to the firm and keeping for himself a bonus from a client, over and above the reduced fee that he caused the firm to accept in the case; (2) failing to inform the firm of an unemployment benefits client's potential whistleblower action, directing that the client's case be closed out, and proceeding to represent the client and settle the whistleblower action after he left the firm; and (3) taking five other clients without the firm's knowledge by omitting them from the list of clients he took. Id. at 383. We conclude that, similar to the conduct in Shankman, Winters' and Yonker's conduct in copying client files and maintaining possession of client files without the Mulholland Firm's permission violated rule 4–8.4(c). Accordingly, the referee's recommendation as to this issue is disapproved.

The Bar next argues that the same conduct that violated rules 4–8.4(b) and (c) also violated rule 4–8.4(d). Rule 4–8.4(d) states, in pertinent part, that a lawyer "shall not engage in conduct in connection with the practice of law that is prejudicial to the administration of justice." R. Regulating Fla. Bar 4–8.4(d). The Bar argues that because Respondents' conduct was dishonest, it was inherently prejudicial to the administration of justice in violation of this rule. We agree. Although the Court has held that this rule "applies only when a lawyer engages in misconduct while employed in a legal capacity," *Fla. Bar v. Brake*, 767 So.2d 1163, 1168 (Fla.2000) (emphasis added), we conclude that because Respondents' misconduct in this case occurred in their capacities as associate attorneys of the Mulholland Firm, it was sufficiently "in connection with the practice of law" to be covered by this rule. Accordingly, we disapprove the referee's recommendation that Respondents be found not guilty of violating rule 4–8.4(d).

II. DISCIPLINE

The standard of review for a referee's recommendation as to discipline is as follows:

> In reviewing a referee's recommended discipline, the Court's scope of review is broader than that afforded to the referee's findings of fact because, ultimately, it is our responsibility to order the appropriate sanction. See *Fla. Bar v. Anderson*, 538 So.2d 852, 854 (Fla.1989); see also art. V, 15, Fla. Const. However, generally speaking this Court will not second-guess the referee's recommended discipline as long as it has a reasonable basis in existing caselaw and the Standards for Imposing Lawyer Sanctions. See *Fla. Bar v. Temmer*, 753 So.2d 555, 558 (Fla.1999).

Fla. Bar v. Ratiner, 46 So.3d 35, 39 (Fla.2010). Here, the referee recommended that Respondents be found guilty of violating only rule 4–7.10(f) and rule 3–4.3 and as a sanction, recommended that Respondents be admonished.

As explained above, we conclude that Respondents' misconduct also violated rules 4–8.4(b), 4–8.4(c), and 4–8.4(d). When these additional rule violations are considered, it is clear that the referee's recommendation of an admonishment is not supported.

We conclude that under the caselaw and standards, the appropriate sanction for Respondent Winters is a ninety-one-day suspension, and the appropriate sanction for Respondent Yonker is a sixty-day suspension. Standards for Imposing Lawyer Sanctions 5.12 and 7.2 provide, respectively, that suspension is appropriate "when a lawyer knowingly engages in criminal conduct ... that seriously adversely reflects on the lawyer's fitness to practice law" or "when a lawyer knowingly engages in conduct that is a violation of a duty owed as a professional and causes injury or potential injury to a client, the public, or the legal system." See also *Shankman*, 908 So.2d at 387 (imposing ninety-one-day suspension where attorney received bonus from client after causing firm to accept reduced fee, failed to disclose bonus to his partners in law firm, failed to make full disclosure to partners regarding clients he took to another law firm, divided fees with nonlawyers, and failed to timely file response to summary judgment motion); *Fla. Bar v. Kossow*, 912 So.2d 544, 548 (Fla.2005) (imposing thirty-day suspension where attorney represented clients outside of firm where he was employed and kept fees for himself, lied about his activities, and used firm resources in his representation of outside clients); *Fla. Bar v. Arcia*, 848 So.2d 296, 300 (Fla.2003) (imposing three-year suspension where attorney represented clients outside of firm where he was employed and kept fees for himself in violation of his employment agreement, solicited clients or potential clients by intercepting phone calls directed to firm, deposited fees from firm clients into separate account for his own professional association, intercepted firm mail in order to take checks made to his own professional association, induced firm clients to pay fees directly to him and his own professional association by preparing misleading documents and stationery, and used firm resources during office hours to conduct his fraudulent activities); *Fla. Bar v. Cox*, 655 So.2d 1122, 1123 (Fla.1995) (imposing thirty-day suspension where attorney represented clients outside of firm where he was employed and kept some of the fees for himself, corresponded with and billed outside clients on firm stationery, and initially lied about his activities when confronted).

CONCLUSION

Accordingly, William Henry Winters is hereby suspended from the practice of law for ninety-one days. Marc Edward Yonker is suspended from the practice of law for sixty days. The suspensions will be effective thirty days from the filing of this opinion so that Respondents can close out their practice and protect the interests of existing clients. If either Respondent notifies this Court in writing that he is no longer practicing and does not need the thirty days to protect existing clients, this Court will enter an order making his suspension effective immediately. Respondents shall fully comply with Rule Regulating the Florida Bar 3–5.1(h). Respondent Winters shall accept no new business from the date this opinion is filed until he is reinstated. Respondent Yonker shall accept no new business from the date this opinion is filed until his suspension is completed.

Judgment is entered for The Florida Bar, 651 East Jefferson Street, Tallahassee, Florida 32399–2300, for recovery of costs from William Henry Winters and Marc Edward Yonker, jointly and severally, in the amount of $24,750.00, for which sum let execution issue.

It is so ordered.

Questions for Discussion

1.   If Winters wanted to leave to start his own firm, what was the proper course of conduct?

2.   Why would they have continued to use the third attorney's name on the letterhead after he informed them he was not joining? Do you think the third attorney had relationships with clients they wanted?

3.   Why do you think the two lawyers didn't receive the same discipline?

The Florida Bar v. Berthiaume, 78 So. 3d 503 (Fla. 2011)

. . . .

FACTS

The Florida Bar filed a disciplinary complaint alleging that Respondent Berthiaume violated the Rules Regulating the Florida Bar by serving a fraudulent subpoena on a bank. A referee was appointed. After holding hearings, in which the referee considered testimony and evidence, the referee submitted a report to the Court with the following findings and recommendations.

On September 25, 2004, Respondent signed and served by United States mail a document entitled "Subpoena Duces Tecum" on Pelican Bank. The purported subpoena directed the bank to produce the records of Respondent's client, specifically seeking information regarding checks that the client had written to Respondent from the client's account at the bank. Previously, the bank had not honored the checks. The fraudulent subpoena stated: "If you fail to produce these records and the above requested information as described, you may be held in contempt of court, punishable by a fine or incarceration or both." There was no pending case and the purported subpoena was not authorized by law. The bank refused to honor the false subpoena, and a lawyer for the Bank filed a Bar complaint regarding Respondent's conduct.

The referee found by clear and convincing evidence that Respondent was responsible for the language in the fraudulent subpoena, including the language threatening incarceration and contempt. Respondent designed the purposefully misleading subpoena to cause the bank to produce the records, even though she did not have any legal authority for the subpoena. Further, Respondent knowingly and deliberately sent the false subpoena.

Based on these factual findings, the referee recommended finding Respondent guilty of violating Rule Regulating the Florida Bar 4–8.4(d) (a lawyer shall not engage in conduct in connection with the practice of law that is prejudicial to the administration of justice). The referee accurately noted that all members of the legal profession must conduct themselves responsibly and professionally to preserve the integrity of our system. As the referee stated, it is unacceptable for a member of The Florida Bar to knowingly and deliberately utilize a fraudulent subpoena to threaten a third party with incarceration or mislead them to produce documents.

The referee recommended that Respondent be found not guilty of the alleged violations of rules 4–4.1 (in the course of representing a client, a lawyer shall not knowingly make a false statement of material fact or law to a third person), 4–4.4 (in representing a client, a lawyer shall not use means that have no substantial purpose other than to embarrass, delay, or burden a third person or knowingly use methods of obtaining evidence that violate the legal rights of such a person), and 4–8.4(c) (a lawyer shall not engage in conduct involving dishonesty, fraud, deceit, or misrepresentation).

In recommending a sanction, the referee relied on Florida Standards for Imposing Lawyer Sanctions 6.22, "Abuse of the Legal Process" (suspension is appropriate when a lawyer knowingly violates a court order or rule, and causes injury or potential injury to a client or a party, or causes interference or potential interference with a legal proceeding), and 7.2, "Violations of Other Duties Owed as a Professional" (suspension is appropriate when a lawyer knowingly engages in conduct that is a violation of a duty owed as a professional and causes injury or potential injury to a client, the public, or the legal system).

The referee did not find any factors in aggravation. With regard to mitigating factors, the referee found Florida Standards for Imposing Lawyer Sanctions 9.32(a) (absence of a prior disciplinary record), 9.32(f) (inexperience in the practice of law), 9.32(g) (character or reputation), and 9.32(j) (interim rehabilitation). In addition, the referee noted that Respondent has provided pro bono representation to disadvantaged individuals through Florida Rural Legal Services. The referee stated that if Respondent did not have the mitigating factor of pro bono service, the recommended sanction would have been more severe. Further, subsequent to the misconduct, Respondent twice submitted to a voluntary LOMAS review. She also participated in the Professionalism Workshop and Ethics School courses.

The referee recommended the sanction of a ten-day suspension and awarded costs to the Bar in the amount of $13,528.92. The Bar sought review of the referee's report. The Bar challenges the referee's recommendations that Respondent be found not guilty of violating rule 4–8.4(c) and that a ten-day suspension is the appropriate sanction. Respondent filed a cross-petition challenging the referee's report. Respondent asserts that various rulings by the referee prevented her from presenting her case in defense and that the appropriate sanction is a public reprimand.

ANALYSIS

I. Respondent Asserts that the Referee Erred by Ruling Against Respondent on Several Issues, Which Prevented Respondent From Presenting Her Case.

As for the first issue on review, Respondent claims that the referee erred by ruling against Respondent's requests to depose witnesses and introduce evidence allegedly showing that the Bar failed to abide by the Rules Regulating the Florida Bar. Respondent argues that the rulings prohibited her from mounting a proper defense in the disciplinary proceeding.

Respondent's fundamental argument is that the referee did not permit her to take certain depositions. Pursuant to Rule Regulating the Florida Bar 3–7.6(f)(2), "[d]iscovery shall be available to the parties in accordance with the Florida Rules of Civil Procedure." In civil cases and in Bar disciplinary cases, trial courts' and referees' decisions regarding discovery are discretionary and are only reviewed for an abuse of discretion. See *Fla. Bar v. Lobasz*, 64 So.3d 1167, 1171 (Fla.2011); *Vega v. CSCS Int'l, N.V.*, 795 So.2d 164, 167 (Fla. 3d DCA 2001). In this case, the record shows that the referee did not abuse her discretion when she decided not to allow Respondent to take the depositions.

The referee repeatedly allowed Respondent to present her argument that the Bar engaged in misconduct. The referee considered Respondent's repetitious allegations, even when the same arguments were presented in different forms (i.e., a motion to dismiss, an amended motion for affirmative defenses). The mere fact that the referee ruled against Respondent does not demonstrate that the referee erred or prohibited Respondent from presenting a defense. In fact, the record shows just the opposite—the referee permitted Respondent to repeatedly present these arguments. In her report, the referee discussed the issues and even stated that "this has been a lengthy prosecution" and that a "large amount of time was spent in this proceeding dealing with multiple challenges by Respondent to the authority of The Florida Bar to prosecute Respondent." Report of Referee at 12. Thus, Respondent was not prevented from presenting a defense before the referee.

Next, Respondent continues to assert that in a previous proceeding, the Bar's Designated Reviewer had a conflict of interest and should not have been permitted to present the investigation to the initial grievance committee and the Board of Governors. However, Respondent's current argument is meritless. In that initial case, the parties agreed to a dismissal without prejudice. As that case was jointly dismissed by the Bar and

Respondent, and thereafter a different grievance committee considered the investigation, Respondent has already been provided with the appropriate relief. Any possible taint or bias that might have created a conflict during the first proceeding was removed. In addition, as Respondent made these arguments before the referee, she was not prevented from presenting her defense.

Further, the Bar served its complaint in the initial case against Respondent in February 2007. This is the case that was dismissed without prejudice "so that a new grievance committee could be assigned the case for a new, taint free investigation." Report of Referee at 12. Despite Respondent's current assertions, the Bar was specifically authorized to bring a second case against Respondent. The Bar did not violate the Rules Regulating the Florida Bar by bringing another case, in September 2008, against Respondent that included new allegations of misconduct. As Respondent had agreed that the first case could be dismissed without prejudice, she is mischaracterizing the history of the proceedings by claiming that the Bar was not authorized to bring the second case. Also, Respondent made these arguments before the referee, so her instant claim that she was prevented from presenting a defense is without merit.

In addition, Respondent asserts that a question by a member of the second grievance committee, Andrew Epstein, showed bias and prejudice that warranted the recusal of the entire grievance committee. Epstein had asked a witness about the nature of her relationship with Respondent, stating that his inquiry went to the issue of the witness's possible bias. Respondent has repeatedly raised this allegation of bias and prejudice. She sought to have Epstein recuse himself. He did not. She asked the second grievance committee to be recused. It did not. The chair of the grievance committee did not grant her additional request for recusal. Before the referee, Respondent raised this claim again, moving to dismiss the Bar's complaint, arguing that the grievance committee and Epstein should have recused themselves. The referee denied her motion. She then recast these arguments in the form of an Answer and Affirmative Defenses, raising the issue as a defense that the Bar engaged in misconduct. The referee considered her various arguments and ruled on them. Thereafter, Respondent filed a motion to amend her affirmative defenses, which the referee denied. Despite the referee's repeated consideration and rulings on this very issue, Respondent then sought to depose certain people, including Epstein. The referee ruled against Respondent and did not permit her to conduct the depositions. Courts have authority to control discovery in all aspects in order to prevent harassment and undue invasion of privacy. *S. Fla. Blood Service, Inc. v. Rasmussen*, 467 So.2d 798 (Fla. 3d DCA 1985), approved, 500

So.2d 533 (Fla.1987). The record clearly shows that the referee allowed Respondent to present her arguments repeatedly. The record suggests that the referee denied Respondent's request to take the depositions in order to control the case and move forward.

Accordingly, for the above reasons, we conclude that the referee did not engage in an abuse of discretion by denying Respondent's request to take the depositions. We further conclude that Respondent was not prevented from presenting a defense in the proceedings.

> II.   Whether Respondent Should be Found Guilty of Violating Rule 4–8.4(c).

As for the second issue, the Bar challenges the referee's recommendation that Respondent be found not guilty of violating rule 4–8.4(c) (a lawyer shall not engage in conduct involving dishonesty, fraud, deceit, or misrepresentation). The Bar asserts that the referee should have recommended finding Respondent guilty of violating rule 4–8.4(c) because she knowingly sent an unauthorized subpoena to the bank that was clearly misleading and designed to obtain the bank's records of a client.

The referee found that Respondent sent a document titled "Subpoena Duces Tecum" to the bank. The document directed the bank to produce the financial records of Respondent's client, even though Respondent did not have authority to request the records. Respondent asserts that she made a mistake and that the document was not intended to look like a subpoena. However, the document plainly stated: "If you fail to produce these records and the above requested information as described, you may be held in contempt of court, punishable by a fine or incarceration or both." It also contained the phrase "civil action." The referee stated:

> I find by clear and convincing evidence that Respondent is responsible for including language threatening incarceration and contempt in the purported subpoena which was clearly designed to cause the Bank to produce the records without legal authority. The language in the purported subpoena was clearly misleading. Respondent knowingly and deliberately sent the purported subpoena with the offending language. (Emphasis added.)

Report of Referee at 3. Respondent signed this fraudulent subpoena when she knew that she did not have a case pending against her client.

Although the referee made these factual findings, she recommended that

Respondent be found not guilty of violating rule 4– 8.4(c) (a lawyer shall not engage in conduct involving dishonesty, fraud, deceit, or misrepresentation). Respondent argues that the referee is supported in recommending that she is not guilty because the Bar did not prove that Respondent engaged in fraud. This argument is misguided because there is no requirement that fraud must be proven to show that a respondent violated the rule. In fact, conduct involving any element, such as dishonesty, deceit, or misrepresentation, can result in a violation of rule 4–8.4(c).

In *Florida Bar v. Forrester*, 818 So.2d 477, 481 (Fla.2002), the Court approved the referee's recommended finding of a violation of rule 4–8.4(c) for a respondent who had engaged in misrepresentation but not fraud. During a deposition, Forrester made an intentional misrepresentation concerning the location of an exhibit when asked whether she had it. Although Forrester accurately replied, "I'm not seeing it," Forrester's answer was intentionally misleading because she knew the document was located by her briefcase and she deliberately failed to disclose that information to opposing counsel. Forrester engaged in an intentional misrepresentation, not fraud, and was found guilty of violating rule 4–8.4(c).

Similarly, in *Florida Bar v. Nicnick*, 963 So.2d 219, 223–24 (Fla.2007), Nicnick deliberately and knowingly concealed a signed settlement agreement (involving child support arrearages) from opposing counsel. Nicnick's misconduct was intentional, and his failure to share the purported settlement agreement with opposing counsel constituted a deceitful act. By its very nature, the act of omission demonstrated by concealing a relevant document is deceptive. As in Forrester, the Court in Nicnick did not refer to fraud. In Nicnick, the Court spoke of deception, 963 So.2d at 224, and approved the referee's recommendation that Nicnick be found guilty of violating rule 4–8.4(c).

Although the Bar did not seek to prove that Respondent engaged in fraud, the facts, record, and case law show that Respondent is guilty of violating rule 4–8.4(c) due to her intentional misrepresentation and deceitful conduct. See, e.g., *Fla. Bar v. Miller*, 863 So.2d 231 (Fla.2003) (finding respondent violated rule 4–8.4(c) by deliberately concealing that he was aware of the existence of the Equal Employment Opportunity Commission's first notice of client's right to sue, where the respondent's intentional failure to disclose a crucial piece of evidence was not treated as "fraud"). Respondent engaged in deceit and misrepresentation by deliberately crafting and mailing the fraudulent subpoena that was "clearly designed to cause the bank to produce the records without legal authority." Report of Referee at 3.

The Court has repeatedly stated that the referee's factual findings must be sufficient under the applicable rules to support the recommendations as to guilt. See Fla. Bar v. Shoureas, 913 So.2d 554, 557–58 (Fla.2005). In this case, the referee's factual findings do not support the recommendation of not guilty. Accordingly, we disapprove the referee's recommendation that Respondent be found not guilty of violating rule 4–8.4(c). Because the record and the referee's findings show that Respondent "knowingly and deliberately sent the purported subpoena with the offending language," which was "clearly designed to cause the bank to produce the records without legal authority," and thus "clearly misleading" (Report of Referee at 3), we find Respondent guilty of violating rule 4–8.4(c).

III.   Whether the Referee's Recommended Discipline Should be Approved.

As for the third issue, The Florida Bar challenges the referee's recommended sanction of a ten-day suspension, arguing that the appropriate sanction is a ninety-one-day suspension. In reviewing a referee's recommended discipline, this Court's scope of review is broader than that afforded to the referee's findings of fact because, ultimately, it is the Court's responsibility to order the appropriate sanction. *Fla. Bar v. Anderson*, 538 So.2d 852, 854 (Fla.1989); see also art. V, § 15, Fla. Const. However, generally speaking this Court will not second-guess the referee's recommended discipline as long as it has a reasonable basis in existing case law and the Florida Standards for Imposing Lawyer Sanctions. *Fla. Bar v. Temmer*, 753 So.2d 555, 558 (Fla.1999).

On review, we find Respondent guilty of violating rule 4–8.4(c). In addition, we approve the referee's recommendation that she be found guilty of violating rule 4–8.4(d). In considering violations of rules 4–8.4(c) and 4–8.4(d), we have explicitly stated that "basic, fundamental dishonesty ... is a serious flaw, which cannot be tolerated [because] '[d]ishonesty and a lack of candor cannot be tolerated by a profession that relies on the truthfulness of its members.' " *Fla. Bar v. Rotstein*, 835 So.2d 241, 246 (Fla.2002) (quoting *Fla. Bar v. Korones*, 752 So.2d 586, 591 (Fla.2000)); see also *Fla. Bar v. Head*, 27 So.3d 1 (Fla.2010). Respondent has engaged in serious misconduct—she abused the subpoena power, which is a power of the court, for her personal investigation. Such dishonest conduct demonstrates the utmost disrespect for the court and is destructive to the legal system as a whole.

In Forrester, discussed above, Forrester engaged in misrepresentation and was guilty of violating rule 4–8.4(c). Thus, her misdeeds and Respondent's misconduct are similar. Forrester knowingly and intentionally removed and concealed a document for a period of time during a deposition. Although Forrester was given more than one opportunity to return the document, she did not do so until she was confronted by opposing counsel. The Court imposed a sixty-day suspension, followed by one year of probation. By comparison, Respondent's misconduct is significantly more serious than Forrester's behavior. Respondent abused the subpoena power for her personal it would provide her with the financial records of her client, when she had no authority to seek this confidential information. Because Respondent's misconduct is more egregious than Forrester's, she merits a more substantial sanction than Forrester's sixty-day suspension.

In Nicnick, discussed above, Nicnick was guilty of violating rule 4–8.4(c) for deliberately and knowingly concealing a signed settlement agreement from opposing counsel. The Court imposed a ninety-one-day suspension. Respondent's misconduct is as serious as Nicnick's concealment of a document. Respondent created and mailed a fraudulent subpoena to the bank. A subpoena is backed by the authority of the court to enforce the commands of the subpoena. Courts enforce lawful subpoenas through their contempt powers. Creating a false subpoena commanding compliance usurps the judicial prerogative and violates the sanctity of court proceedings. Respondent's misrepresentation and deceit, which violated rules 4–8.4(c) and 4–8.4(d), warrant the same sanction imposed in Nicnick, a ninety-one-day suspension.

We find that the referee's recommended sanction of a ten-day suspension does not have a reasonable basis in existing case law. See Nicnick; Forrester. We disapprove the recommended sanction and, based on case law, conclude that a ninety-one- day suspension is the appropriate sanction.

CONCLUSION

Accordingly, we approve the referee's findings of fact and award of costs. We disapprove the referee's recommendation that Respondent be found not guilty of violating rule 4–8.4(c). We find Respondent guilty of violating rule 4–8.4(c). We approve the referee's other recommendations as to guilt. Further, we disapprove the referee's recommendation of a ten-day suspension. Michelle Erin Berthiaume is hereby suspended from the practice of law for ninety-one days. The suspension will be effective thirty days from the filing of this opinion so that Berthiaume can close out her practice and protect the interests of existing clients. If Berthiaume notifies this Court in writing that she is no longer practicing and does not need the thirty days to protect existing clients, this Court will enter an order making the suspension effective immediately. Michelle Erin Berthiaume shall fully comply with Rule Regulating the Florida Bar 3–5.1(g). Further, Berthiaume shall accept no new business from the date this opinion is filed until she is reinstated.

Judgment is entered for The Florida Bar, 651 East Jefferson Street, Tallahassee, Florida 32399–2300, for recovery of costs from Michelle Erin Berthiaume in the amount of $13,528.92, for which sum let execution issue.

It is so ordered.

Questions for Discussion

1.   Would it have been a difference result if the Subpoena did not threaten incarceration or contempt? Why? Why not?

2.   What should Berthiaume have done if her client bounced checks to pay her retainer fee?

CHAPTER 11
CANDOR TOWARD TRIBUNAL
RULE 4-3.3

Rule 4-3.3 governs lawyer conduct before the tribunal. A tribunal is not simply a matter before a judge in the courtroom. The term is much more broad. The Rule defines a tribunal as: "a court, an arbitrator in a binding arbitration proceeding, or a legislative body, administrative agency, or other body acting in an adjudicative capacity."

A lawyer may not make a "false statement of fact or law to a tribunal or fail to correct a false statement of material fact or law previously made to the tribunal by the lawyer."

Furthermore, the Rule requires the Lawyer to disclose a "material fact to a tribunal when disclosure is necessary to avoid assisting a criminal or fraudulent act by the client." The lawyer must also refuse to offer evidence "the lawyer knows is false," including testimony.

If a witness called by the lawyer, including the client, has "offered material evidence and the lawyer comes to know of its falsity, the lawyer shall take reasonable remedial measures including, if necessary, disclosure to the tribunal."

Finally, the Rule also requires the lawyer disclose legal authority "in the controlling jurisdiction" adverse to the client's position. Comments of the Rule explain that "[a] lawyer is not required to make a disinterested exposition of the law, but must recognize the existence of pertinent legal authorities." The Rule balances advocacy with honesty and fairness. A lawyer is not permitted to trick the trier of fact simply for the benefit of his client.

In *The Florida Bar v. Germain*, 957 So.2d 613 (Fla., 2007) the lawyer had become part owner in a building and shared space with another lawyer. After a dispute, Germain filed several pleadings in various injunction cases alleging his building partner, the other lawyer, had a loaded gun and that he was a convicted felon. He later signed an affidavit stating that he remembered the gun had been removed several years before.

In several court filings, Germain called the neighboring lawyer a "felon" and "cunning." He went as far as accusing him of killing an elderly woman. In a consolidated Bar complaint, Germain was before the Bar for being held in contempt for continuing to interrupt the judge and was cited for two counts of direct criminal contempt.

Based on the egregious conduct of Germain, the Court suspended him from the practice of law for a period of one year and before he may be permitted to apply for readmission, he must be evaluated by a mental health professional and follow the treatment plan suggested.

The Florida Bar v. Germain, 957 So.2d 613 (Fla. 2007)

FACTUAL BACKGROUND

This case arose from a dispute between Germain and Michael C. Norvell concerning ownership of a building called the Lake Law Center (the building) and the employment of James Cardona, who was a paralegal first for Germain and then for Norvell. In November 2002, Germain executed a promissory note for $100,000 for Norvell in exchange for a one-third ownership of the building, where Germain and Norvell operated separate law firms. In April 2003, Norvell offered to purchase Germain's interest for $100,000. Germain rejected the offer.

In March 2004, Germain fired Cardona, his paralegal. The following month, Norvell increased his offer for Germain's interest in the building to $140,000. He also offered, in writing, to sell his two-thirds share to Germain for $280,000. Germain tentatively accepted the offer to purchase Norvell's interest, but was unable to obtain financing.

That same month, on April 17, Germain filed a police report alleging that Norvell had physically attacked him. The officer reported seeing a "large contusion on Mr. Germain's arm along with several slight abrasions." On April 19, Norvell entered one of the offices in the building, removed Germain's files, and sat behind the desk and in front of the computer. Germain and Norvell disputed ownership of that office. That same day, Cardona reported to work at the building, as Norvell had hired him. Cardona and Germain argued. Germain physically escorted Cardona off the premises.

The next day, April 20, Germain delivered a "no trespass" warning to Cardona's mother. Germain placed a lock on the door to the disputed office and placed a no-trespass warning on the door. The following day, Norvell removed the door from its hinges and entered the office. Germain called the police, who responded. Germain accused Cardona of trespassing even though he knew Cardona had Norvell's permission to be there and that Norvell owned two-thirds of the building. Germain then filed against

Norvell a Petition for Injunction for Protection against Repeat Violence (Norvell Petition). In it, Germain swore that Norvell had a "hand gun with ammunition in our office." The court entered a temporary injunction against Norvell.

Germain also filed against Cardona a Petition for Injunction for Protection against Repeat Violence (Cardona Petition). In it, Germain alleged that "Cardona is stalking me and is trying to sabotage my law practice." The petition did not allege any acts of violence or repeat violence by Cardona, as those terms are defined in section 784.046(4)(a)-(b), Florida Statutes (2004), rendering the petition meritless. Cardona responded by filing against Germain a Petition for Injunction for Protection against Repeat Violence (Germain Petition).

A week later Norvell filed a suit for partition of the building and other relief (Partition Action). Germain filed an emergency motion in which he swore that "Norvell is also a convicted felon and Germain has personally observed Norvell handle a loaded pistol in the office."

On June 18, 2004, Germain and Norvell entered into a settlement agreement in the Partition Action. Germain agreed to withdraw the Norvell Petition and to execute an affidavit about the firearm allegation (June 18 Affidavit). The June 18 Affidavit stated: "after some thought, I recall that the pistol was actually in possession of the office paralegal, Rebecca S. Skipper and not Michael C. Norvell." It also stated: "At no time, was the gun ever in Norvell's office or in Norvell's possession" and "[t]hat sometime in 2001 Rebecca S. Skipper removed the gun from the office." Germain signed it under oath.

A few days later, Cardona filed a motion to dismiss the Cardona Petition. The motion also asked the court to award him $30,390 in attorney's fees as a sanction against Germain for filing a frivolous petition. The court held a hearing on the motion. Germain subpoenaed the police officer who took Germain's trespassing complaint, but the court would not allow the officer or Germain to testify. The court did allow Germain to proffer the testimony. The court dismissed the petition, finding that it "does not allege facts supporting an injunction for protection against repeat violence, and the facts proffered by petitioner failed to establish a basis for such an injunction. There was no evidence of violence or imminent fear of violence by respondent toward petitioner."

On July 1, 2004, Norvell paid Germain $140,000 for his one-third share of the building. Two weeks later, the court entered an amended order dismissing the Cardona Petition, denying Germain's motion for reconsideration, and granting Cardona's motion for sanctions. The court found Germain's claims were "so clearly devoid of merit both on the facts and the law as to be completely untenable."

A week later Germain filed a motion to disqualify the judge in the Cardona Petition case. The motion made sworn allegations that the judge should be disqualified, in part, because of a conflict of interest presented by his relationship with Lennon Bowen, an attorney, and Bowen's relationship with Cardona. Two days later he filed a motion for reconsideration of the Cardona Petition's dismissal, arguing the dismissal was improper without an evidentiary hearing. Germain swore the Cardona Petition was not frivolous because "convicted felon Michael C. Norvell's possession of a gun gun [sic] in the office is not frivolous."

Seven months later, in March 2005, Germain again moved the trial court to set aside the order dismissing the Cardona Petition. The motion alleged that the judge who dismissed the petition, who was no longer presiding over the case, had been Chief Assistant State Attorney when Germain sued the State Attorney years before and that the judge, as an assistant state attorney, prosecuted Germain in a contempt proceeding a few years later. According to Germain, Bowen, who had represented Cardona in prior proceedings, was the judge's campaign manager when the judge dismissed the petition. Germain also alleged the judge had solicited a campaign contribution from him while the petition was pending and that the solicitation was "inappropriate, if not illegal." In fact, Bowen was not the judge's campaign manager and never represented Cardona. The solicitation was a mass-mailed invitation to a fund-raising event mailed by a host committee, not the judge.

In several pleadings, in hearings before the trial court and the referee, and in his brief filed in this Court, Germain referred to Norvell as "a convicted felon," "cunning," "devious," and "diabolical." He accused Norvell of killing an elderly client and threatening to kill him. Germain referred to Cardona as "a fugitive" and accused him of trespassing, stalking, and stealing. He described them as "two convicted criminals vouching for each other."

The referee found "that no reasonable person would have feared that Norvell would kill, and that no reasonable person would have had a fear that would justify giving a false statement under oath." He also found the violence between Norvell and Germain had declined over time and that Germain had willingly remained in the space-sharing arrangement with

Norvell.

The second Bar complaint arose from Germain's actions in State v. Guerreo, No. 2004–CF–2140 (Fla. 5th Jud. Cir. Oct. 26, 2004) (order of contempt). Germain represented the defendant in a proceeding in September 2004. During that proceeding, the judge warned Germain that he was going to cite Germain for contempt if he continued to interrupt him. Despite the warning, Germain interrupted twice more. The judge cited him for two counts of direct criminal contempt. After a hearing, the judge found

Germain guilty of two counts of contempt and fined him $100. Germain paid the $100, but filed a motion for reconsideration. The trial judge dismissed the order of contempt, but refused to order the refund of Germain's $100 fine.

RULE VIOLATIONS

The referee concluded that Germain's conduct violated rule 4–3.1 (failing to assert only meritorious claims and contentions), rule 4–3.3(a)(1) (making a false statement of material fact or law to a tribunal), rule 4–3.4(c) (knowingly disobeying an obligation under the rules of a tribunal), 4–3.5(c) (engaging in conduct intended to disrupt tribunal), and rule 4–8.4(d) (engaging in conduct in connection with the practice of law that is prejudicial to the administration of justice) (three counts) of the Rules Regulating the Florida Bar.

The referee found four aggravating factors: (1) previous discipline, including a public reprimand in 1997 for making disparaging remarks in several instances about opposing counsel and a judge and failing to follow the rulings of a trial judge; (2) a pattern of misconduct as established by the earlier misconduct of a similar nature; (3) multiple offenses; and (4) refusal to acknowledge the wrongful nature of his conduct. The referee found three mitigating factors: (1) absence of a dishonest or selfish motive; (2) personal or emotional problems; and (3) physical or mental disability or impairment.

RECOMMENDATION OF DISCIPLINE

The referee recommended a ninety-one-day suspension, followed by one year of probation after reinstatement; an evaluation by a Bar-approved mental health professional and abiding by any recommended treatment or counseling, continuing through the probationary period; and reimbursement of the Bar's costs. The referee relied on Florida Standards for Imposing Lawyer Sanctions 6.12, 6.22, and 8.2, as well as Florida Bar v. Adams, 641 So.2d 399 (Fla.1994).

Germain petitioned for review of the report. He contends the referee erred in excluding evidence of Norvell's alleged exploitation of an elderly client, challenges several of the findings, questions the application of two of the aggravating factors, and argues that the referee erred in failing to find several additional mitigating factors. He also takes issue with the recommendations of a mental health evaluation and ninety-one-day suspension.

ANALYSIS

We first address the exclusion of evidence issue. A referee's admission of evidence is reviewed for abuse of discretion. *Fla. Bar v. Rotstein*, 835 So.2d 241, 244 (Fla.2002). In this case, the referee excluded testimony about Norvell's alleged actions involving an elderly client. Germain argues that this evidence was relevant to whether his fear of Norvell was reasonable and well-grounded, to support his claim that he signed the June 18 Affidavit under duress.

Assuming that Germain's allegations are true, the facts that Norvell unethically made himself a beneficiary under his client's will and then decided to remove her from life support does not tend to prove that he coerced Germain to execute the June 18 Affidavit. The referee did not abuse his discretion in excluding it. See § 90.404(2)(a), Fla. Stat. (2005) (providing that similar fact evidence of other crimes, wrongs, or acts is inadmissible when relevant solely to prove bad character or propensity). Moreover, any error would have been harmless. There is competent, substantial evidence in the record that Germain did not sign the June 18 Affidavit under duress. Germain never advised the court that he had been coerced into signing it. He never sought to have the settlement overturned or set aside. He never filed a police report to the effect that Norvell unlawfully possessed a gun. Germain accused Norvell of having a gun in the office only in civil pleadings and civil hearings. These were not the actions of someone who believed he was in danger. Accordingly, we approve the referee's decision to exclude this evidence.

We next consider the factual findings Germain challenges. The party contending that the referee's findings of fact and conclusions as to guilt are erroneous carries the burden of demonstrating that there is no evidence in the record to support those findings or that the record evidence clearly contradicts the conclusions. *Fla. Bar v. Carlon*, 820 So.2d 891, 898 (Fla.2002). Specifically, Germain challenges the following findings: (1) the Cardona Petition was frivolous; (2) Germain's comments concerning the trial judge, Norvell, and Cardona were inappropriate; (3) Germain misled the police officer by not telling him that Cardona had Norvell's permission to be on the premises of the building; (4) Germain made false statements under oath; (5) Germain was not under duress when he executed the June 18 Affidavit; and (6) Norvell's violence toward Germain had declined over time.

Germain points to contradictory evidence in the record or, presumably, in his proffers, to support his claims of error. He nevertheless fails to meet his burden to demonstrate that there is no evidence in the record to support the referee's findings. The findings are supported in large part by the facts to which Germain stipulated.

In the June 18 Affidavit, Germain stated under oath that Norvell never possessed the gun, the gun was in the possession of a paralegal, and the paralegal had removed the gun from the office in 2001. Yet, both before and after June 18, 2004, Germain filed pleadings alleging that Norvell had a gun in the office. He tries to defend the fact that he lied under oath, either in the June 18 Affidavit or in the pleadings filed before and after it, by claiming that Norvell coerced him to sign the affidavit. The referee found that "no reasonable person" would have been in fear of his life and that "no reasonable person" would have felt compelled to lie under oath.

Germain's failure to advise the court that he signed the affidavit under duress is compelling evidence that he was not coerced into signing it. The assertion of duress has other flaws, however. Accusing Norvell of having possession of a gun in subsequent civil pleadings was inconsistent with his purported fear of Norvell. Further, if the building was worth $700,000, as Germain claimed in his brief, Norvell would not have offered to sell Germain his two-thirds interest for $280,000. For that matter, Germain would have been able to obtain financing for $280,000 if the collateral had been worth over twice that amount.

Germain's points concerning the other disputed factual findings are equally flawed and boil down to credibility assessments. As the referee is in a unique position to assess witness credibility, this Court will not overturn his judgment absent clear and convincing evidence. See, e.g., *Fla. Bar v. Carricarte*, 733 So.2d 975, 978 (Fla.1999). There is no evidence that the referee's judgment is incorrect in this case. Accordingly, we approve these factual findings.

Germain also argues the referee erred in finding the aggravating factor of previous discipline based upon a finding that he had been publicly reprimanded for disparaging remarks about a judge. He also challenges the aggravating factor of refusal to acknowledge the wrongful nature of his conduct. Finally, he faults the referee for failing to find the following mitigating factors: (1) imposition of other penalties or sanctions; (2) remorse; and (3) remoteness of prior offenses.

Like other factual findings, a referee's findings of mitigation and aggravation carry a presumption of correctness and will be upheld unless clearly erroneous or without support in the record. *Fla. Bar v. Arcia*, 848 So.2d 296 (Fla.2003). A referee's failure to find that an aggravating factor or mitigating factor applies is due the same deference. See Fla. Bar v. Morse, 784 So.2d 414, 415–16 (Fla.2001); *Fla. Bar v. Bustamante*, 662 So.2d 687, 687 (Fla.1995); *Fla. Bar v. Hecker*, 475 So.2d 1240, 1242 (Fla.1985). Germain fails to meet his burden.

Competent, substantial evidence supports the referee's findings. As to the mitigating factor that other penalties already have been imposed, Germain paid Cardona $15,000 to settle an attorney's fee award greater than $30,000. Thus, his payment was less than half the amount awarded. Moreover, the Cardona Petition is only a small part of the conduct resulting in discipline. The

$100 fine Germain paid in the criminal contempt-of-court case is also just a small part of this case. In light of all of Germain's misconduct, we cannot say the referee erred in failing to find that the imposition of these penalties or sanctions constituted mitigation.

Similarly, Germain presented little or no evidence of remorse upon which the referee could have based a finding of this mitigating factor. While Germain claims he apologized, both verbally and in writing, to the judge in the criminal contempt-of- court case, there is nothing to suggest he experienced any true remorse for his conduct, other than that his conduct cost him money. It is clear from his arguments that he still considers himself an innocent victim, first of Norvell and Cardona and then of the Bar, and still believes that all of his conduct was appropriate and justified.

The mitigating factor of the remoteness of prior offenses also does not apply. On June 28, 2001, the Court ordered Florida Bar diversion in Case No. SC96944. This case was resolved one year before Germain became embroiled with Norvell as a co-owner of the building and only three years before most of the misconduct at issue here. Four years before the Florida Bar diversion, this Court publicly reprimanded Germain in Case No. SC90589. See *Fla. Bar v. Germain*, 705 So.2d 11 (Fla.1997) (table).

These same facts support the finding of the aggravating factor of previous discipline. In 1997, we publicly reprimanded Germain for making disparaging comments about opposing counsel and failing to comply with a trial court order. (Although the Bar dismissed the charge that he made disparaging comments about opposing counsel and a trial judge, the aggravating factor of previous discipline still applies.) The aggravating factor of previous discipline does not require the previous offense to be of the same nature. Rather, previous discipline for the same kind of misconduct establishes a pattern of misconduct or multiple offenses or increases the weight given to the previous discipline factor.

Germain's argument that he should not be penalized for continuing to assert his innocence in these proceedings is a closer question. The Court has held that "it is improper for a referee to base the severity of a recommended punishment on an attorney's refusal to admit alleged misconduct or on 'lack of remorse' presumed from such refusal." *Fla. Bar v. Lipman*, 497 So.2d 1165, 1168 (Fla.1986); see also *Fla. Bar v. Karten*, 829 So.2d 883, 889–90 (Fla.2002); *Fla. Bar v. Mogil*, 763 So.2d 303, 312 (Fla.2000); *Fla. Bar v. Corbin*, 701 So.2d 334, 337 (Fla.1997).

At first glance, these cases seem to be in conflict with the Court's decision in *Florida Bar v. Gersten*, 707 So.2d 711 (Fla.1998). Upon closer examination, however, we conclude they are not. In Gersten, the respondent continued to refuse to comply with a court order to submit to the taking of his sworn statement after the order had been affirmed on appeal. Whether the respondent had an obligation to comply with the court's order was a legal issue, not a factual one. In Lipman, Karten, Mogil, and Corbin the respondents disputed the factual findings that they had engaged in the conduct giving rise to the rule violations. These were pure findings of fact.

The situation here is like that in Gersten, and unlike the situations in Lipman, Karten, Mogil, and Corbin. Germain has stipulated to most of the facts. He does not dispute that he engaged in the conduct. He nevertheless continues to assert that his actions did not constitute unethical conduct. These are legal issues. With a minimum of legal research, Germain could have discovered that his conduct did constitute unethical conduct and either curtailed his activities or avoided them altogether. Where the issue rests on a legal question, the aggravating factor of failing to acknowledge the wrongfulness of the conduct clearly applies. Accordingly, we approve the referee's findings concerning aggravating and mitigating factors.

Lastly, we address the recommendation of discipline. Germain argues that the recommendation of a mental health evaluation violates due process because he had no notice that his mental health was at issue. He also argues that the recommendation of a ninety-one-day suspension is improper, first, because he engaged in no misconduct and, second, because it is too severe.

In reviewing a referee's recommended discipline, this Court's scope of review is broader than that afforded to the referee's findings of fact because it is ultimately the Court's responsibility to order the appropriate sanction. *Fla. Bar v. Miller*, 863 So.2d 231, 235 (Fla.2003); *Fla. Bar v. Anderson*, 538 So.2d 852, 854 (Fla.1989); see also art. V, 15, Fla. Const. Generally, the Court will not second-guess a referee's recommended discipline as long as it has a reasonable basis in existing case law and the Florida Standards for Imposing Lawyer Sanctions. Miller, 863 So.2d at 235; *Fla. Bar v. Temmer*, 753 So.2d 555, 558 (Fla.1999).

The nature of Germain's arguments, the unusual series of events giving rise to this case, and Germain's inability to grasp the problematic nature of his conduct are enough to raise the issue of Germain's mental stability. The real issue, however, is whether Germain was or should have been aware that his mental state was at issue. See *Carricarte*, 733 So.2d at 979 (approving recommendation of mental health evaluation where Bar counsel mentioned a mental health evaluation in his closing argument at the conclusion of the guilt phase of the hearing).

Germain's own theory of defense made his mental state an issue. He claimed he was the victim of several vicious, unprovoked attacks and that he was in fear for his life when he signed the June 18 Affidavit. In addition, the referee's first report, which preceded the sanctions phase of the hearing, stated: "the undersigned finds that no reasonable person would have feared that Norvell would kill, and that no reasonable person would have a fear that would justify giving a false statement under oath." (Emphasis added.) The referee made several findings concerning the incidents of violence between Norvell and Germain and concluded that "the violence in these incidents declined over time. It is notable that after the July 2002 incident, Respondent willingly remained in the space-sharing arrangement with Norvell."

These findings and Germain's own arguments were sufficient to put Germain on notice that his mental state was at issue. Accordingly, we approve the recommendation for a mental health evaluation.

Next, we consider the appropriate discipline for Germain's misconduct. As set forth above, we will not second-guess a referee's recommended discipline as long as it has a reasonable basis in existing caselaw and the Florida Standards for Imposing Lawyer Sanctions. Having reviewed the standards, the cases involving similar misconduct, and the aggravating and mitigating factors found by the referee, we disapprove the referee's recommendation of a ninety-one-day suspension and instead suspend Germain for one year.

Standards 6.12, 6.22, and 8.2, which the referee cited, all support a suspension. 3 To determine the proper length, we obtain guidance from our previous cases. In Adams, 641 So.2d 399, in a letter and at a hearing before a judge the respondent accused three opposing counsel of attempting to suborn perjury. None of the attorneys had done so; although there was cause for respondent to suspect one of the attorneys, there was no basis to suspect the others. This Court suspended him for ninety days. Our opinion does not mention aggravating or mitigating factors or previous discipline.

When we consider that Germain was previously disciplined for the same kind of misconduct and that he lied under oath and engaged in other misconduct, it is clear that a longer suspension is warranted here than in Adams. The Court views cumulative misconduct more seriously than isolated instances. *Carlon*, 820 So.2d at 899. This is the second time Germain comes before the Court for making disparaging comments about other professionals. These circumstances alone support the recommended ninety-one-day suspension.

However, that Germain lied under oath convinces us that an even longer suspension is warranted.

This court considers a lawyer who intentionally lies under oath to have committed an extremely serious offense. Our condemnation of this type of misconduct is not of recent vintage. In *Dodd v. Florida Bar*, 118 So.2d 17, 19 (Fla.1960), this Court stated:

No breach of professional ethics, or of the law, is more harmful to the administration of justice or more hurtful to the public appraisal of the legal profession than the knowledgeable use by an attorney of false testimony in the judicial process.

We have warned that such conduct warrants severe discipline and have dealt harshly with those who commit this offense.

Fla. Bar v. Cibula, 725 So.2d 360, 364 (Fla.1999) (suspending an attorney for ninety-one days after he lied under oath during two court hearings held in connection with alimony obligations); see also *Fla. Bar v. Nunes*, 734 So.2d 393 (Fla.1999) (imposing a three-year suspension for filing a frivolous lawsuit, continuing to represent clients after being discharged, making disparaging remarks about judges and opposing counsel, and making false representations to a tribunal, among other things); *Fla. Bar v. Klausner*, 721 So.2d 720 (Fla.1998) (imposing a three-year suspension for forging signatures on documents submitted to the court and lying about the misconduct to the court and in a sworn statement to an investigator with the state attorney's office, among other things); *Fla. Bar v. Vining*, 707 So.2d 670 (Fla.1998) (imposing a three-year suspension for misrepresentations in a stipulation submitted to the court while seeking funds in the court registry); *Fla. Bar v. Segal*, 663 So.2d 618, 622 (Fla.1995) (imposing a three-year suspension for making a false statement in a petition for discharge submitted to the probate court); *Fla. Bar v. Kleinfeld*, 648 So.2d 698 (Fla.1994) (imposing a three-year suspension for making false statements in an affidavit seeking disqualification of a judge in a contempt hearing against the attorney, among other things); *Fla. Bar v. O'Malley*, 534 So.2d 1159, 1162 (Fla.1988) (imposing a three-year suspension for false testimony in a suit against the attorney for return of bond collateral entrusted to him).

These cases support a three-year suspension. Nevertheless, in light of the mitigating factors found by the referee (absence of a dishonest or selfish motive, personal or emotional problems, and physical or mental disability or impairment), we impose a suspension of one year.

CONCLUSION

For the reasons stated above, Mark F. Germain is hereby suspended from the practice of law for one year. The suspension will be effective thirty days from the filing of this opinion so that Germain can close out his practice and protect the interests of existing clients. If Germain notifies this Court in writing that he is no longer practicing and does not need the thirty days to protect existing clients, this Court will enter an order making the suspension effective immediately. Germain shall accept no new business from the date of this opinion until he is reinstated to the practice of law.

Before his reinstatement, Germain must submit proof that he has been evaluated by a licensed mental health professional approved by The Florida Bar, has complied with any recommended treatment or counseling, and is either continuing in treatment or counseling or has satisfactorily completed such treatment or counseling.

Judgment is entered for The Florida Bar, 651 East Jefferson Street, Tallahassee, Florida 32399–2300, for recovery of costs from Mark F. Germain in the amount of $4,485.84, for which sum let execution issue.

It is so ordered.

Questions for Discussion

1.   What was the best course of action that Germain could have taken if he wanted to sever his ties with his building partner?

2.   Did Norvell act within the Rules of Professional Responsibility?

3.   Was Germain remorseful for his conduct? Did that play a factor in his discipline?

CHAPTER 12
FAIRNESS TO OPPOSING PARTY
AND COUNSEL
RULE 4-3.4

Rule 4-3.4 is far reaching as to the scope of its requirements in representing a client. It bestows requirements on the lawyers pre-suit, during litigation and also at trial.

The Rule prohibits the lawyers from "obstruct[ing] another party's access to evidence" by altering, destroying or concealing a document or other material that the lawyer "knows or reasonably should know" is relevant to a pending matter or foreseeable matter.

The lawyer may not fabricate evidence, assist or induce a witness in testifying falsely, or knowingly disobey an obligation under the Rules of a tribunal.

Furthermore, the Rule prohibits the lawyer from making frivolous discovery requests and failing to comply with proper discovery requests.

During trial, the lawyer may not make statements of his personal opinion about the credibility of the witness, the justness of the cause, guilt or innocence of a person or assert personal knowledge of facts that are at issue unless testifying as a witness.

With the advance of technology and the creation of social media over the last several years, this Rule has been the subject of recent cases involving the discovery of social media and what a lawyer can and cannot advise a client about it.

The Florida Bar issued a recent proposed ethics opinion dated January 23, 2015, regarding a lawyer's advice to clients with respect to removing posts, photographs, videos and other information from their social media accounts. The opinion cautions lawyers and their advice to their clients regarding social media and references the requirements of Rule 4-3.4. The opinion states that "a lawyer may advise the client pre-litigation to remove information from a social media page, regardless of its relevance to a reasonably foreseeable proceeding, as long as the removal does not violate any substantive law regarding preservation and/or spoliation of evidence."

The ethics opinion sites several cases involving discovery of social media in various jurisdictions including a case in Virginia where the lawyer was sanctioned $542,000 for directing a client to delete photographs from their social media page and signing discovery responses stating the accounts did not exist.

PROFESSIONAL ETHICS OF THE FLORIDA BAR
PROPOSED ADVISORY OPINION 14-1
January 23, 2015

A Florida Bar member has asked the committee regarding the ethical obligations on advising clients to "clean up" their social media pages before litigation is filed to remove embarrassing information that the lawyer believes is not material to the litigation matter. The inquirer asks the following 4 questions:

1) Pre-litigation, may a lawyer advise a client to remove posts, photos, videos, and information from social media pages/accounts that are related directly to the incident for which the lawyer is retained?

2) Pre-litigation, may a lawyer advise a client to remove posts, photos, videos, and information from social media pages/accounts that are not related directly to the incident for which the lawyer is retained?

3) Pre-litigation, may a lawyer advise a client to change social media pages/accounts privacy settings to remove the pages/accounts from public view?

4) Pre-litigation, must a lawyer advise a client not to remove posts, photos, videos and information whether or not directly related to the litigation if the lawyer has advised the client to set privacy settings to not allow public access?

Rule 4-3.4(a) is applicable and states as follows:

A lawyer must not:

(a) unlawfully obstruct another party's access to evidence or otherwise unlawfully alter, destroy, or conceal a document or other material that the lawyer knows or reasonably should know is relevant to a pending or a reasonably foreseeable proceeding; nor counsel or assist another person to do any such act;

The comment to the rule provides further guidance:

The procedure of the adversary system contemplates that the evidence in a case is to be marshalled competitively by the contending parties. Fair competition in the adversary system is secured by prohibitions against destruction or concealment of evidence, improperly influencing witnesses, obstructive tactics in discovery procedure, and the like.

Documents and other items of evidence are often essential to establish a claim or defense. Subject to evidentiary privileges, the right of an opposing party, including the government, to obtain evidence through discovery or subpoena is an important procedural right. The exercise of that right can be frustrated if relevant material is altered, concealed, or destroyed. Applicable law in many jurisdictions makes it an offense to destroy material for the purpose of impairing its availability in a pending proceeding or one whose commencement can be foreseen. Falsifying evidence is also generally a criminal offense. Subdivision (a) applies to evidentiary material generally, including computerized information.

The committee is of the opinion that the representation in this inquiry involves a "reasonably foreseeable proceeding" as the client has hired the lawyer, presumably to determine whether the client has a viable claim and pursue the claim if viable. However, under the rule, the proper inquiry is whether information on a client's social media page is relevant to that reasonably foreseeable proceeding, rather than whether information is "related directly" or "not related directly" to the client's matter. Information that is not "related directly" to the incident giving rise to the need for legal representation may still be relevant. However, what is relevant requires a factual, case-by-case determination. In Florida, the second District Court of Appeal has determined that normal discovery principles apply to social media, and that information sought to be discovered from social media must be "(1) relevant to the case's subject matter, and (2) admissible in court or reasonably calculated to lead to evidence that is admissible in court." *Root v. Balfour Beatty Construction, Inc.*,132 So.3d 867, 869-70 (Fla. 2nd DCA 2014).

What constitutes an "unlawful" obstruction, alteration, destruction, or concealment of evidence is a legal question, outside the scope of an ethics opinion. The committee is aware of cases addressing the issue of discovery or spoliation relating to social media, but in these cases, the issue arose in the course of discovery after litigation commenced. See, *Allied Concrete Co. v. Lester*, 736 S.E.2d 699 (Va. 2013) (Sanctions of $542,000 imposed against lawyer and $180,000 against the client for spoliation when client, at lawyer's direction, deleted photographs from client's social media page, the client deleted the accounts, and the lawyer signed discovery requests that the client did not have the accounts); *Gatto v. United Airlines*, 2013 WL 1285285, Case No. 10-cv-1090-ES-SCM (U.S. Dist. Ct. NJ March 25, 2013) (Adverse inference instruction, but no monetary sanctions, against plaintiff who deactivated his social media accounts, which then became unavailable, after the defendants requested access); *Romano v. Steelcase, Inc.* 907 N.Y.S.2d 650 (NY 2010) (Court granted request for access to plaintiff's MySpace and Facebook pages, including private and deleted pages, when plaintiff's physical condition was at issue and information on the pages is inconsistent with her purported injuries based on information about plaintiff's activities available on the public pages of her MySpace and Facebook pages). In the disciplinary context, at least one lawyer has been suspended for 5 years for advising a client to clean up Facebook page, causing the removal of photographs and other material after a request for production had been made. In the Matter of *Matthew B. 69   Murray*, 2013 WL 5630414, VSB Docket Nos. 11-070-088405 and 11-070-088422 (Virginia State Bar Disciplinary Board July 17, 2013).

The New York County Lawyers Association has issued NYCLA Ethics Opinion 745 (2013) addressing the issue. The opinion concludes that lawyers may advise their clients to use the highest level of privacy settings on their social media pages and may advise clients to remove information from social media pages unless the lawyer has a duty to preserve information under law and there is no violation of law relating to spoliation of evidence. Other states have since come to similar conclusions. See, e.g., North Carolina Formal Ethics Opinion 5 (attorney must advise client about information on social media if information is relevant and material to the client's representation and attorney may advise client to remove information on social media if not spoliation or otherwise illegal); Pennsylvania Bar Association Opinion 2014-300 (attorney may advise client to delete information from client's social media provided that this does not constitute spoliation or is otherwise illegal, but must take appropriate action to preserve the information); and Philadelphia Bar Association Professional Guidance Committee Opinion 2014-5 (attorney may advise a client to change the privacy settings on the client's social media page but may not instruct client to destroy any relevant content on the page). Subsequent to the publication of the opinion, the New York State Bar Association's Commercial and Federal Litigation Section adopted Social Media Ethics Guidelines. Guideline No. 4.A, citing to the opinion, states as follows:

A lawyer may advise a client as to what content may be maintained or made private on her social media account, as well as to what content may be "taken down" or removed, whether posted by the client or someone else, as long as there is no violation of common law or any statute, rule, or regulation relating to the preservation of information. Unless an appropriate record of the social media information or data is preserved, a party or nonparty may not delete information from a social media profile that is subject to a duty to preserve. [Footnote omitted.]

The committee agrees with the NYCLA that a lawyer may advise a client to use the highest level of privacy setting on the client's social media pages.

The committee also agrees that a lawyer may advise the client pre-litigation to remove information from a social media page, regardless of its relevance to a reasonably foreseeable proceeding, as long as the removal does not violate any substantive law regarding preservation and/or spoliation of evidence. The committee is of the opinion that if the lawyer does so, an appropriate record of the social media information or data must be preserved if the information or data is known by the lawyer or reasonably should be known by the lawyer to be relevant to the reasonably foreseeable proceeding.

The committee is of the opinion that the general obligation of competence may require the inquirer to advise the client regarding removal of relevant information from the client's social media pages, including whether removal would violate any legal duties regarding preservation of evidence, regardless of the privacy settings. If a client specifically asks the inquirer regarding removal of information, the lawyer's advice must comply with Rule 4-3.4(a). What information on a social media page is relevant to reasonably foreseeable litigation is a factual question that must be determined on a case-by-case basis.

In summary, a lawyer may advise that a client change privacy settings on the client's social media pages so that they are not publicly accessible. Provided that there is no violation of the rules or substantive law pertaining to the preservation and/or spoliation of evidence, a lawyer also may advise that a client remove information relevant to the foreseeable proceeding from social media pages as long as an appropriate record of the social media information or data is preserved.

Nucci v. Target Corp., No. 4D14-138, 2015 WL 71726 (Fla. Dist. Ct. App. Jan. 7, 2015)

….

In a personal injury case, Maria Nucci petitions for certiorari relief to quash a December 12, 2013 order compelling discovery of photographs from her Facebook account. The photographs sought were reasonably calculated to lead to the discovery of admissible evidence and Nucci's privacy interest in them was minimal, if any. Because the discovery order did not amount to a departure from the essential requirements of law, we deny the petition.

In her personal injury lawsuit, Nucci claimed that on February 4, 2010, she slipped and fell on a foreign substance on the floor of a Target store. In the complaint, she alleged the following:

- Suffered bodily injury
- Experienced pain from the injury
- Incurred medical, hospital, and nursing expenses, suffered physical handicap
- Suffered emotional pain and suffering
- Lost earnings
- Lost the ability to earn money
- Lost or suffered a diminution of ability to enjoy her life
- Suffered aggravation of preexisting injuries
- Suffered permanent or continuing injuries
- Will continue to suffer the losses and impairment in the future

Target took Nucci's deposition on September 4, 2013. Before the deposition, Target's lawyer viewed Nucci's Facebook profile and saw that it contained 1,285 photographs. At the deposition, Nucci objected to disclosing her Facebook photographs. Target's lawyer examined Nucci's Facebook profile two days after the deposition and saw that it listed only 1,249 photographs. On September 9, 2013, Target moved to compel inspection of Nucci's Facebook profile. Target wrote to Nucci and asked that she not destroy further information posted on her social media websites. Target argued that it was entitled to view the profile because Nucci's lawsuit put her physical and mental condition at issue.

Nucci's response to the motion explained that, since its creation, her Facebook page had been on a privacy setting that prevented the general public from having access to her account. She claimed that she had a reasonable expectation of privacy regarding her Facebook information and that Target's access would invade that privacy right. In addition, Nucci argued that Target's motion was an overbroad fishing expedition.

On October 17, 2013, the trial court conducted a hearing on Target's motion to compel. At the hearing, Target showed the court photographs from a surveillance video in which Nucci could be seen walking with two purses on her shoulders or carrying two jugs of water. Again, Target argued that because Nucci had put her physical condition at question, the relevancy of the Facebook photographs outweighed Nucci's right to privacy. It also argued that there was no constitutional right to privacy in photographs posted on Facebook. The circuit court denied Target's motion to compel, in part because the request was "vague, overly broad and unduly burdensome."

Target responded to the court's ruling by filing narrower, more focused discovery requests. Target served Nucci with a set of Electronic Media Interrogatories, with four questions. It also served a Request for Production of Electronic Media, requesting nine items. In response to the interrogatories, Nucci objected on the grounds of (1) privacy; (2) items not readily accessible; and (3) relevance.

As to the Request for Production, Nucci raised the same three objections and additionally argued that the request was (4) overbroad; (5) brought solely to harass; (6) "over[ly] burdensome;" (7) "unduly burdensome"; and (9) unduly vague. Nucci raised only these general claims and no objections specifically directed at any particular photograph.

Target moved that the trial court disallow Nucci's objections. At a hearing on the motion, Target conceded that its request for production should be limited to photographs depicting Nucci. After a hearing on the motion, the trial court granted Target's motion in part and denied it in part. On December 12, 2013, the trial court compelled answers to the following interrogatories:

    1.   Identify all social/professional networking websites that Plaintiff is registered with currently (such as Facebook, MySpace, LinkedIn, Meetup.com, MyLife, etc.)

    2.   Please list the number and service carrier associated with each cellular telephone used by the Plaintiff and/or registered in the Plaintiff's name (this includes all numbers registered to and/or used by the Plaintiff under a "family plan" or similar service) at the time of loss and currently.

The order also compelled production of the following items:

1.   For each social networking account listed in response to the interrogatories, please provide copies or screenshots of all photographs associated with that account during the two (2) years prior to the date of loss.

2.   For each social networking account listed in the interrogatories, provide copies or screenshots of all photographs associated with that account from the date of loss to present.

3.   For each cell phone listed in the interrogatories, please provide copies or screenshots of all photographs associated with that account during the two years prior to the date of loss.

4.   For each cellular phone listed in response to the interrogatories, please provide copies or screenshots of all photographs associated with that account from the date of loss to present.

5.   For each cellular phone listed in the interrogatories, please provide copies of any documentation outlining what calls were made or received on the date of loss.

Nucci argues that the December 12 order departs from the essential requirements of the law because it constitutes an invasion of privacy. Citing to Salvato v. Miley, No. 5:12–CV–635–Oc–10PRL, 2013 WL 2712206 (M.D.Fla. June 11, 2013), which involved a request for e-mails and text messages, she contends that "the mere hope" that the discovery yields relevant evidence is not enough to warrant production. She also argues that the traditional rules of relevancy still apply to a request for social media materials. Nucci additionally asserts that her activation of privacy settings demonstrates an invocation of federal law. See Ehling v. Monmouth–Ocean Hosp. Serv. Corp., 961 F.Supp.2d 659, 665 (D.N.J.2013). Relying upon Ehling, Nucci argues that her private Facebook posts were covered by the Federal Stored Communications Act ("SCA"), 18 U.S.C. §§ 2701–2712, and were not therefore discoverable. We note that Nucci objected below to all disclosure; she did not attempt to limit disclosure of the photographs by establishing discrete guidelines. See Reid v. Ingerman Smith LLP, No. CV 2012–0307(ILG)(MDG), 2012 WL 6720752, at *2 (E.D.N.Y. Dec. 27, 2012); E.E.O.C. v. Simply Storage Mgmt., LLC, 270 F.R.D. 430, 436 (S.D.Ind.2010).

In its response, Target points out, as it did below, that surveillance videos show Nucci carrying heavy bags, jugs of water, and doing other physical acts, suggesting that her claim of serious personal injury is suspect.

Target suggests that the material ordered is relevant to Nucci's claim of injury in that it allows a comparison of her current physical condition and limitations to her physical condition and quality of life before the date of the slip and fall. In its response to this Court, Target concedes that the order is limited to photographs depicting Nucci from the two years before the date of the incident to the present. It argues that the trial court did not grant unfettered access because it did not compel the production of passwords to her social networking accounts.

As to material injury or harm, Target points out that Nucci has not claimed that production of any particular photograph or other identifiable material will cause her damage or embarrassment. Citing to *Davenport v. State Farm Mutual Automobile Insurance Co.*, No. 3:11–cv–632–J–JBT, 2012 WL 555759 (M.D.Fla. Feb. 21, 2012), Target contends that the content of social networking

sites is not privileged or protected by the right to privacy. It notes that Facebook's terms and conditions explain that, regardless of a user's intentions, the material contained in a post could be disseminated by Facebook at its discretion or under court order.

Finally, Target argues that in the context of a civil lawsuit, Florida courts can compel a party to release relevant records from social networking sites without implicating or violating the SCA.

Discussion

This case stands at the intersection of a litigant's privacy interests in social media postings and the broad discovery allowed in Florida in a civil case. Consideration of four factors leads to the conclusion that Nucci's petition for certiorari should be denied. First, certiorari relief is available in only a narrow class of cases and this case does not meet the stringent requirements for certiorari relief. Second, the scope of discovery in civil cases is broad and discovery rulings by trial courts are reviewed under an abuse of discretion standard. Third, the information sought—photographs of Nucci posted on Nucci's social media sites—is highly relevant. Fourth, Nucci has but a limited privacy interest, if any, in pictures posted on her social networking sites.

Nucci's petition challenges only the discovery of photographs from social networking sites, such as Facebook. Thus, the order compelling the answers to interrogatories and production pertaining to a cellular phone are not at issue. Similarly, our ruling in this case covers neither communications other than photographs exchanged through electronic means nor access to other types of information contained on social networking sites.

....

The Broad Scope of Discovery

A "part[y] may obtain discovery regarding any matter, not privileged, that is relevant to the subject matter of the pending action, whether it relates to the claim or defense of the party seeking discovery or the claim or defense of any other party."Fla. R. Civ. P. 1.280(b)(1)."It is not ground for objection that the information sought will be inadmissible at the trial if the information sought appears reasonably calculated to lead to the discovery of admissible evidence." Id. (emphasis added).Florida Rule of Civil Procedure 1.350(a) includes electronically stored information within the scope of discovery. 2 An outer limit of discovery is that "'litigants are not entitled to carte blanche discovery of irrelevant material.'" *Life Care Ctrs. of Am. v. Reese*, 948 So.2d 830, 832 (Fla. 5th DCA 2007) (quoting *Tanchel v. Shoemaker*, 928 So.2d 440, 442 (Fla. 5th DCA 2006)). Because the permissible scope of discovery is so broad, a "trial court is given wide discretion in dealing with discovery matters, and unless there is a clear abuse of that discretion, the appellate court will not disturb the trial court's order." *Alvarez v. Cooper Tire & Rubber Co.*, 75 So.3d 789, 793 (Fla. 4th DCA 2011) (direct appeal of discovery issue). It is because of this wide discretion accorded to trial judges that it is difficult to establish certiorari jurisdiction of discovery orders.

In a personal injury case where the plaintiff is seeking intangible damages, the fact-finder is required to examine the quality of the plaintiff's life before and after the accident to determine the extent of the loss. From testimony alone, it is often difficult for the fact-finder to grasp what a plaintiff's life was like prior to an accident. It would take a great novelist, a Tolstoy, a Dickens, or a Hemingway, to use words to summarize the totality of a prior life. If a photograph is worth a thousand words, there is no better portrayal of what an individual's life was like than those photographs the individual has chosen to share through social media before the occurrence of an accident causing injury. Such photographs are the equivalent of a "day in the life" slide show produced by the plaintiff before the existence of any motive to manipulate reality. The photographs sought here are thus powerfully relevant to the damage issues in the lawsuit. The relevance of the photographs is enhanced, because the post- accident surveillance videos of Nucci suggest that her injury claims are suspect and that she may not be an accurate reporter of her pre-accident life or of the quality of her life since then. The production order is not overly broad under the circumstances, as it is limited to the two years prior to the incident up to the present; the photographs sought are easily accessed and exist in electronic form, so compliance with the order is not onerous.

The Right of Privacy

To curtail the broad scope of discovery allowed in civil litigation, Nucci asserts a right of privacy. However, the relevance of the photographs overwhelms Nucci's minimal privacy interest in them.

The Florida Constitution expressly protects an individual's right to privacy. SeeArt. I, § 23, Fla. Const. ("Every natural person has the right to be let alone and free from governmental intrusion into the person's private life except as otherwise provided herein."). This right is broader than the right to privacy implied in the Federal Constitution. *Berkeley*, 699 So.2d at 790. The right to privacy in the Florida Constitution "ensures that individuals are able 'to determine for themselves when, how and to what extent information about them is communicated to others.'" *Shaktman v. State*, 553 So.2d 148, 150 (Fla.1989) (quoting A. Westin, Privacy and Freedom 7 (1967)).

Before the right to privacy attaches, there must exist a legitimate expectation of privacy. *Winfield v. Div. of Pari–Mutuel Wagering, Dep't of Bus. Regulation*, 477 So.2d 544, 547 (Fla.1985). Once a legitimate expectation of privacy is shown, the burden is on the party seeking disclosure to show the invasion is warranted by a compelling interest and that the least intrusive means are used. Id. In the civil discovery context, courts must engage in a balancing test, weighing the need for

the discovery against the privacy interests. *Rasmussen v. S. Fla. Blood Serv., Inc.*, 500 So.2d 533, 535 (Fla.1987). If the person raising the privacy bar establishes the existence of a legitimate expectation of privacy, the party seeking to obtain the private information has the burden of establishing need sufficient to outweigh the privacy interest. *Berkeley*, 699 So.2d at 791–92.

In a thoughtful opinion, a Palm Beach County circuit judge has summarized the nature of social networking sites as follows:

Social networking sites, such as Facebook, are free websites where an individual creates a "profile" which functions as a personal web page and may include, at the user's discretion, numerous photos and a vast array of personal information including age, employment, education, religious and political views and various recreational interests. *Trail v. Lesko*, [No. GD–10–017249,] 2012 WL 2864004 (Pa.Com.Pl. July 5, 2012). Once a user joins a social networking site, he or she can use the site to search for "friends" and create linkages to others based on similar interests. Kelly Ann Bub, Comment, Privacy's Role in the Discovery of Social Networking Site Information, 64 SMU L.Rev. 1433, 1435 (2011).

Through the use of these sites, "users can share a variety of materials with friends or acquaintances of their choosing, including tasteless jokes, updates on their love lives, poignant reminiscences, business successes, petty complaints, party photographs, news about their children, or anything else they choose to disclose." Bruce E. Boyden, Comment, Oversharing: Facebook Discovery and the Unbearable Sameness of Internet Law, 65 Ark. L.Rev. 39, 42 (2012). As a result, social networking sites can provide a "treasure trove" of information in litigation. Christopher B. Hopkins, Discovery of Facebook Contents in Florida Cases, 31 No. 2 Trial Advoc. Q. 14 (2012).

Levine v. Culligan of Fla., Inc., Case No. 50–2011–CA–010339–XXXXMB, 2013 WL 1100404, at *2–*3 (Fla. 15th Cir.Ct. Jan. 29, 2013).

We agree with those cases concluding that, generally, the photographs posted on a social networking site are neither privileged nor protected by any right of privacy, regardless of any privacy settings that the user may have established. See *Davenport v. State Farm Mut. Auto. Ins. Co.*, No. 3:11–cv–632–J–JBT, 2012 WL 555759, at *1 (M.D.Fla. Feb. 21, 2012); see also *Patterson v. Turner Constr. Co.*, 88 A.D.3d 617, 931 N.Y.S.2d 311, 312 (N.Y.App.2011) (holding that the "postings on plaintiff's online Facebook account, if relevant, are not shielded from discovery merely because plaintiff used the service's privacy settings to restrict access"). Such posted photographs are unlike medical records or communications with one's attorney, where disclosure is confined to narrow, confidential relationships. Facebook itself does not guarantee privacy. *Romano v. Steelcase, Inc.*, 30 Misc.3d 426, 907 N.Y.S.2d 650, 656 (N.Y.Sup.Ct.2010). By creating a Facebook account, a user acknowledges that her personal information would be shared with others.Id. at 657. "Indeed, that is the very nature and purpose of these social networking sites else they would cease to exist."Id.

Because "information that an individual shares through social networking web-sites like Facebook may be copied and disseminated by another," the expectation that such information is private, in the traditional sense of the word, is not a reasonable one. *Beswick v. N.W. Med. Ctr., Inc.*, No. 07–020592 CACE(03), 2011 WL 7005038 (Fla. 17th Cir.Ct. Nov. 3, 2011). As one federal judge has observed,

Even had plaintiff used privacy settings that allowed only her "friends" on Facebook to see postings, she "had no justifiable expectation that h[er] 'friends' would keep h[er] profile private...." *U.S. v. Meregildo*, 2012 WL 3264501, at *2 (S.D.N.Y.2012). In fact, "the wider h[er] circle of 'friends,' the more likely [her] posts would be viewed by someone [s]he never expected to see them."Id. Thus, as the Second Circuit has recognized, legitimate expectations of privacy may be lower in e-mails or other Internet transmissions. *U.S. v. Lifshitz*, 369 F.3d 173, 190 (2d Cir.2004) (contrasting privacy expectation of e-mail with greater expectation of privacy of materials located on a person's computer).

Reid v. Ingerman Smith LLP, No. CV2012–0307(ILG)(MDG), 2012 WL 6720752, at *2 (E.D.N.Y. Dec. 27, 2012); see also

Tompkins v. Detroit Metro. Airport, 278 F.R.D. 387, 388 (E.D.Mich.2012) (holding that "material posted on a 'private' Facebook page, that is accessible to a selected group of recipients but not available for viewing by the general public, is generally not privileged, nor is it protected by common law or civil law notions of privacy"); *Mailhoit v. Home Depot U.S.A., Inc.*, 285 F.R.D. 566, 570 (C.D.Cal.2012) (indicating that social networking site content is neither privileged nor protected, but recognizing that party requesting discovery must make a threshold showing that such discovery is reasonably calculated to lead to admissible evidence).

We distinguish this case from *Root v. Balfour Beatty Construction, LLC*, 132 So.3d 867 (Fla. 2d DCA 2014). That case involved a claim filed by a mother on behalf of her three-year-old son who was struck by a vehicle. Unlike this case, where the trial court ordered the production of photographs from the plaintiff's Facebook account, the court in Balfour ordered the production of a much broader swath of Facebook material without any temporal limitation—postings, statuses, photos, "likes," or videos—that relate to the mother's relationships with all of her children, not just the three year old, and with "other family members, boyfriends, husbands, and/or significant others, both prior to, and following the accident."Id. at 869. The second district determined that "social media evidence is discoverable," but held that the ordered discovery was "overbroad" and compelled "the production of personal information ... not relevant to" the mother's claims. Id. at 868, 870. The court found that this was the type of "carte blanche" irrelevant discovery the Florida Supreme Court has sought to guard against. Id. at 870; Langston, 655 So.2d at 95 ("[W]e do not believe that a litigant is entitled carte blanche to irrelevant discovery.") The discovery ordered in this case is narrower in scope and, as set forth above, is calculated to lead to evidence that is admissible in court.

Finally, we reject the claim that the Stored Communications Act, 18 U.S.C. §§ 2701–2712, has any application to this case. Generally, the "SCA prevents 'providers' of communication services from divulging private communications to certain entities and/or individuals." *Quon v. Arch Wireless Operating Co., Inc.*, 529 F.3d 892, 900 (9th Cir.2008), rev'd on other grounds by *City of Ontario, Cal. v. Quon*, 560 U.S. 746, 130 S.Ct. 2619, 177 L.Ed.2d 216 (2010) (citation omitted). The act does not apply to individuals who use the communications services provided. See, e.g., *Flagg v. City of Detroit*, 252 F.R.D. 346, 349 (E.D.Mich.2008) (ruling that the SCA does not preclude civil discovery of a party's electronically stored communications which remain within the party's control even if they are maintained by a non-party service provider).

Finding no departure from the essential requirements of law, we deny the petition for certiorari.

Root v. Balfour Beatty Const., LLC, 132 So.3d 867 (Fla. 2014)

....

Tonia Root, individually and on behalf of Gage Root, seeks certiorari review of the circuit court's discovery order approving a magistrate's recommendations and requiring Root to produce copies of postings on her Facebook account. Root argues that the order departs from the essential requirements of the law because it allows discovery that is overbroad and compels the production of personal information that is not relevant to her claims. We agree and grant the petition.

The underlying action is a negligence action filed by Root against the City of Cape Coral, a construction contractor, and subcontractors (Defendants) for damages Root's three-year-old son Gage suffered when he was struck by an oncoming vehicle in front of a construction site. The accident occurred while Gage was under the care of his seventeen-year-old aunt.

Root alleged that Defendants were negligent for failing to use reasonable care in keeping the construction site safe for pedestrians. Root also raised derivative claims for loss of parental consortium. Defendants raised affirmative defenses including negligent entrustment of Gage by Root, the aunt's failure to supervise, and the driver's negligence.

The discovery order at issue requires Root to produce copies of postings on her Facebook account which include the following:

(i.) Any counseling or psychological care obtained by Tonia Root before or after the accident;

....

(o.) Any and all postings, statuses, photos, "likes" or videos related to Tonia Root's

i.   Relationships with Gage or her other children, both prior to, and following, the accident;

ii.   Relationships with other family members, boyfriends, husbands, and/or significant others, both prior to, and following the accident;

iii.   Mental health, stress complaints, alcohol use or other substance use, both prior to and after, the accident;

....

(v.) Facebook account postings relating to any lawsuit filed after the accident by Tonia Root or others[.] These categories are in addition to fifteen other categories of information which Root concedes is discoverable.

Root argues that the order departs from the essential requirements of the law because the above-listed categories are overbroad and the order requires the production of personal information that is irrelevant and not likely to lead to the discovery of admissible evidence. Defendants disagree and also argue that Root has not established certiorari jurisdiction in this court because she has not alleged irreparable harm arising from the discovery order.

We begin our analysis with Defendants' jurisdictional argument. In order to confer certiorari jurisdiction, a petitioner is required to establish irreparable harm that is material and not remediable on postjudgment appeal. *Allstate Ins. Co. v. Langston*, 655 So.2d 91, 94 (Fla.1995); *Parkway Bank v. Fort Myers*

Armature Works, Inc., 658 So.2d 646, 649 (Fla. 2d DCA 1995). An order compelling the production of discovery that implicates privacy rights demonstrates irreparable harm. *Fla. First Fin. Group, Inc. v. De Castro*, 815 So.2d 789, 791 (Fla. 4th DCA 2002) (citing *Rasmussen v. S. Fla. Blood Serv., Inc.*, 500 So.2d 533, 536–37 (Fla.1987)); see also *Holland v. Barfield*, 35 So.3d 953, 956 (Fla. 5th DCA 2010) (holding that a discovery order requiring disclosure of private information on a computer hard drive and cell phone SIM card demonstrated irreparable harm). Additionally, an order that entitles a party to carte blanche discovery of irrelevant material demonstrates the type of irreparable harm that may be remedied via petition for writ of certiorari. See *Langston*, 655 So.2d at 95. We conclude that Root has appropriately invoked our certiorari jurisdiction.

On the merits, trial courts around the country have repeatedly determined that social media evidence is discoverable. See

Christopher B. Hopkins & Tracy T. Segal, Discovery of Facebook Content in Fla. Cases, 31 No. 2 Trial Advoc. Q. 14, 14 (Spring 2012). And the Florida Rules of Civil Procedure were amended in 2012 to provide guidelines regarding the production of electronically stored information. See Fla. R. Civ. P. 1.350 committee notes (2012 amend.). As one federal court has stated, discovery of information on social networking sites simply requires applying "basic discovery principles in a novel context." *E.E.O.C. v. Simply Storage Mgmt., LLC*, 270 F.R.D. 430, 434 (S.D.Ind.2010).

Under the basic principles for evaluating discovery in Florida, the party seeking discovery must establish that it is (1) relevant to the case's subject matter, and (2) admissible in court or reasonably calculated to lead to evidence that is admissible in court. Fla. R. Civ. P. 1.280(b)(1); Langston, 655 So.2d at 94. We agree with Root that at present, Defendants have not met this burden as to the requested discovery.

Root's complaint contains claims on behalf of Gage for negligence as to each defendant and Root's derivative claims for loss of parental consortium. Defendants responded with several affirmative defenses including negligent entrustment of Gage by Root, the aunt's failure to supervise, and the driver's negligence. As to Gage's claims for negligence, none of the objected- to discovery pertains to the accident itself. Similarly, none of the objected-to discovery pertains to Defendants' affirmative defenses. Instead, the discovery relates to Root's past and present personal relationships with all her children, other family members, and significant others; Root's past and present mental health, stress complaints, and use of alcohol or other substances; and lawsuits of any nature filed by Root or others after the accident.

The requested discovery also appears at this time to be irrelevant to Root's claims for loss of consortium. Although Root's deposition has been taken, Defendants do not point to anything claimed by her in support of their contention that the requested information is relevant and discoverable. Generally, any such discovery should have been limited to that related to the impact of Gage's injury upon Root. See *United States v. Dempsey*, 635 So.2d 961, 965 (Fla.1994) ("[W]e define loss of 'consortium' to include the loss of companionship, society, love, affection, and solace of the injured child, as well as ordinary day-to-day services that the child would have rendered.").

Moreover, the scope of the discovery compelled in categories (i) and (o)(i, ii, iii, v) regarding Root's relationships with her entire family and significant others, her mental health history, her substance use history, and her litigation history appears to be the type of carte blanche discovery the supreme court sought to guard against in Langston. See *Russell v. Stardust Cruisers, Inc.*, 690 So.2d 743, 745 (Fla. 5th DCA 1997) (observing that while an individual's health, life expectancy, and habits are at issue and broad discovery is allowed, a court must still determine which records would be relevant and the court should take protective measures, such as an in camera inspection, to prevent disclosure of irrelevant matters); see also *Higgins v. Koch Dev. Corp.*, No. 3:11–cv–81–RLY–WGH, 2013 WL 3366278, at *3 (S.D.Ind. July 5, 2013) (holding that the defendant was entitled to discovery of the plaintiffs' Facebook pages limited to the specific material that is relevant to the plaintiffs' claims).

Significantly, one defendant's argument to the magistrate who heard the discovery issues supports Root's contention that the requested discovery constitutes a fishing expedition. The defendant's attorney stated, "These are all things that we would like to look under the hood, so to speak, and figure out whether that's even a theory worth exploring." Even the magistrate acknowledged that relevancy might be a problem, noting that "95 percent, or 99 percent of this may not be relevant." The magistrate also expressed some misgivings at the possibility that large amounts of material might have to be reviewed in camera.

In summary, based on the current posture of the case we conclude that the portion of the order permitting the discovery of categories (i) and (o)(i, ii, iii, v) must be quashed. Should further developments in the litigation suggest that the requested information may be discoverable, the trial court may have to review the material in camera and fashion appropriate limits and protections regarding the discovery. See *Alterra Healthcare Corp. v. Estate of Shelley*, 827 So.2d 936, 945–46 (Fla.2002); *Russell*, 690 So.2d at 745; see also Michael B. Pullano & Matthew G. Laver, Discovery Rulings Increasingly Unfriendly to Facebook Users' Privacy Rights, 82 U.S.L.W. 867, 892–95 (Dec. 17, 2013) (discussing various approaches courts have taken to ensure that Facebook material requested in discovery is not overbroad). Accordingly, we grant Root's petition for writ of certiorari and quash the discovery order as it pertains to categories (i) and (o)(i, ii, iii, v).

Petition granted; order quashed in part.

Questions for Discussion

1.　What should you tell your clients about social media before a lawsuit? During litigation?

2.　How can you insure your clients know not to delete or destroy this type of information?

3.　Why the different rulings in Nucci and the Root case?

4.　Is it clear what is discoverable from your clients social media?

Jason C. King

APPENDIX

Rules Regulating the Florida Bar:
Rules of Professional Conduct
Rules Regulating Trust Accounts
&
Florida Bar Discipline Statistics

RULES OF PROFESSIONAL CONDUCT
PREAMBLE: A LAWYER'S RESPONSIBILITIES

A lawyer, as a member of the legal profession, is a representative of clients, an officer of the legal system, and a public citizen having special responsibility for the quality of justice.

As a representative of clients, a lawyer performs various functions. As an adviser, a lawyer provides a client with an informed understanding of the client's legal rights and obligations and explains their practical implications. As an advocate, a lawyer zealously asserts the client's position under the rules of the adversary system. As a negotiator, a lawyer seeks a result advantageous to the client but consistent with requirements of honest dealing with others. As an evaluator, a lawyer acts by examining a client's legal affairs and reporting about them to the client or to others.

In addition to these representational functions, a lawyer may serve as a third-party neutral, a nonrepresentational role helping the parties to resolve a dispute or other matter. Some of these rules apply directly to lawyers who are or have served as third-party neutrals. See, e.g., rules 4-1.12   and 4-2.4. In addition, there are rules that apply to lawyers who are not active in the practice of law or to practicing lawyers even when they are acting in a nonprofessional capacity. For example, a lawyer who commits fraud in the conduct of a business is subject to discipline for engaging in conduct involving dishonesty, fraud, deceit, or misrepresentation. See rule 4-8.4.

In all professional functions a lawyer should be competent, prompt, and diligent. A lawyer should maintain communication with a client concerning the representation. A lawyer should keep in confidence information relating to representation of a client except so far as disclosure is required or permitted by the Rules of Professional Conduct or by law.

A lawyer's conduct should conform to the requirements of the law, both in professional service to clients and in the lawyer's business and personal affairs. A lawyer should use the law's procedures only for legitimate purposes and not to harass or intimidate others. A lawyer should demonstrate respect for the legal system and for those who serve it, including judges, other lawyers, and public officials. While it is a lawyer's duty, when necessary, to challenge the rectitude of official action, it is also a lawyer's duty to uphold legal process.

As a public citizen, a lawyer should seek improvement of the law, access to the legal system, the administration of justice, and the quality of service rendered by the legal profession. As a member of a learned profession, a lawyer should cultivate knowledge of the law beyond its use for clients, employ that knowledge in reform of the law, and work to strengthen legal education. In addition, a lawyer should further the public's understanding of and confidence in the rule of law and the justice system, because legal institutions in a constitutional democracy depend on popular participation and support to maintain their authority. A lawyer should be mindful of deficiencies in the administration of justice and of the fact that the poor, and sometimes persons who are not poor, cannot afford adequate legal assistance. Therefore, all lawyers should devote professional time and resources and use civic influence to ensure equal access to our system of justice for all those who because of economic or social barriers cannot afford or secure adequate legal counsel. A lawyer should aid the legal profession in pursuing these objectives and should help the bar regulate itself in the public interest.

Many of the lawyer's professional responsibilities are prescribed in the Rules of Professional Conduct and in substantive and procedural law. A lawyer is also guided by personal conscience and the approbation of professional peers. A lawyer should strive to attain the highest level of skill, to improve the law and the legal profession, and to exemplify the legal profession's ideals of public service.

A lawyer's responsibilities as a representative of clients, an officer of the legal system, and a public citizen are usually harmonious. Zealous advocacy is not inconsistent with justice. Moreover, unless violations of law or injury to another or another's property is involved, preserving client confidences ordinarily serves the public interest because people are more likely to seek legal advice, and thereby heed their legal obligations, when they know their communications will be private.

In the practice of law conflicting responsibilities are often encountered. Difficult ethical problems may arise from a conflict between a lawyer's responsibility to a client and the lawyer's own sense of personal honor, including obligations to society and the legal profession. The Rules of Professional Conduct often prescribe terms for resolving such conflicts. Within the framework of these rules, however, many difficult issues of professional discretion can arise. Such issues must be resolved through the exercise of sensitive professional and moral judgment guided by the basic principles underlying the rules. These principles include the lawyer's obligation to protect and pursue a client's legitimate interests, within the bounds of the law, while maintaining a professional, courteous, and civil attitude toward all persons involved in the legal system.

Lawyers are officers of the court and they are responsible to the judiciary for the propriety of their professional activities. Within that context, the legal profession has been granted powers of self-government. Self-regulation helps maintain the legal profession's independence from undue government domination. An independent legal profession is an important force in preserving government under law, for abuse of legal authority is more readily challenged by a profession whose members are not dependent on the executive and legislative branches of government for the right to practice. Supervision by an independent judiciary, and conformity with the rules the judiciary adopts for the profession, assures both independence and responsibility.

Thus, every lawyer is responsible for observance of the Rules of Professional Conduct. A lawyer should also aid in securing their observance by other lawyers. Neglect of these responsibilities compromises the independence of the profession and the public interest that it serves.

Scope:

The Rules of Professional Conduct are rules of reason. They should be interpreted with reference to the purposes of legal representation and of the law itself. Some of the rules are imperatives, cast in the terms of "shall" or "shall not." These define proper conduct for purposes of professional discipline. Others, generally cast in the term "may," are permissive and define areas under the rules in which the lawyer has discretion to exercise professional judgment. No disciplinary action should be taken when the lawyer chooses not to act or acts within the bounds

of such discretion. Other rules define the nature of relationships between the lawyer and others. The rules are thus partly obligatory and disciplinary and partly constitutive and descriptive in that they define a lawyer's professional role.

The comment accompanying each rule explains and illustrates the meaning and purpose of the rule. The comments are intended only as guides to interpretation, whereas the text of each rule is authoritative. Thus, comments, even when they use the term "should," do not add obligations to the rules but merely provide guidance for practicing in compliance with the rules.

The rules presuppose a larger legal context shaping the lawyer's role.

That context includes court rules and statutes relating to matters of licensure, laws defining specific obligations of lawyers, and substantive and procedural law in general. Compliance with the rules, as with all law in an open society, depends primarily upon understanding and voluntary compliance, secondarily upon reinforcement by peer and public opinion, and finally, when necessary, upon enforcement through disciplinary proceedings. The rules do not, however, exhaust the moral and ethical considerations that should inform a lawyer, for no worthwhile human activity can be completely defined by legal rules. The rules simply provide a framework for the ethical practice of law. The comments are sometimes used to alert lawyers to their responsibilities under other law.

Furthermore, for purposes of determining the lawyer's authority and responsibility, principles of substantive law external to these rules determine whether a client-lawyer relationship exists. Most of the duties flowing from the client-lawyer relationship attach only after the client has requested the lawyer to render legal services and the lawyer has agreed to do so. But there are some duties, such as that of confidentiality under rule 4-1.6, which attach when the lawyer agrees to consider whether a client-lawyer relationship shall be established. See rule 4-1.18. Whether a client-lawyer relationship exists for any specific purpose can depend on the circumstances and may be a question of fact.

Failure to comply with an obligation or prohibition imposed by a rule is a basis for invoking the disciplinary process. The rules presuppose that disciplinary assessment of a lawyer's conduct will be made on the basis of the facts and circumstances as they existed at the time of the conduct in question in recognition of the fact that a lawyer often has to act upon uncertain or incomplete evidence of the situation. Moreover, the rules presuppose that whether discipline should be imposed for a violation, and the severity of a sanction, depend on all the circumstances, such as the willfulness and seriousness of the violation, extenuating factors, and whether there have been previous violations.

Violation of a rule should not itself give rise to a cause of action against a lawyer nor should it create any presumption in such a case that a legal duty has been breached. In addition, violation of a rule does not necessarily warrant any other nondisciplinary remedy, such as disqualification of a lawyer in pending litigation. The rules are designed to provide guidance to lawyers and to provide a structure for regulating conduct through disciplinary agencies. They are not designed to be a basis for civil liability. Furthermore, the purpose of the rules can be subverted when they are invoked by opposing parties as procedural weapons. The fact that a rule is a just basis for a lawyer's self-assessment, or for sanctioning a lawyer under the administration of a disciplinary authority, does not imply that an antagonist in a collateral proceeding or

transaction has standing to seek enforcement of the rule. Accordingly, nothing in the rules should be deemed to augment any substantive legal duty of lawyers or the extra-disciplinary consequences of violating such duty. Nevertheless, since the rules do establish standards of conduct by lawyers, a lawyer's violation of a rule may be evidence of a breach of the applicable standard of conduct.

Terminology:

"Belief" or "believes" denotes that the person involved actually supposed the fact in question to be true. A person's belief may be inferred from circumstances.

"Consult" or "consultation" denotes communication of information reasonably sufficient to permit the client to appreciate the significance of the matter in question.

"Confirmed in writing," when used in reference to the informed consent of a person, denotes informed consent that is given in writing by the person or a writing that a lawyer promptly transmits to the person confirming an oral informed consent. See "informed consent" below. If it is not feasible to obtain or transmit the writing at the time the person gives informed consent, then the lawyer must obtain or transmit it within a reasonable time thereafter.

"Firm" or "law firm" denotes a lawyer or lawyers in a law partnership, professional corporation, sole proprietorship, or other association authorized to practice law; or lawyers employed in the legal department of a corporation or other organization.

"Fraud" or "fraudulent" denotes conduct having a purpose to deceive and not merely negligent misrepresentation or failure to apprise another of relevant information.

"Informed consent" denotes the agreement by a person to a proposed course of conduct after the lawyer has communicated adequate information and explanation about the material risks of and reasonably available alternatives to the proposed course of conduct.

"Knowingly," "known," or "knows" denotes actual knowledge of the fact in question. A person's knowledge may be inferred from circumstances.

"Lawyer" denotes a person who is a member of The Florida Bar or otherwise authorized to practice in any court of the State of Florida.

"Partner" denotes a member of a partnership and a shareholder in a law firm organized as a professional corporation, or a member of an association authorized to practice law.

"Reasonable" or "reasonably" when used in relation to conduct by a lawyer denotes the conduct of a reasonably prudent and competent lawyer.

"Reasonable belief" or "reasonably believes" when used in reference to a lawyer denotes that the lawyer believes the matter in question and that the circumstances are such that the belief is reasonable.

"Reasonably should know" when used in reference to a lawyer denotes that a lawyer of reasonable prudence and competence would ascertain the matter in question.

"Screened" denotes the isolation of a lawyer from any participation in a matter through the timely imposition of procedures within a firm that are reasonably adequate under the circumstances to protect information that the isolated lawyer is obligated to protect under these rules or other law.

"Substantial" when used in reference to degree or extent denotes a material matter of clear and weighty importance.

"Tribunal" denotes a court, an arbitrator in a binding arbitration proceeding, or a legislative body, administrative agency, or other body acting in an adjudicative capacity. A legislative body, administrative agency, or other body acts in an adjudicative capacity when a neutral official, after the presentation of evidence or legal argument by a party or parties, will render a binding legal judgment directly affecting a party's interests in a particular matter.

"Writing" or "written" denotes a tangible or electronic record of a communication or representation, including handwriting, typewriting, printing, photostating, photography, audio or video recording, and e-mail. A "signed" writing includes an electronic sound, symbol or process attached to or logically associated with a writing and executed or adopted by a person with the intent to sign the writing.

Comment

Confirmed in writing

If it is not feasible to obtain or transmit a written confirmation at the time the client gives informed consent, then the lawyer must obtain or transmit it within a reasonable time thereafter. If a lawyer has obtained a client's informed consent, the lawyer may act in reliance on that consent so long as it is confirmed in writing within a reasonable time thereafter.

Firm

Whether 2 or more lawyers constitute a firm above can depend on the specific facts. For example, 2 practitioners who share office space and occasionally consult or assist each other ordinarily would not be regarded as constituting a firm. However, if they present themselves to the public in a way that suggests that they are a firm or conduct themselves as a firm, they should be regarded as a firm for purposes of the rules. The terms of any formal agreement between associated lawyers are relevant in determining whether they are a firm, as is the fact that they have mutual access to information concerning the clients they serve. Furthermore, it is relevant in doubtful cases to consider the underlying purpose of the rule that is involved. A group of lawyers could be regarded as a firm for purposes of the rule that the same lawyer should not represent opposing parties in litigation, while it might not be so regarded for purposes of the rule that information acquired by 1 lawyer is attributed to another.

With respect to the law department of an organization, including the government, there is ordinarily no question that the members of the department constitute a firm within the meaning

of the Rules of Professional Conduct. There can be uncertainty, however, as to the identity of the client. For example, it may not be clear whether the law department of a corporation represents a subsidiary or an affiliated corporation, as well as the corporation by which the members of the department are directly employed. A similar question can arise concerning an unincorporated association and its local affiliates.

Similar questions can also arise with respect to lawyers in legal aid and legal services organizations. Depending upon the structure of the organization, the entire organization or different components of it may constitute a firm or firms for purposes of these rules.

Fraud

When used in these rules, the terms "fraud" or "fraudulent" refer to conduct that has a purpose to deceive. This does not include merely negligent misrepresentation or negligent failure to apprise another of relevant information. For purposes of these rules, it is not necessary that anyone has suffered damages or relied on the misrepresentation or failure to inform.

Informed consent

Many of the Rules of Professional Conduct require the lawyer to obtain the informed consent of a client or other person (e.g., a former client or, under certain circumstances, a prospective client) before accepting or continuing representation or pursuing a course of conduct. See, e.g., rules 4-1.2(c), 4-1.6(a), 4-1.7(b), and 4-1.18. The communication necessary to obtain such consent will vary according to the rule involved and the circumstances giving rise to the need to obtain informed consent. The lawyer must make reasonable efforts to ensure that the client or other person possesses information reasonably adequate to make an informed decision. Ordinarily, this will require communication that includes a disclosure of the facts and circumstances giving rise to the situation, any explanation reasonably necessary to inform the client or other person of the material advantages and disadvantages of the proposed course of conduct and a discussion of the client's or other person's options and alternatives. In some circumstances it may be appropriate for a lawyer to advise a client or other person to seek the advice of other counsel. A lawyer need not inform a client or other person of facts or implications already known to the client or other person; nevertheless, a lawyer who does not personally inform the client or other person assumes the risk that the client or other person is inadequately informed and the consent is invalid. In determining whether the information and explanation provided are reasonably adequate, relevant factors include whether the client or other person is experienced in legal matters generally and in making decisions of the type involved, and whether the client or other person is independently represented by other counsel in giving the consent. Normally, such persons need less information and explanation than others, and generally a client or other person who is independently represented by other counsel in giving the consent should be assumed to have given informed consent.

Obtaining informed consent will usually require an affirmative response by the client or other person. In general, a lawyer may not assume consent from a client's or other person's silence. Consent may be inferred, however, from the conduct of a client or other person who has reasonably adequate information about the matter. A number of rules state that a person's consent be confirmed in writing. See, e.g., rule 4-1.7(b). For a definition of "writing" and

"confirmed in writing," see terminology above. Other rules require that a client's consent be obtained in a writing signed by the client. See, e.g., rule 4-1.8(a). For a definition of "signed," see terminology above.

Screened

This definition applies to situations where screening of a personally disqualified lawyer is permitted to remove imputation of a conflict of interest under rules 4-1.11, 4-1.12, or 4-1.18.

The purpose of screening is to assure the affected parties that confidential information known by the personally disqualified lawyer remains protected. The personally disqualified lawyer should acknowledge the obligation not to communicate with any of the other lawyers in the firm with respect to the matter. Similarly, other lawyers in the firm who are working on the matter should be informed that the screening is in place and that they may not communicate with the personally disqualified lawyer with respect to the matter. Additional screening measures that are appropriate for the particular matter will depend on the circumstances. To implement, reinforce, and remind all affected lawyers of the presence of the screening, it may be appropriate for the firm to undertake such procedures as a written undertaking by the screened lawyer to avoid any communication with other firm personnel and any contact with any firm files or other materials relating to the matter, written notice and instructions to all other firm personnel forbidding any communication with the screened lawyer relating to the matter, denial of access by the screened lawyer to firm files or other materials relating to the matter, and periodic reminders of the screen to the screened lawyer and all other firm personnel.

In order to be effective, screening measures must be implemented as soon as practicable after a lawyer or law firm knows or reasonably should know that there is a need for screening.

Amended July 23, 1992, effective Jan. 1, 1993 (605 So.2d 252); amended March 23, 2006, effective May 22,
2006 (SC04-2246), (933 So.2d 417).

4-1. CLIENT-LAWYER RELATIONSHIP
RULE 4-1.1 COMPETENCE

A lawyer shall provide competent representation to a client. Competent representation requires the legal knowledge, skill, thoroughness, and preparation reasonably necessary for the representation.

Comment

Legal knowledge and skill

In determining whether a lawyer employs the requisite knowledge and skill in a particular matter, relevant factors include the relative complexity and specialized nature of the matter, the lawyer's general experience, the lawyer's training and experience in the field in question, the preparation and study the lawyer is able to give the matter, and whether it is feasible to refer the matter to, or associate or consult with, a lawyer of established competence in the field in question. In many instances the required proficiency is that of a general practitioner. Expertise in a particular field of law may be required in some circumstances.

A lawyer need not necessarily have special training or prior experience to handle legal problems of a type with which the lawyer is unfamiliar. A newly admitted lawyer can be as competent as a practitioner with long experience. Some important legal skills, such as the analysis of precedent, the evaluation of evidence and legal drafting, are required in all legal problems. Perhaps the most fundamental legal skill consists of determining what kind of legal problems a situation may involve, a skill that necessarily transcends any particular specialized knowledge. A lawyer can provide adequate representation in a wholly novel field through necessary study. Competent representation can also be provided through the association of a lawyer of established competence in the field in question.

In an emergency a lawyer may give advice or assistance in a matter in which the lawyer does not have the skill ordinarily required where referral to or consultation or association with another lawyer would be impractical. Even in an emergency, however, assistance should be limited to that reasonably necessary in the circumstances, for ill-considered action under emergency conditions can jeopardize the client's interest.

A lawyer may accept representation where the requisite level of competence can be achieved by reasonable preparation. This applies as well to a lawyer who is appointed as counsel for an unrepresented person. See also rule 4-6.2.

Thoroughness and preparation

Competent handling of a particular matter includes inquiry into and analysis of the factual and legal elements of the problem, and use of methods and procedures meeting the standards of competent practitioners. It also includes adequate preparation. The required attention and preparation are determined in part by what is at stake; major litigation and complex transactions ordinarily require more extensive treatment than matters of lesser complexity and consequence. The lawyer should consult with the client about the degree of thoroughness and the level of preparation required as well as the estimated costs involved under the circumstances.

Maintaining competence

To maintain the requisite knowledge and skill, a lawyer should keep abreast of changes in the law and its practice, engage in continuing study and education, and comply with all continuing legal education requirements to which the lawyer is subject.

Amended March 23, 2006, effective May 22, 2006 (SC04-2246), (933 So.2d 417) So.2d 417)

. . . .

RULE 4-1.3 DILIGENCE

A lawyer shall act with reasonable diligence and promptness in representing a client.

Comment

A lawyer should pursue a matter on behalf of a client despite opposition, obstruction, or personal inconvenience to the lawyer and take whatever lawful and ethical measures are required to vindicate a client's cause or endeavor. A lawyer must also act with commitment and dedication to the interests of the client and with zeal in advocacy upon the client's behalf. A lawyer is not bound, however, to press for every advantage that might be realized for a client. For example, a lawyer may have authority to exercise professional discretion in determining the means by which a matter should be pursued. See rule 4-1.2. The lawyer's duty to act with reasonable diligence does not require the use of offensive tactics or preclude the treating of all persons involved in the legal process with courtesy and respect.

A lawyer's workload must be controlled so that each matter can be handled competently.

Perhaps no professional shortcoming is more widely resented than procrastination. A client's interests often can be adversely affected by the passage of time or the change of conditions; in extreme instances, as when a lawyer overlooks a statute of limitations, the client's legal position may be destroyed. Even when the client's interests are not affected in substance, however, unreasonable delay can cause a client needless anxiety and undermine confidence in the lawyer. A lawyer's duty to act with reasonable promptness, however, does not preclude the lawyer from agreeing to a reasonable request for a postponement that will not prejudice the lawyer's client.

Unless the relationship is terminated as provided in rule 4-1.16, a lawyer should carry through to conclusion all matters undertaken for a client. If a lawyer's employment is limited to a specific matter, the relationship terminates when the matter has been resolved. If a lawyer has served a client over a substantial period in a variety of matters, the client sometimes may assume that the lawyer will continue to serve on a continuing basis unless the lawyer gives notice of withdrawal. Doubt about whether a client-lawyer relationship still exists should be clarified by the lawyer, preferably in writing, so that the client will not mistakenly suppose the lawyer is looking after the client's affairs when the lawyer has ceased to do so. For example, if a lawyer has handled a judicial or administrative proceeding that produced a result adverse to the client and the lawyer and the client have not agreed that the lawyer will handle the matter on appeal, the lawyer must consult with the client about the possibility of appeal before relinquishing responsibility for the matter. See rule 4-1.4(a)(2). Whether the lawyer is obligated to prosecute the appeal for the client depends on the scope of the representation the lawyer has agreed to provide to the client. See rule 4-1.2.

Comment amended July 23, 1992, effective Jan. 1, 1993 (605 So.2d 252); March 23, 2006, effective May 22,
2006 (SC04-2246), (933 So.2d 417).

RULE 4-1.4 COMMUNICATION

(a)   Informing Client of Status of Representation. A lawyer shall:

(1)   promptly inform the client of any decision or circumstance with respect to which the client's informed consent, as defined in terminology, is required by these rules;

(2)   reasonably consult with the client about the means by which the client's objectives are to be accomplished;

(3)   keep the client reasonably informed about the status of the matter;

(4)   promptly comply with reasonable requests for information; and

(5)   consult with the client about any relevant limitation on the lawyer's conduct when the lawyer knows or reasonably should know that the client expects assistance not permitted by the Rules of Professional Conduct or other law.

(b)   Duty to Explain Matters to Client. A lawyer shall explain a matter to the extent reasonably necessary to permit the client to make informed decisions regarding the representation.

Comment

Reasonable communication between the lawyer and the client is necessary for the client to effectively participate in the representation.

Communicating with client

If these rules require that a particular decision about the representation be made by the client, subdivision (a)(1) requires that the lawyer promptly consult with and secure the client's consent prior to taking action unless prior discussions with the client have resolved what action the client wants the lawyer to take. For example, a lawyer who receives from opposing counsel an offer of settlement in a civil controversy or a proffered plea bargain in a criminal case must promptly inform the client of its substance unless the client has previously indicated that the proposal will be acceptable or unacceptable or has authorized the lawyer to accept or to reject the offer. See rule 4-1.2(a).

Subdivision (a)(2) requires the lawyer to reasonably consult with the client about the means to be used to accomplish the client's objectives. In some situations – depending on both the importance of the action under consideration and the feasibility of consulting with the client – this duty will require consultation prior to taking action. In other circumstances, such as during a trial when an immediate decision must be made, the exigency of the situation may require the lawyer to act without prior consultation. In such cases the lawyer must nonetheless act reasonably to inform the client of actions the lawyer has taken on the client's behalf. Additionally, subdivision (a)(3) requires that the lawyer keep the client reasonably informed about the status of the matter, such as significant developments affecting the timing or the substance of the representation.

A lawyer's regular communication with clients will minimize the occasions on which a client will need to request information concerning the representation. When a client makes a reasonable request for information, however, subdivision (a)(4) requires prompt compliance with the request, or if a prompt response is not feasible, that the lawyer, or a member of the lawyer's staff, acknowledge receipt of the request and advise the client when a response may be expected.

Explaining matters

The client should have sufficient information to participate intelligently in decisions concerning the objectives of the representation and the means by which they are to be pursued, to the extent the client is willing and able to do so.

Adequacy of communication depends in part on the kind of advice or assistance that is involved. For example, when there is time to explain a proposal made in a negotiation, the lawyer should review all important provisions with the client before proceeding to an agreement. In litigation a lawyer should explain the general strategy and prospects of success and ordinarily should consult the client on tactics that are likely to result in significant expense or to injure or coerce others. On the other hand, a lawyer ordinarily will not be expected to describe trial or negotiation strategy in detail. The guiding principle is that the lawyer should fulfill reasonable client expectations for information consistent with the duty to act in the client's best interests and the client's overall requirements as to the character of representation. In certain circumstances, such as when a lawyer asks a client to consent to a representation affected by a conflict of interest, the client must give informed consent, as defined in terminology.

Ordinarily, the information to be provided is that appropriate for a client who is a comprehending and responsible adult. However, fully informing the client according to this standard may be impracticable, for example, where the client is a child or suffers from mental disability. See rule 4-1.14. When the client is an organization or group, it is often impossible or inappropriate to inform every one of its members about its legal affairs; ordinarily, the lawyer should address communications to the appropriate officials of the organization. See rule 4-1.13. Where many routine matters are involved, a system of limited or occasional reporting may be arranged with the client.

Withholding information

In some circumstances, a lawyer may be justified in delaying transmission of information when the client would be likely to react imprudently to an immediate communication. Thus, a lawyer might withhold a psychiatric diagnosis of a client when the examining psychiatrist indicates that disclosure would harm the client. A lawyer may not withhold information to serve the lawyer's own interest or convenience or the interests or convenience of another person. Rules or court orders governing litigation may provide that information supplied to a lawyer may not be disclosed to the client. Rule 4-3.4(c) directs compliance with such rules or orders.

Amended July 23, 1992, effective Jan. 1, 1993 (605 So.2d 252); March 23, 2006, effective May 22, 2006
(SC04-2246), (933 So.2d 417).

RULE 4-1.5 FEES AND COSTS FOR LEGAL SERVICES

(a)   Illegal, Prohibited, or Clearly Excessive Fees and Costs. An attorney shall not enter into an agreement for, charge, or collect an illegal, prohibited, or clearly excessive fee or cost, or a fee generated by employment that was obtained through advertising or solicitation not in compliance with the Rules Regulating The Florida Bar. A fee or cost is clearly excessive when:

(1)   after a review of the facts, a lawyer of ordinary prudence would be left with a definite and firm conviction that the fee or the cost exceeds a reasonable fee or cost for services provided to such a degree as to constitute clear overreaching or an unconscionable demand by the attorney; or

(2)   the fee or cost is sought or secured by the attorney by means of intentional misrepresentation or fraud upon the client, a nonclient party, or any court, as to either entitlement to, or amount of, the fee.

(b)   Factors to Be Considered in Determining Reasonable Fees and Costs.

(1)   Factors to be considered as guides in determining a reasonable fee include:

(A)   the time and labor required, the novelty, complexity, and difficulty of the questions involved, and the skill requisite to perform the legal service properly;

(B)   the likelihood that the acceptance of the particular employment will preclude other employment by the lawyer;

(C)   the fee, or rate of fee, customarily charged in the locality for legal services of a comparable or similar nature;

(D)   the significance of, or amount involved in, the subject matter of the representation, the responsibility involved in the representation, and the results obtained;

(E)   the time limitations imposed by the client or by the circumstances and, as between attorney and client, any additional or special time demands or requests of the attorney by the client;

(F)   the nature and length of the professional relationship with the client;

(G)   the experience, reputation, diligence, and ability of the lawyer or lawyers performing the service and the skill, expertise, or efficiency of effort reflected in the actual providing of such services; and

(H)   whether the fee is fixed or contingent, and, if fixed as to amount or rate, then whether the client's ability to pay rested to any significant degree on the outcome of the representation.

(2)   Factors to be considered as guides in determining reasonable costs include:

(A)   the nature and extent of the disclosure made to the client about the costs;

(B)   whether a specific agreement exists between the lawyer and client as to the costs a client is expected to pay and how a cost is calculated that is charged to a client;

(C)   the actual amount charged by third party providers of services to the attorney;

(D)   whether specific costs can be identified and allocated to an individual client or a reasonable basis exists to estimate the costs charged;

(E)   the reasonable charges for providing in-house service to a client if the cost is an in-house charge for services; and

(F)   the relationship and past course of conduct between the lawyer and the client.

All costs are subject to the test of reasonableness set forth in subdivision (a) above. When the parties have a written contract in which the method is established for charging costs, the costs charged thereunder shall be presumed reasonable.

(c)   Consideration of All Factors. In determining a reasonable fee, the time devoted to the representation and customary rate of fee need not be the sole or controlling factors. All factors set forth in this rule should be considered, and may be applied, in justification of a fee higher or lower than that which would result from application of only the time and rate factors.

(d)   Enforceability of Fee Contracts. Contracts or agreements for attorney's fees between attorney and client will ordinarily be enforceable according to the terms of such contracts or agreements, unless found to be illegal, obtained through advertising or solicitation not in compliance with the Rules Regulating The Florida Bar, prohibited by this rule, or clearly excessive as defined by this rule.

(e)   Duty to Communicate Basis or Rate of Fee or Costs to Client. When the lawyer has not regularly represented the client, the basis or rate of the fee and costs shall be communicated to the client, preferably in writing, before or within a reasonable time after commencing the representation. A fee for legal services that is nonrefundable in any part shall be confirmed in writing and shall explain the intent of the parties as to the nature and amount of the nonrefundable fee. The test of reasonableness found in subdivision (b), above, applies to all fees for legal services without regard to their characterization by the parties.

The fact that a contract may not be in accord with these rules is an issue between the attorney and client and a matter of professional ethics, but is not the proper basis for an action or defense by an opposing party when fee-shifting litigation is involved.

(f)   Contingent Fees. As to contingent fees:

(1)   A fee may be contingent on the outcome of the matter for which the service is rendered, except in a matter in which a contingent fee is prohibited by subdivision (f)(3) or by law. A contingent fee agreement shall be in writing and shall state the method by which the fee is to be determined, including the percentage or percentages that shall accrue to the lawyer in the event

of settlement, trial, or appeal, litigation and other expenses to be deducted from the recovery, and whether such expenses are to be deducted before or after the contingent fee is calculated. Upon conclusion of a contingent fee matter, the lawyer shall provide the client with a written statement stating the outcome of the matter and, if there is a recovery, showing the remittance to the client and the method of its determination.

(2)   Every lawyer who accepts a retainer or enters into an agreement, express or implied, for compensation for services rendered or to be rendered in any action, claim, or proceeding whereby the lawyer's compensation is to be dependent or contingent in whole or in part upon the successful prosecution or settlement thereof shall do so only where such fee arrangement is reduced to a written contract, signed by the client, and by a lawyer for the lawyer or for the law firm representing the client. No lawyer or firm may participate in the fee without the consent of the client in writing. Each participating lawyer or law firm shall sign the contract with the client and shall agree to assume joint legal responsibility to the client for the performance of the services in question as if each were partners of the other lawyer or law firm involved. The client shall be furnished with a copy of the signed contract and any subsequent notices or consents. All provisions of this rule shall apply to such fee contracts.

(3)   A lawyer shall not enter into an arrangement for, charge, or collect:

(A)   any fee in a domestic relations matter, the payment or amount of which is contingent upon the securing of a divorce or upon the amount of alimony or support, or property settlement in lieu thereof; or

(B)   a contingent fee for representing a defendant in a criminal case.

(4)   A lawyer who enters into an arrangement for, charges, or collects any fee in an action or claim for personal injury or for property damages or for death or loss of services resulting from personal injuries based upon tortious conduct of another, including products liability claims, whereby the compensation is to be dependent or contingent in whole or in part upon the successful prosecution or settlement thereof shall do so only under the following requirements:

(A)   The contract shall contain the following provisions:

(i)   "The undersigned client has, before signing this contract, received and read the statement of client's rights and understands each of the rights set forth therein. The undersigned client has signed the statement and received a signed copy to refer to while being represented by the undersigned attorney(s)."

(ii)   "This contract may be cancelled by written notification to the attorney at any time within 3 business days of the date the contract was signed, as shown below, and if cancelled the client shall not be obligated to pay any fees to the attorney for the work performed during that time. If the attorney has advanced funds to others in representation of the client, the attorney is entitled to be reimbursed for such amounts as the attorney has reasonably advanced on behalf of the client."

(B)   The contract for representation of a client in a matter set forth in subdivision (f)(4) may provide for a contingent fee arrangement as agreed upon by the client and the lawyer, except as limited by the following provisions:

(i)   Without prior court approval as specified below, any contingent fee that exceeds the following standards shall be presumed, unless rebutted, to be clearly excessive:

a.Before the filing of an answer or the demand for appointment of arbitrators or, if no answer is filed or no demand for appointment of arbitrators is made, the expiration of the time period provided for such action:

1.   33 1/3% of any recovery up to $1 million; plus

2.   30% of any portion of the recovery between $1 million and $2 million; plus

3.   20% of any portion of the recovery exceeding $2 million.

b.   After the filing of an answer or the demand for appointment of arbitrators or, if no answer is filed or no demand for appointment of arbitrators is made, the expiration of the time period provided for such action, through the entry of judgment:

1.   40% of any recovery up to $1 million; plus

2.   30% of any portion of the recovery between $1 million and $2 million; plus

3.   20% of any portion of the recovery exceeding $2 million.

c.If all defendants admit liability at the time of filing their answers and request a trial only on damages:

1.   33 1/3% of any recovery up to $1 million; plus

2.   20% of any portion of the recovery between $1 million and $2 million; plus

3.   15% of any portion of the recovery exceeding $2 million.

d.   An additional 5% of any recovery after institution of any appellate proceeding is filed or post-judgment relief or action is required for recovery on the judgment.

(ii)   If any client is unable to obtain an attorney of the client's choice because of the limitations set forth in subdivision (f)(4)(B)(i), the client may petition the court in which the matter would be filed, if litigation is necessary, or if such court

will not accept jurisdiction for the fee division, the circuit court wherein the cause of action arose, for approval of any fee contract between the client and an attorney of the client's choosing. Such authorization shall be given if the court determines the client has a complete understanding of the client's rights and the terms of the proposed contract. The application for authorization of such a contract can be filed as a separate proceeding before suit or simultaneously with the filing of a complaint. Proceedings thereon may occur before service on the defendant and this aspect of the file may be sealed. A petition under this subdivision shall contain a certificate showing service on the client and, if the petition is denied, a copy of the petition and order denying the petition shall be served on The Florida Bar in Tallahassee by the member of the bar who filed the petition. Authorization of such a contract shall not bar subsequent inquiry as to whether the fee actually claimed or charged is clearly excessive under subdivisions (a) and (b).

(iii)   Subject to the provisions of 4-1.5(f)(4)(B)(i) and (ii) a lawyer who enters into an arrangement for, charges, or collects any fee in an action or claim for medical liability whereby the compensation is dependent or contingent in whole or in part upon the successful prosecution or settlement thereof shall provide the language of article I, section 26 of the Florida Constitution to the client in writing and shall orally inform the client that:

a.Unless waived, in any medical liability claim involving a contingency fee, the claimant is entitled to receive no less than 70% of the first $250,000 of all damages received by the claimant, exclusive of reasonable and customary costs, whether received by judgment, settlement, or otherwise, and regardless of the number of defendants. The claimant is entitled to 90% of all damages in excess of $250,000, exclusive of reasonable and customary costs and regardless of the number of defendants.

b.   If a lawyer chooses not to accept the representation of a client under the terms of article I, section 26 of the Florida Constitution, the lawyer shall advise the client, both orally and in writing of alternative terms, if any, under which the lawyer would accept the representation of the client, as well as the client's right to seek representation by another lawyer willing to accept the representation under the terms of article I, section 26 of the Florida Constitution, or a lawyer willing to accept the representation on a fee basis that is not contingent.

c.If any client desires to waive any rights under article I, section 26 of the Florida Constitution in order to obtain a lawyer of the client's choice, a client may do so by waiving such rights in writing, under oath, and in the form provided in this rule. The lawyer shall provide each client a copy of the written waiver and shall afford each client a full and complete opportunity to understand the rights being waived as set forth in the waiver. A copy of the waiver, signed by each client and lawyer, shall be given to each client to retain, and the lawyer shall keep a copy in the lawyer's file pertaining to the client. The waiver shall be retained by the lawyer with the written fee contract and

closing statement under the same conditions and requirements provided in 4- 1.5(f)(5).

WAIVER OF THE CONSTITUTIONAL RIGHT PROVIDED IN ARTICLE I, SECTION 26 OF THE FLORIDA CONSTITUTION

On November 2, 2004, voters in the State of Florida approved The Medical Liability Claimant's Compensation Amendment that was identified as Amendment 3 on the ballot. The amendment is set forth below:

The Florida Constitution

Article I, Section 26 is created to read "Claimant's right to fair compensation." In any medical liability claim involving a contingency fee, the claimant is entitled to receive no less than 70% of the first $250,000 in all damages received by the claimant, exclusive of reasonable and customary costs, whether received by judgment, settlement or otherwise, and regardless of the number of defendants. The claimant is entitled to 90% of all damages in excess of $250,000, exclusive of reasonable and customary costs and regardless of the number of defendants. This provision is self-executing and does not require implementing legislation.

The undersigned client understands and acknowledges that (initial each provision):

I have been advised that signing this waiver releases an important constitutional right; and

I have been advised that I may consult with separate counsel before signing this waiver; and that I may request a hearing before a judge to further explain this waiver; and

By signing this waiver I agree to an increase in the attorney fee that might otherwise be owed if the constitutional provision listed above is not waived. Without prior court approval, the increased fee that I agree to may be up to the maximum contingency fee percentages set forth in Rule Regulating The Florida Bar 4-1.5(f)(4)(B)(i). Depending on the circumstances of my case, the maximum agreed upon fee may range from

33 1/3% to 40% of any recovery up to $1 million; plus 20% to 30% of any portion of the recovery between $1 million and $2 million; plus 15% to 20% of any recovery exceeding $2 million; and

I have three (3) business days following execution of this waiver in which to cancel this waiver; and

I wish to engage the legal services of the lawyers or law firms listed below in an action or claim for medical liability the fee for which is contingent in whole or in part upon the successful prosecution or settlement thereof, but I am unable to do so because of the provisions of the constitutional limitation set forth above. In consideration of the lawyers' or law firms' agreements to represent me and my desire to employ the lawyers or law firms listed below, I hereby knowingly, willingly, and voluntarily waive any and all rights and privileges that I may have under the constitutional provision set forth above, as apply to the contingency fee agreement only. Specifically, I waive the percentage restrictions that are the subject of the

constitutional provision and confirm the fee percentages set forth in the contingency fee agreement; and

I have selected the lawyers or law firms listed below as my counsel of choice in this matter and would not be able to engage their services without this waiver; and I expressly state that this waiver is made freely and voluntarily, with full knowledge of its terms, and that all questions have been answered to my satisfaction.

ACKNOWLEDGMENT BY CLIENT FOR PRESENTATION TO THE COURT

The undersigned client hereby acknowledges, under oath, the following:

I have read and understand this entire waiver of my rights under the constitutional provision set forth above.

I am not under the influence of any substance, drug, or condition (physical, mental, or emotional) that interferes with my understanding of this entire waiver in which I am entering and all the consequences thereof.

I have entered into and signed this waiver freely and voluntarily.

I authorize my lawyers or law firms listed below to present this waiver to the appropriate court, if required for purposes of approval of the contingency fee agreement. Unless the court requires my attendance at a hearing for that purpose, my lawyers or law firms are authorized to provide this waiver to the court for its consideration without my presence.

Dated this day of   ,   .

By:

CLIENT

Sworn to and subscribed before me this   day of   ,   by
         , who is personally known to me, or has produced the following identification: .

Notary Public

My Commission Expires:

Dated this day of   ,   .

By:

ATTORNEY

(C)   Before a lawyer enters into a contingent fee contract for representation of a client in a matter set forth in this rule, the lawyer shall provide the client with a copy of the statement of client's rights and shall afford the client a full and complete opportunity to understand each of the rights as set forth therein. A copy of the

statement, signed by both the client and the lawyer, shall be given to the client to retain and the lawyer shall keep a copy in the client's file. The statement shall be retained by the lawyer with the written fee contract and closing statement under the same conditions and requirements as subdivision (f)(5).

(D)   As to lawyers not in the same firm, a division of any fee within subdivision (f)(4) shall be on the following basis:

(i)   To the lawyer assuming primary responsibility for the legal services on behalf of the client, a minimum of 75% of the total fee.

(ii)   To the lawyer assuming secondary responsibility for the legal services on behalf of the client, a maximum of 25% of the total fee. Any fee in excess of 25% shall be presumed to be clearly excessive.

(iii)   The 25% limitation shall not apply to those cases in which 2 or more lawyers or firms accept substantially equal active participation in the providing of legal services. In such circumstances counsel shall apply to the court in which the matter would be filed, if litigation is necessary, or if such court will not accept jurisdiction for the fee division, the circuit court wherein the cause of action arose, for authorization of the fee division in excess of 25%, based upon a sworn petition signed by all counsel that shall disclose in detail those services to be performed. The application for authorization of such a contract may be filed as a separate proceeding before suit or simultaneously with the filing of a complaint, or within 10 days of execution of a contract for division of fees when new counsel is engaged. Proceedings thereon may occur before service of process on any party and this aspect of the file may be sealed. Authorization of such contract shall not bar subsequent inquiry as to whether the fee actually claimed or charged is clearly excessive. An application under this subdivision shall contain a certificate showing service on the client and, if the application is denied, a copy of the petition and order denying the petition shall be served on The Florida Bar in Tallahassee by the member of the bar who filed the petition. Counsel may proceed with representation of the client pending court approval.

(iv)   The percentages required by this subdivision shall be applicable after deduction of any fee payable to separate counsel retained especially for appellate purposes.

(5)   In the event there is a recovery, upon the conclusion of the representation, the lawyer shall prepare a closing statement reflecting an itemization of all costs and expenses, together with the amount of fee received by each participating lawyer or law firm. A copy of the closing statement shall be executed by all participating lawyers, as well as the client, and each shall receive a copy. Each participating lawyer shall retain a copy of the written fee contract and closing statement for 6 years after execution of the closing statement. Any contingent fee contract and closing statement shall be available for inspection at reasonable times by the client, by any other person upon judicial order, or by the appropriate disciplinary agency.

(6)   In cases in which the client is to receive a recovery that will be paid to the client on a future structured or periodic basis, the contingent fee percentage shall be calculated only on the cost of the structured verdict or

settlement or, if the cost is unknown, on the present money value of the structured verdict or settlement, whichever is less. If the damages and the fee are to be paid out over the long term future schedule, this limitation does not apply. No attorney may negotiate separately with the defendant for that attorney's fee in a structured verdict or settlement when separate negotiations would place the attorney in a position of conflict.

(g)   Division of Fees Between Lawyers in Different Firms. Subject to the provisions of subdivision (f)(4)(D), a division of fee between lawyers who are not in the same firm may be made only if the total fee is reasonable and:

(1)   the division is in proportion to the services performed by each lawyer; or

(2)   by written agreement with the client:

(A)   each lawyer assumes joint legal responsibility for the representation and agrees to be available for consultation with the client; and

(B)   the agreement fully discloses that a division of fees will be made and the basis upon which the division of fees will be made.

(h)   Credit Plans. A lawyer or law firm may accept payment under a credit plan. No higher fee shall be charged and no additional charge shall be imposed by reason of a lawyer's or law firm's participation in a credit plan.

(i)   Arbitration Clauses. A lawyer shall not make an agreement with a potential client prospectively providing for mandatory arbitration of fee disputes without first advising that person in writing that the potential client should consider obtaining independent legal advice as to the advisability of entering into an agreement containing such mandatory arbitration provisions. A lawyer shall not make an agreement containing such mandatory arbitration provisions unless the agreement contains the following language in bold print:

NOTICE: This agreement contains provisions requiring arbitration of fee disputes. Before you sign this agreement you should consider consulting with another lawyer about the advisability of making an agreement with mandatory arbitration requirements. Arbitration proceedings are ways to resolve disputes without use of the court system. By entering into agreements that require arbitration as the way to resolve fee disputes, you give up (waive) your right to go to court to resolve those disputes by a judge or jury. These are important rights that should not be given up without careful consideration.

STATEMENT OF CLIENT'S RIGHTS FOR CONTINGENCY FEES

Before you, the prospective client, arrange a contingent fee agreement with a lawyer, you should understand this statement of your rights as a client. This

statement is not a part of the actual contract between you and your lawyer, but, as a prospective client, you should be aware of these rights:

1.   There is no legal requirement that a lawyer charge a client a set fee or a percentage of money recovered in a case. You, the client, have the right to talk with your lawyer about the proposed fee and to bargain about the rate or percentage as in any other contract. If you do not reach an agreement with 1 lawyer you may talk with other lawyers.

2.   Any contingent fee contract must be in writing and you have 3 business days to reconsider the contract. You may cancel the contract without any reason if you notify your lawyer in writing within 3 business days of signing the contract. If you withdraw from the contract within the first 3 business days, you do not owe the lawyer a fee although you may be responsible for the lawyer's actual costs during that time. If your lawyer begins to represent you, your lawyer may not withdraw from the case without giving you notice, delivering necessary papers to you, and allowing you time to employ another lawyer. Often, your lawyer must obtain court approval before withdrawing from a case. If you discharge your lawyer without good cause after the 3-day period, you may have to pay a fee for work the lawyer has done.

3.   Before hiring a lawyer, you, the client, have the right to know about the lawyer's education, training, and experience. If you ask, the lawyer should tell you specifically about the lawyer's actual experience dealing with cases similar to yours. If you ask, the lawyer should provide information about special training or knowledge and give you this information in writing if you request it.

4.   Before signing a contingent fee contract with you, a lawyer must advise you whether the lawyer intends to handle your case alone or whether other lawyers will be helping with the case. If your lawyer intends to refer

the case to other lawyers, the lawyer should tell you what kind of fee sharing arrangement will be made with the other lawyers. If lawyers from different law firms will represent you, at least 1 lawyer from each law firm must sign the contingent fee contract.

5.	If your lawyer intends to refer your case to another lawyer or counsel with other lawyers, your lawyer should tell you about that at the beginning. If your lawyer takes the case and later decides to refer it to another lawyer or to associate with other lawyers, you should sign a new contract that includes the new lawyers. You, the client, also have the right to consult with each lawyer working on your case and each lawyer is legally responsible to represent your interests and is legally responsible for the acts of the other lawyers involved in the case.

6.	You, the client, have the right to know in advance how you will need to pay the expenses and the legal fees at the end of the case. If you pay a deposit in advance for costs, you may ask reasonable questions about how the money will be or has been spent and how much of it remains unspent. Your lawyer should give a reasonable estimate about future necessary costs. If your lawyer agrees to lend or advance you money to prepare or research the case, you have the right to know periodically how much money your lawyer has spent on your behalf. You also have the right to decide, after consulting with your lawyer, how much money is to be spent to prepare a case. If you pay the expenses, you have the right to decide how much to spend. Your

lawyer should also inform you whether the fee will be based on the gross amount recovered or on the amount recovered minus the costs.

7.	You, the client, have the right to be told by your lawyer about possible adverse consequences if you lose the case. Those adverse consequences might include money that you might have to pay to your lawyer for costs and liability you might have for attorney's fees, costs, and expenses to the other side.

8.	You, the client, have the right to receive and approve a closing statement at the end of the case before you pay any money. The statement must list all of the financial details of the entire case, including the amount recovered, all expenses, and a precise statement of your lawyer's fee. Until you approve the closing statement your lawyer cannot pay any money to anyone, including you, without an appropriate order of the court. You also have the right to have every lawyer or law firm working on your case sign this closing statement.

9.   You, the client, have the right to ask your lawyer at reasonable intervals how the case is progressing and to have these questions answered to the best of your lawyer's ability.

10.   You, the client, have the right to make the final decision regarding settlement of a case. Your lawyer must notify you of all offers of settlement before and after the trial.   Offers during the trial must be immediately communicated and you should consult with your lawyer regarding whether to accept a settlement. However, you must make the final decision to accept or reject a settlement.

11.   If at any time you, the client, believe that your lawyer has charged an excessive or illegal fee, you have the right to report the matter to The Florida Bar, the agency that oversees the practice and behavior of all lawyers in Florida. For information on how to reach The Florida Bar, call 850/561-5600, or contact the local bar association. Any disagreement between you and your lawyer about a fee can be taken to court and you may wish to hire another lawyer to help you resolve this disagreement. Usually fee disputes must be handled in a separate lawsuit, unless your fee contract provides for arbitration.   You can request, but may not require, that a provision for arbitration (under Chapter 682, Florida Statutes, or under the fee arbitration rule of the Rules Regulating The Florida Bar) be included in your fee contract.

Date: Date:

Client Signature   Attorney Signature

Comment

Bases or rate of fees and costs

When the lawyer has regularly represented a client, they ordinarily will have evolved an understanding concerning the basis or rate of the fee. The conduct of the lawyer and client in prior relationships is relevant when analyzing the requirements of this rule. In a new client- lawyer relationship, however, an understanding as to the fee should be promptly established. It

is not necessary to recite all the factors that underlie the basis of the fee but only those that are directly involved in its computation. It is sufficient, for example, to state the basic rate is an hourly charge or a fixed amount or an estimated amount, or to identify the factors that may be taken into account in finally fixing the fee. Although hourly billing or a fixed fee may be the most common bases for computing fees in an area of practice, these may not be the only bases for computing fees. A lawyer should, where appropriate, discuss alternative billing methods with the client. When developments occur during the representation that render an earlier estimate substantially inaccurate, a revised estimate should be provided to the client. A written statement concerning the fee reduces the possibility of misunderstanding. Furnishing the client with a simple memorandum or a copy of the lawyer's customary fee schedule is sufficient if the basis or rate of the fee is set forth.

General overhead should be accounted for in a lawyer's fee, whether the lawyer charges hourly, flat, or contingent fees. Filing fees, transcription, and the like should be charged to the client at the actual amount paid by the lawyer. A lawyer may agree with the client to charge a reasonable amount for in-house costs or services. In-house costs include items such as copying, faxing, long distance telephone, and computerized research. In-house services include paralegal services, investigative services, accounting services, and courier services. The lawyer should sufficiently communicate with the client regarding the costs charged to the client so that the client understands the amount of costs being charged or the method for calculation of those costs. Costs appearing in sufficient detail on closing statements and approved by the parties to the transaction should meet the requirements of this rule.

Rule 4-1.8(e) should be consulted regarding a lawyer's providing financial assistance to a client in connection with litigation.

Lawyers should also be mindful of any statutory, constitutional, or other requirements or restrictions on attorney's fees.

In order to avoid misunderstandings concerning the nature of legal fees, written documentation is required when any aspect of the fee is nonrefundable. A written contract provides a method to resolve misunderstandings and to protect the lawyer in the event of continued misunderstanding. Rule 4-1.5 (e) does not require the client to sign a written document memorializing the terms of the fee. A letter from the lawyer to the client setting forth the basis or rate of the fee and the intent of the parties in regard to the nonrefundable nature of the fee is sufficient to meet the requirements of this rule.

All legal fees and contracts for legal fees are subject to the requirements of the Rules Regulating The Florida Bar. In particular, the test for reasonableness of legal fees found in rule 4-1.5(b) applies to all types of legal fees and contracts related to them.

Terms of payment

A lawyer may require advance payment of a fee but is obliged to return any unearned portion. See rule 4-1.16(d). A lawyer is not, however, required to return retainers that, pursuant to an agreement with a client, are not refundable. A lawyer may accept property in payment for services, such as an ownership interest in an enterprise, providing this does not involve

acquisition of a proprietary interest in the cause of action or subject matter of the litigation contrary to rule 4-1.8(i). However, a fee paid in property instead of money may be subject to special scrutiny because it involves questions concerning both the value of the services and the lawyer's special knowledge of the value of the property.

An agreement may not be made whose terms might induce the lawyer improperly to curtail services for the client or perform them in a way contrary to the client's interest. For example, a lawyer should not enter into an agreement whereby services are to be provided only up to a stated amount when it is foreseeable that more extensive services probably will be required, unless the situation is adequately explained to the client. Otherwise, the client might have to bargain for further assistance in the midst of a proceeding or transaction. However, it is proper to define the extent of services in light of the client's ability to pay. A lawyer should not exploit a fee arrangement based primarily on hourly charges by using wasteful procedures. When there is doubt whether a contingent fee is consistent with the client's best interest, the lawyer should offer the client alternative bases for the fee and explain their implications. Applicable law may impose limitations on contingent fees, such as a ceiling on the percentage.

Prohibited contingent fees

Subdivision (f)(3)(A) prohibits a lawyer from charging a contingent fee in a domestic relations matter when payment is contingent upon the securing of a divorce or upon the amount of alimony or support or property settlement to be obtained. This provision does not preclude a contract for a contingent fee for legal representation in connection with the recovery of post- judgment balances due under support, alimony, or other financial orders because such contracts do not implicate the same policy concerns.

Contingent fee regulation

Subdivision (e) is intended to clarify that whether the lawyer's fee contract complies with these rules is a matter between the lawyer and client and an issue for professional disciplinary enforcement. The rules and subdivision (e) are not intended to be used as procedural weapons or defenses by others. Allowing opposing parties to assert noncompliance with these rules as a defense, including whether the fee is fixed or contingent, allows for potential inequity if the opposing party is allowed to escape responsibility for their actions solely through application of these rules.

Rule 4-1.5(f)(4) should not be construed to apply to actions or claims seeking property or other damages arising in the commercial litigation context.

Rule 4-1.5(f)(4)(B) is intended to apply only to contingent aspects of fee agreements. In the situation where a lawyer and client enter a contract for part noncontingent and part contingent attorney's fees, rule 4-1.5(f)(4)(B) should not be construed to apply to and prohibit or limit the noncontingent portion of the fee agreement. An attorney could properly charge and retain the noncontingent portion of the fee even if the matter was not successfully prosecuted or if the noncontingent portion of the fee exceeded the schedule set forth in rule 4-1.5(f)(4)(B). Rule 4- 1.5(f)(4)(B) should, however, be construed to apply to any additional contingent portion of such a contract when considered together with earned noncontingent fees. Thus, under such a contract

a lawyer may demand or collect only such additional contingent fees as would not cause the total fees to exceed the schedule set forth in rule 4-1.5(f)(4)(B).

The limitations in rule 4-1.5(f)(4)(B)(i)c. are only to be applied in the case where all the defendants admit liability at the time they file their initial answer and the trial is only on the issue of the amount or extent of the loss or the extent of injury suffered by the client. If the trial involves not only the issue of damages but also such questions as proximate cause, affirmative defenses, seat belt defense, or other similar matters, the limitations are not to be applied because of the contingent nature of the case being left for resolution by the trier of fact.

Rule 4-1.5(f)(4)(B)(ii) provides the limitations set forth in subdivision (f)(4)(B)(i) may be waived by the client upon approval by the appropriate judge. This waiver provision may not be used to authorize a lawyer to charge a client a fee that would exceed rule 4-1.5(a) or (b). It is contemplated that this waiver provision will not be necessary except where the client wants to retain a particular lawyer to represent the client or the case involves complex, difficult, or novel questions of law or fact that would justify a contingent fee greater than the schedule but not a contingent fee that would exceed rule 4-1.5(b).

Upon a petition by a client, the trial court reviewing the waiver request must grant that request if the trial court finds the client: (a) understands the right to have the limitations in rule 4-1.5(f)(4)(B) applied in the specific matter; and (b) understands and approves the terms of the proposed contract. The consideration by the trial court of the waiver petition is not to be used as an opportunity for the court to inquire into the merits or details of the particular action or claim that is the subject of the contract.

The proceedings before the trial court and the trial court's decision on a waiver request are to be confidential and not subject to discovery by any of the parties to the action or by any other
individual or entity except The Florida Bar. However, terms of the contract approved by the trial court may be subject to discovery if the contract (without court approval) was subject to discovery under applicable case law or rules of evidence.

Rule 4-1.5(f)(4)(B)(iii) is added to acknowledge the provisions of Article 1, Section 26 of the Florida Constitution, and to create an affirmative obligation on the part of an attorney contemplating a contingency fee contract to notify a potential client with a medical liability claim of the limitations provided in that constitutional provision. This addition to the rule is adopted prior to any judicial interpretation of the meaning or scope of the constitutional provision and this rule is not intended to make any substantive interpretation of the meaning or scope of that provision. The rule also provides that a client who wishes to waive the rights of the constitutional provision, as those rights may relate to attorney's fees, must do so in the form contained in the rule.

Rule 4-1.5(f)(6) prohibits a lawyer from charging the contingent fee percentage on the total, future value of a recovery being paid on a structured or periodic basis. This prohibition does not apply if the lawyer's fee is being paid over the same length of time as the schedule of payments to the client.

Contingent fees are prohibited in criminal and certain domestic relations matters. In domestic relations cases, fees that include a bonus provision or additional fee to be determined at a later time and based on results obtained have been held to be impermissible contingency fees and therefore subject to restitution and disciplinary sanction as elsewhere stated in these Rules Regulating The Florida Bar.

Fees that provide for a bonus or additional fees and that otherwise are not prohibited under the Rules Regulating The Florida Bar can be effective tools for structuring fees. For example, a fee contract calling for a flat fee and the payment of a bonus based on the amount of property retained or recovered in a general civil action is not prohibited by these rules. However, the bonus or additional fee must be stated clearly in amount or formula for calculation of the fee (basis or rate). Courts have held that unilateral bonus fees are unenforceable. The test of reasonableness and other requirements of this rule apply to permissible bonus fees.

Division of fee

A division of fee is a single billing to a client covering the fee of 2 or more lawyers who are not in the same firm. A division of fee facilitates association of more than 1 lawyer in a matter in which neither alone could serve the client as well, and most often is used when the fee is contingent and the division is between a referring lawyer and a trial specialist. Subject to the provisions of subdivision (f)(4)(D), subdivision (g) permits the lawyers to divide a fee on either the basis of the proportion of services they render or by agreement between the participating lawyers if all assume responsibility for the representation as a whole and the client is advised and does not object. It does require disclosure to the client of the share that each lawyer is to receive. Joint responsibility for the representation entails the obligations stated in rule 4-5.1 for purposes of the matter involved.

Disputes over fees

Since the fee arbitration rule (chapter 14) has been established by the bar to provide a procedure for resolution of fee disputes, the lawyer should conscientiously consider submitting to it. Where law prescribes a procedure for determining a lawyer's fee, for example, in representation of an executor or administrator, a class, or a person entitled to a reasonable fee as part of the measure of damages, the lawyer entitled to such a fee and a lawyer representing another party concerned with the fee should comply with the prescribed procedure.

Referral fees and practices

A secondary lawyer shall not be entitled to a fee greater than the limitation set forth in rule 4-1.5(f)(4)(D)(ii) merely because the lawyer agrees to do some or all of the following: (a) consults with the client; (b) answers interrogatories; (c) attends depositions; (d) reviews pleadings; (e) attends the trial; or (f) assumes joint legal responsibility to the client. However, the provisions do not contemplate that a secondary lawyer who does more than the above is necessarily entitled to a larger percentage of the fee than that allowed by the limitation.

The provisions of rule 4-1.5(f)(4)(D)(iii) only apply where the participating lawyers have for purposes of the specific case established a co-counsel relationship. The need for court approval of a referral fee arrangement under rule 4-1.5(f)(4)(D)(iii) should only occur in a small

percentage of cases arising under rule 4-1.5(f)(4) and usually occurs prior to the commencement of litigation or at the onset of the representation. However, in those cases in which litigation has been commenced or the representation has already begun, approval of the fee division should be sought within a reasonable period of time after the need for court approval of the fee division arises.

In determining if a co-counsel relationship exists, the court should look to see if the lawyers have established a special partnership agreement for the purpose of the specific case or matter. If such an agreement does exist, it must provide for a sharing of services or responsibility and the fee division is based upon a division of the services to be rendered or the responsibility assumed. It is contemplated that a co-counsel situation would exist where a division of responsibility is based upon, but not limited to, the following: (a) based upon geographic considerations, the lawyers agree to divide the legal work, responsibility, and representation in a convenient fashion. Such a situation would occur when different aspects of a case must be handled in different locations; (b) where the lawyers agree to divide the legal work and representation based upon their particular expertise in the substantive areas of law involved in the litigation; or (c) where the lawyers agree to divide the legal work and representation along established lines of division, such as liability and damages, causation and damages, or other similar factors.

The trial court's responsibility when reviewing an application for authorization of a fee division under rule 4-1.5(f)(4)(D)(iii) is to determine if a co-counsel relationship exists in that particular case. If the court determines a co-counsel relationship exists and authorizes the fee division requested, the court does not have any responsibility to review or approve the specific amount of the fee division agreed upon by the lawyers and the client.

Rule 4-1.5(f)(4)(D)(iv) applies to the situation where appellate counsel is retained during the trial of the case to assist with the appeal of the case. The percentages set forth in subdivision (f)(4)(D) are to be applicable after appellate counsel's fee is established. However, the effect should not be to impose an unreasonable fee on the client.

Credit Plans

Credit plans include credit cards. If a lawyer accepts payment from a credit plan for an advance of fees and costs, the amount must be held in trust in accordance with chapter 5, Rules Regulating The Florida Bar, and the lawyer must add the lawyer's own money to the trust account in an amount equal to the amount charged by the credit plan for doing business with the credit plan.

Amended: Oct. 20, 1987, effective Jan. 1, 1988 (519 So.2d 971); Oct. 26, 1989 (550 So.2d 1120); Dec. 21,
1990, effective Jan. 1, 1991 (571 So.2d 451); July 23, 1992, effective Jan. 1, 1993 (605 So.2d 252); Oct. 20,
1994 (644 So.2d 282); July 20, 1995 (658 So.2d 930); Sept. 24, 1998, effective Oct. 1, 1998 (718 So.2d 1179);
March 23, 2000 (763 So.2d 1002); Feb. 8, 2001 (795 So.2d 1); April 25, 2002 (820 So.2d 210); May 20, 2004
(SC03-705); corrected opinion issued July 7, 2004, (875 So.2d 448); October 6, 2005, effective January 1,
2006 (SC05-206), (916 So.2d 655); March 23, 2006, effective May 22, 2006 (SC04-2246), (933 So.2d 417);
September 28, 2006, effective September 28, 2006 (SC05-1150), (939 So.2d 1032); December 20, 2007,
effective March 1, 2008 (SC06-736), (978 So.2d 91); November 19, 2009, effective February 1, 2010 (SC08-
1890) (34 Fla.L.Weekly S628a). Amended April 12, 2012, effective July 1, 2012 (SC10-1967).

RULE 4-1.6 CONFIDENTIALITY OF INFORMATION

(a)   Consent Required to Reveal Information. A lawyer must not reveal information relating to representation of a client except as stated in subdivisions (b), (c), and (d), unless the client gives informed consent.

(b)   When Lawyer Must Reveal Information. A lawyer must reveal such information to the extent the lawyer reasonably believes necessary:

(1)   to prevent a client from committing a crime; or

(2)   to prevent a death or substantial bodily harm to another.

(c)   When Lawyer May Reveal Information. A lawyer may reveal such information to the extent the lawyer reasonably believes necessary:

(1)   to serve the client's interest unless it is information the client specifically requires not to be disclosed;

(2)   to establish a claim or defense on behalf of the lawyer in a controversy between the lawyer and client;

(3)   to establish a defense to a criminal charge or civil claim against the lawyer based upon conduct in which the client was involved;

(4)   to respond to allegations in any proceeding concerning the lawyer's representation of the client; or

(5)   to comply with the Rules Regulating the Florida Bar.

(d)   Exhaustion of Appellate Remedies. When required by a tribunal to reveal such information, a lawyer may first exhaust all appellate remedies.

(e)   Limitation on Amount of Disclosure.   When disclosure is mandated or permitted, the lawyer must disclose no more information than is required to meet the requirements or accomplish the purposes of this rule.

Comment

The lawyer is part of a judicial system charged with upholding the law. One of the lawyer's functions is to advise clients so that they avoid any violation of the law in the proper exercise of their rights.

This rule governs the disclosure by a lawyer of information relating to the representation of a client during the lawyer's representation of the client. See rule 4-1.18 for the lawyer's duties with respect to information provided to the lawyer by a prospective client, rule 4-1.9(c) for the lawyer's duty not to reveal information relating to the lawyer's prior representation of a former

client, and rules 4-1.8(b) and 4-1.9(b) for the lawyer's duties with respect to the use of such information to the disadvantage of clients and former clients.

A fundamental principle in the client-lawyer relationship is that, in the absence of the client's informed consent, the lawyer must not reveal information relating to the representation. See terminology for the definition of informed consent. This contributes to the trust that is the hallmark of the client-lawyer relationship. The client is thereby encouraged to seek legal assistance and to communicate fully and frankly with the lawyer even as to embarrassing or legally damaging subject matter. The lawyer needs this information to represent the client effectively and, if necessary, to advise the client to refrain from wrongful conduct. Almost without exception, clients come to lawyers in order to determine their rights and what is, in the complex of laws and regulations, deemed to be legal and correct. Based upon experience, lawyers know that almost all clients follow the advice given, and the law is upheld.

The principle of confidentiality is given effect in 2 related bodies of law, the attorney-client privilege (which includes the work product doctrine) in the law of evidence and the rule of confidentiality established in professional ethics. The attorney-client privilege applies in judicial and other proceedings in which a lawyer may be called as a witness or otherwise required to produce evidence concerning a client. The rule of client-lawyer confidentiality applies in situations other than those where evidence is sought from the lawyer through compulsion of law. The confidentiality rule applies not merely to matters communicated in confidence by the client but also to all information relating to the representation, whatever its source. A lawyer may not disclose such information except as authorized or required by the Rules Regulating the Florida Bar or by law. However, none of the foregoing limits the requirement of disclosure in subdivision (b). This disclosure is required to prevent a lawyer from becoming an unwitting accomplice in the fraudulent acts of a client. See also Scope.

The requirement of maintaining confidentiality of information relating to representation applies to government lawyers who may disagree with the policy goals that their representation is designed to advance.

Authorized disclosure

A lawyer is impliedly authorized to make disclosures about a client when appropriate in carrying out the representation, except to the extent that the client's instructions or special circumstances limit that authority. In litigation, for example, a lawyer may disclose information by admitting a fact that cannot properly be disputed or in negotiation by making a disclosure that facilitates a satisfactory conclusion.

Lawyers in a firm may, in the course of the firm's practice, disclose to each other information relating to a client of the firm, unless the client has instructed that particular information be confined to specified lawyers.

Disclosure adverse to client

The confidentiality rule is subject to limited exceptions. In becoming privy to information about a client, a lawyer may foresee that the client intends serious harm to another person. However, to the extent a lawyer is required or permitted to disclose a client's purposes, the client

will be inhibited from revealing facts that would enable the lawyer to counsel against a wrongful course of action. While the public may be protected if full and open communication by the client is encouraged, several situations must be distinguished.

First, the lawyer may not counsel or assist a client in conduct that is criminal or fraudulent. See rule 4-1.2(d). Similarly, a lawyer has a duty under rule 4-3.3(a)(4) not to use false evidence. This duty is essentially a special instance of the duty prescribed in rule 4-1.2(d) to avoid assisting a client in criminal or fraudulent conduct.

Second, the lawyer may have been innocently involved in past conduct by the client that was criminal or fraudulent. In such a situation the lawyer has not violated rule 4-1.2(d), because to "counsel or assist" criminal or fraudulent conduct requires knowing that the conduct is of that character.

Third, the lawyer may learn that a client intends prospective conduct that is criminal. As stated in subdivision (b)(1), the lawyer must reveal information in order to prevent such consequences. It is admittedly difficult for a lawyer to "know" when the criminal intent will actually be carried out, for the client may have a change of mind.

Subdivision (b)(2) contemplates past acts on the part of a client that may result in present or future consequences that may be avoided by disclosure of otherwise confidential communications. Rule 4-1.6(b)(2) would now require the lawyer to disclose information reasonably necessary to prevent the future death or substantial bodily harm to another, even though the act of the client has been completed.

The lawyer's exercise of discretion requires consideration of such factors as the nature of the lawyer's relationship with the client and with those who might be injured by the client, the lawyer's own involvement in the transaction, and factors that may extenuate the conduct in question. Where practical the lawyer should seek to persuade the client to take suitable action. In any case, a disclosure adverse to the client's interest should be no greater than the lawyer reasonably believes necessary to the purpose.

Withdrawal

If the lawyer's services will be used by the client in materially furthering a course of criminal or fraudulent conduct, the lawyer must withdraw, as stated in rule 4-1.16(a)(1).

After withdrawal the lawyer is required to refrain from making disclosure of the client's confidences, except as otherwise provided in rule 4-1.6. Neither this rule nor rule 4-1.8(b) nor rule 4-1.16(d) prevents the lawyer from giving notice of the fact of withdrawal, and the lawyer may also withdraw or disaffirm any opinion, document, affirmation, or the like.

Where the client is an organization, the lawyer may be in doubt whether contemplated conduct will actually be carried out by the organization. Where necessary to guide conduct in connection with the rule, the lawyer may make inquiry within the organization as indicated in rule 4-1.13(b).

Dispute concerning lawyer's conduct

A lawyer's confidentiality obligations do not preclude a lawyer from securing confidential legal advice about the lawyer's personal responsibility to comply with these rules. In most situations, disclosing information to secure such advice will be impliedly authorized for the lawyer to carry out the representation. Even when the disclosure is not impliedly authorized, subdivision (b)(5) permits such disclosure because of the importance of a lawyer's compliance with the Rules of Professional Conduct.

Where a legal claim or disciplinary charge alleges complicity of the lawyer in a client's conduct or other misconduct of the lawyer involving representation of the client, the lawyer may respond to the extent the lawyer reasonably believes necessary to establish a defense. The same is true with respect to a claim involving the conduct or representation of a former client. The lawyer's right to respond arises when an assertion of such complicity has been made. Subdivision (c) does not require the lawyer to await the commencement of an action or proceeding that charges such complicity, so that the defense may be established by responding directly to a third party who has made such an assertion. The right to defend, of course, applies where a proceeding has been commenced. Where practicable and not prejudicial to the lawyer's ability to establish the defense, the lawyer should advise the client of the third party's assertion and request that the client respond appropriately. In any event, disclosure should be no greater than the lawyer reasonably believes is necessary to vindicate innocence, the disclosure should be made in a manner that limits access to the information to the tribunal or other persons having a need to know it, and appropriate protective orders or other arrangements should be sought by the lawyer to the fullest extent practicable.

If the lawyer is charged with wrongdoing in which the client's conduct is implicated, the rule of confidentiality should not prevent the lawyer from defending against the charge. Such a charge can arise in a civil, criminal, or professional disciplinary proceeding and can be based on a wrong allegedly committed by the lawyer against the client or on a wrong alleged by a third person; for example, a person claiming to have been defrauded by the lawyer and client acting together. A lawyer entitled to a fee is permitted by subdivision (c) to prove the services rendered in an action to collect it. This aspect of the rule expresses the principle that the beneficiary of a fiduciary relationship may not exploit it to the detriment of the fiduciary. As stated above, the lawyer must make every effort practicable to avoid unnecessary disclosure of information relating to a representation, to limit disclosure to those having the need to know it, and to obtain protective orders or make other arrangements minimizing the risk of disclosure.

Disclosures otherwise required or authorized

The attorney-client privilege is differently defined in various jurisdictions. If a lawyer is called as a witness to give testimony concerning a client, absent waiver by the client, rule 4- 1.6(a) requires the lawyer to invoke the privilege when it is applicable. The lawyer must comply with the final orders of a court or other tribunal of competent jurisdiction requiring the lawyer to give information about the client.

The Rules of Professional Conduct in various circumstances permit or require a lawyer to disclose information relating to the representation. See rules 4-2.3, 4-3.3, and 4-4.1. In addition

to these provisions, a lawyer may be obligated or permitted by other provisions of law to give information about a client. Whether another provision of law supersedes rule 4-1.6 is a matter of interpretation beyond the scope of these rules, but a presumption should exist against such a supersession.

Former client

The duty of confidentiality continues after the client-lawyer relationship has terminated. See rule 4-1.9 for the prohibition against using such information to the disadvantage of the former client.

Amended July 23, 1992, effective Jan. 1, 1993 (605 So.2d 252); Oct. 20, 1994 (644 So.2d 282); March 23,
2006, effective May 22, 2006 (SC04-2246), (933 So.2d 417); amended July 7, 2011, effective October 1, 2011
(SC10-1968); amended May 29, 2014, effective June 1, 2014 (SC12-2234).

RULE 4-1.7 CONFLICT OF INTEREST; CURRENT CLIENTS

(a)   Representing Adverse Interests. Except as provided in subdivision (b), a lawyer must not represent a client if:

(1)   the representation of 1 client will be directly adverse to another client; or

(2)   there is a substantial risk that the representation of 1 or more clients will be materially limited by the lawyer's responsibilities to another client, a former client or a third person or by a personal interest of the lawyer.

(b)   Informed Consent. Notwithstanding the existence of a conflict of interest under subdivision (a), a lawyer may represent a client if:

(1)   the lawyer reasonably believes that the lawyer will be able to provide competent and diligent representation to each affected client;

(2)   the representation is not prohibited by law;

(3)   the representation does not involve the assertion of a position adverse to another client when the lawyer represents both clients in the same proceeding before a tribunal; and

(4)   each affected client gives informed consent, confirmed in writing or clearly stated on the record at a hearing.

(c)   Explanation to Clients. When representation of multiple clients in a single matter is undertaken, the consultation must include an explanation of the implications of the common representation and the advantages and risks involved.

(d)   Lawyers Related by Blood, Adoption, or Marriage. A lawyer related by blood, adoption, or marriage to another lawyer as parent, child, sibling, or spouse must not represent a client in a representation directly adverse to a person who the lawyer knows is represented by the other lawyer except with the client's informed consent, confirmed in writing or clearly stated on the record at a hearing.

(e)   Representation of Insureds.   Upon undertaking the representation of an insured client at the expense of the insurer, a lawyer has a duty to ascertain whether the lawyer will be representing both the insurer and the insured as clients, or only the insured, and to inform both the insured and the insurer regarding the scope of the representation. All other Rules Regulating The Florida Bar related to conflicts of interest apply to the representation as they would in any other situation.

Comment

Loyalty to a client

Loyalty and independent judgment are essential elements in the lawyer's relationship to a client. Conflicts of interest can arise from the lawyer's responsibilities to another client, a former client or a third person, or from the lawyer's own interests. For specific rules regarding certain conflicts of interest, see rule 4-1.8. For former client conflicts of interest, see rule 4-1.9. For conflicts of interest involving prospective clients, see rule 4-1.18. For definitions of "informed consent" and "confirmed in writing," see terminology.

An impermissible conflict of interest may exist before representation is undertaken, in which event the representation should be declined. If such a conflict arises after representation has been undertaken, the lawyer should withdraw from the representation. See rule 4-1.16. Where more than 1 client is involved and the lawyer withdraws because a conflict arises after representation, whether the lawyer may continue to represent any of the clients is determined by rule 4-1.9. As to whether a client-lawyer relationship exists or, having once been established, is continuing, see comment to rule 4-1.3 and scope.

As a general proposition, loyalty to a client prohibits undertaking representation directly adverse to that client's or another client's interests without the affected client's consent. Subdivision (a)(1) expresses that general rule. Thus, a lawyer ordinarily may not act as advocate against a person the lawyer represents in some other matter, even if it is wholly unrelated. On the other hand, simultaneous representation in unrelated matters of clients whose interests are only generally adverse, such as competing economic enterprises, does not require consent of the respective clients. Subdivision (a)(1) applies only when the representation of 1 client would be directly adverse to the other and where the lawyer's responsibilities of loyalty and confidentiality of the other client might be compromised.

Loyalty to a client is also impaired when a lawyer cannot consider, recommend, or carry out an appropriate course of action for the client because of the lawyer's other responsibilities or interests. The conflict in effect forecloses alternatives that would otherwise be available to the client. Subdivision (a)(2) addresses such situations. A possible conflict does not itself preclude the representation. The critical questions are the likelihood that a conflict will eventuate and, if it does, whether it will materially interfere with the lawyer's independent professional judgment in considering alternatives or foreclose courses of action that reasonably should be pursued on behalf of the client. Consideration should be given to whether the client wishes to accommodate the other interest involved.

Consultation and consent

A client may consent to representation notwithstanding a conflict. However, as indicated in subdivision (a)(1) with respect to representation directly adverse to a client and subdivision (a)(2) with respect to material limitations on representation of a client, when a disinterested lawyer would conclude that the client should not agree to the representation under the circumstances, the lawyer involved cannot properly ask for such agreement or provide representation on the basis of the client's consent. When more than 1 client is involved, the question of conflict must be resolved as to each client. Moreover, there may be circumstances where it is impossible to make the disclosure necessary to obtain consent. For example, when the lawyer represents different clients in related matters and 1 of the clients refuses to consent to the disclosure necessary to permit the other client to make an informed decision, the lawyer cannot properly ask the latter to consent.

Lawyer's interests

The lawyer's own interests should not be permitted to have adverse effect on representation of a client. For example, a lawyer's need for income should not lead the lawyer to undertake matters that cannot be handled competently and at a reasonable fee. See rules 4-1.1 and 4-1.5. If the probity of a lawyer's own conduct in a transaction is in serious question, it may be difficult or impossible for the lawyer to give a client detached advice. A lawyer may not allow related business interests to affect representation, for example, by referring clients to an enterprise in which the lawyer has an undisclosed interest.

Conflicts in litigation

Subdivision (a)(1) prohibits representation of opposing parties in litigation. Simultaneous representation of parties whose interests in litigation may conflict, such as co-plaintiffs or co- defendants, is governed by subdivisions (a), (b), and (c). An impermissible conflict may exist by reason of substantial discrepancy in the parties' testimony, incompatibility in positions in relation to an opposing party, or the fact that there are substantially different possibilities of settlement of the claims or liabilities in question. Such conflicts can arise in criminal cases as well as civil. The potential for conflict of interest in representing multiple defendants in a criminal case is so grave that ordinarily a lawyer should decline to represent more than 1 co-defendant. On the other hand, common representation of persons having similar interests is proper if the risk of adverse effect is minimal and the requirements of subdivisions (b) and (c) are met.

Ordinarily, a lawyer may not act as advocate against a client the lawyer represents in some other matter, even if the other matter is wholly unrelated. However, there are circumstances in which a lawyer may act as advocate against a client. For example, a lawyer representing an enterprise with diverse operations may accept employment as an advocate against the enterprise in an unrelated matter if doing so will not adversely affect the lawyer's relationship with the enterprise or conduct of the suit and if both clients consent upon consultation. By the same token, government lawyers in some circumstances may represent government employees in proceedings in which a government agency is the opposing party. The propriety of concurrent representation can depend on the nature of the litigation. For example, a suit charging fraud entails conflict to a degree not involved in a suit for a declaratory judgment concerning statutory interpretation.

A lawyer may represent parties having antagonistic positions on a legal question that has arisen in different cases, unless representation of either client would be adversely affected. Thus, it is ordinarily not improper to assert such positions in cases pending in different trial courts, but it may be improper to do so in cases pending at the same time in an appellate court.

Interest of person paying for a lawyer's service

A lawyer may be paid from a source other than the client, if the client is informed of that fact and consents and the arrangement does not compromise the lawyer's duty of loyalty to the client. See rule 4-1.8(f). For example, when an insurer and its insured have conflicting interests in a matter arising from a liability insurance agreement and the insurer is required to provide special counsel for the insured, the arrangement should assure the special counsel's professional independence. So also, when a corporation and its directors or employees are involved in a controversy in which they have conflicting interests, the corporation may provide funds for separate legal representation of the directors or employees, if the clients consent after consultation and the arrangement ensures the lawyer's professional independence.

Other conflict situations

Conflicts of interest in contexts other than litigation sometimes may be difficult to assess. Relevant factors in determining whether there is potential for adverse effect include the duration and intimacy of the lawyer's relationship with the client or clients involved, the functions being performed by the lawyer, the likelihood that actual conflict will arise, and the likely prejudice to the client from the conflict if it does arise. The question is often one of proximity and degree.

For example, a lawyer may not represent multiple parties to a negotiation whose interests are fundamentally antagonistic to each other, but common representation is permissible where the clients are generally aligned in interest even though there is some difference of interest among them.

Conflict questions may also arise in estate planning and estate administration. A lawyer may be called upon to prepare wills for several family members, such as husband and wife, and, depending upon the circumstances, a conflict of interest may arise. In estate administration the identity of the client may be unclear under the law of some jurisdictions. In Florida, the personal representative is the client rather than the estate or the beneficiaries. The lawyer should make clear the relationship to the parties involved.

A lawyer for a corporation or other organization who is also a member of its board of directors should determine whether the responsibilities of the 2 roles may conflict. The lawyer may be called on to advise the corporation in matters involving actions of the directors. Consideration should be given to the frequency with which such situations may arise, the potential intensity of the conflict, the effect of the lawyer's resignation from the board, and the possibility of the corporation's obtaining legal advice from another lawyer in such situations. If there is material risk that the dual role will compromise the lawyer's independence of professional judgment, the lawyer should not serve as a director.

Conflict charged by an opposing party

Resolving questions of conflict of interest is primarily the responsibility of the lawyer undertaking the representation. In litigation, a court may raise the question when there is reason to infer that the lawyer has neglected the responsibility. In a criminal case, inquiry by the court is generally required when a lawyer represents multiple defendants. Where the conflict is such as clearly to call in question the fair or efficient administration of justice, opposing counsel may properly raise the question. Such an objection should be viewed with caution, however, for it can be misused as a technique of harassment. See scope.

Family relationships between lawyers

Rule 4-1.7(d) applies to related lawyers who are in different firms. Related lawyers in the same firm are also governed by rules 4-1.9 and 4-1.10. The disqualification stated in rule 4- 1.7(d) is personal and is not imputed to members of firms with whom the lawyers are associated. The purpose of Rule 4-1.7(d) is to prohibit representation of adverse interests, unless informed consent is given by the client, by a lawyer related to another lawyer by blood, adoption, or marriage as a parent, child, sibling, or spouse so as to include those with biological or adopted children and within relations by marriage those who would be considered in-laws and stepchildren and stepparents.

Representation of insureds

The unique tripartite relationship of insured, insurer, and lawyer can lead to ambiguity as to whom a lawyer represents. In a particular case, the lawyer may represent only the insured, with the insurer having the status of a non-client third party payor of the lawyer's fees. Alternatively, the lawyer may represent both as dual clients, in the absence of a disqualifying conflict of interest, upon compliance with applicable rules. Establishing clarity as to the role of the lawyer at the inception of the representation avoids misunderstanding that may ethically compromise the lawyer. This is a general duty of every lawyer undertaking representation of a client, which is made specific in this context due to the desire to minimize confusion and inconsistent expectations that may arise.

Consent confirmed in writing or stated on the record at a hearing

Subdivision (b) requires the lawyer to obtain the informed consent of the client, confirmed in writing or clearly stated on the record at a hearing. With regard to being confirmed in writing, such a writing may consist of a document executed by the client or one that the lawyer promptly records and transmits to the client following an oral consent. See terminology. If it is not feasible to obtain or transmit the writing at the time the client gives informed consent, then the lawyer must obtain or transmit it within a reasonable time afterwards. See terminology. The requirement of a writing does not supplant the need in most cases for the lawyer to talk with the client, to explain the risks and advantages, if any, of representation burdened with a conflict of interest, as well as reasonably available alternatives, and to afford the client a reasonable opportunity to consider the risks and alternatives and to raise questions and concerns. Rather, the writing is required in order to impress upon clients the seriousness of the decision the client is being asked to make and to avoid disputes or ambiguities that might later occur in the absence of a writing.

Amended July 23, 1992, effective Jan. 1, 1993 (605 So.2d 252); Jan. 23, 2003, effective July 1, 2003 (838
So.2d 1140); March 23, 2006, effective May 22, 2006 (SC04-2246); revised opinion issued June 29, 2006,

(933 So.2d 417); amended May 29, 2014, effective June 1, 2014 (SC12-2234).

RULE 4-1.8 CONFLICT OF INTEREST; PROHIBITED AND OTHER TRANSACTIONS

(a) Business Transactions With or Acquiring Interest Adverse to Client. A lawyer shall not enter into a business transaction with a client or knowingly acquire an ownership, possessory, security, or other pecuniary interest adverse to a client, except a lien granted by law to secure a lawyer's fee or expenses, unless:

(1) the transaction and terms on which the lawyer acquires the interest are fair and reasonable to the client and are fully disclosed and transmitted in writing to the client in a manner that can be reasonably understood by the client;

(2) the client is advised in writing of the desirability of seeking and is given a reasonable opportunity to seek the advice of independent legal counsel on the transaction; and

(3) the client gives informed consent, in a writing signed by the client, to the essential terms of the transaction and the lawyer's role in the transaction, including whether the lawyer is representing the client in the transaction.

(b) Using Information to Disadvantage of Client. A lawyer shall not use information relating to representation of a client to the disadvantage of the client unless the client gives informed consent, except as permitted or required by these rules.

(c) Gifts to Lawyer or Lawyer's Family. A lawyer shall not solicit any substantial gift from a client, including a testamentary gift, or prepare on behalf of a client an instrument giving the lawyer or a person related to the lawyer any substantial gift unless the lawyer or other recipient of the gift is related to the client. For purposes of this subdivision, related persons include a spouse, child, grandchild, parent, grandparent, or other relative with whom the lawyer or the client maintains a close, familial relationship.

(d) Acquiring Literary or Media Rights. Prior to the conclusion of representation of a client, a lawyer shall not make or negotiate an agreement giving the lawyer literary or media rights to a portrayal or account based in substantial part on information relating to the representation.

(e)   Financial Assistance to Client. A lawyer shall not provide financial assistance to a client in connection with pending or contemplated litigation, except that:

(1)   a lawyer may advance court costs and expenses of litigation, the repayment of which may be contingent on the outcome of the matter; and

(2)   a lawyer representing an indigent client may pay court costs and expenses of litigation on behalf of the client.

(f)   Compensation by Third Party. A lawyer shall not accept compensation for representing a client from one other than the client unless:

(1)   the client gives informed consent;

(2)   there is no interference with the lawyer's independence of professional judgment or with the client-lawyer relationship; and

(3)   information relating to representation of a client is protected as required by rule 4-1.6.

(g)   Settlement of Claims for Multiple Clients. A lawyer who represents 2 or more clients shall not participate in making an aggregate settlement of the claims of or against the clients, or in a criminal case an aggregated agreement as to guilty or nolo contendere pleas, unless each client gives informed consent, in a writing signed by the client. The lawyer's disclosure shall include the existence and nature of all the claims or pleas involved and of the participation of each person in the settlement.

(h)   Limiting Liability for Malpractice. A lawyer shall not make an agreement prospectively limiting the lawyer's liability to a client for malpractice unless permitted by law and the client is independently represented in making the agreement. A lawyer shall not settle a claim for such liability with an unrepresented client or former client without first advising that person in writing that independent representation is appropriate in connection therewith.

(i)   Acquiring Proprietary Interest in Cause of Action. A lawyer shall not acquire a proprietary interest in the cause of action or subject matter of litigation the lawyer is conducting for a client, except that the lawyer may:

(1)   acquire a lien granted by law to secure the lawyer's fee or expenses; and

(2)   contract with a client for a reasonable contingent fee.

(j)   Representation of Insureds. When a lawyer undertakes the defense of an insured other than a governmental entity, at the expense of an insurance company, in regard to an action or claim for personal injury or for property damages, or for death or loss of services resulting from personal injuries based upon tortious conduct, including product liability claims, the Statement of Insured Client's Rights shall be provided to the insured at the commencement of the representation. The lawyer shall sign the statement certifying the date on which the statement was provided to the insured. The lawyer shall keep a copy of the signed statement in the client's file and shall retain a copy of the signed statement for 6 years after the representation is completed. The statement shall be available for inspection at reasonable times by the insured, or by the appropriate disciplinary agency. Nothing in the Statement of Insured Client's Rights shall be deemed to augment or detract from any substantive or ethical duty of a lawyer or affect the extra disciplinary consequences of violating an existing substantive legal or ethical duty; nor shall any matter set forth in the Statement of Insured Client's Rights give rise to an independent

cause of action or create any presumption that an existing legal or ethical duty has been breached.

STATEMENT OF INSURED CLIENT'S RIGHTS

An insurance company has selected a lawyer to defend a lawsuit or claim against you. This Statement of Insured Client's Rights is being given to you to assure that you are aware of your rights regarding your legal representation. This disclosure statement highlights many, but not all, of your rights when your legal representation is being provided by the insurance company.

1.   Your Lawyer. If you have questions concerning the selection of the lawyer by the insurance company, you should discuss the matter with the insurance company and the lawyer. As a client, you have the right to know about the lawyer's education, training, and experience. If you ask, the lawyer should tell you specifically about the lawyer's actual experience dealing with cases similar to yours and give you this information in writing, if you request it. Your lawyer is responsible for keeping you reasonably informed regarding the case and promptly complying with your reasonable

requests for information. You are entitled to be informed of the final disposition of your case within a reasonable time.

2.   Fees and Costs. Usually the insurance company pays all of the fees and costs of defending the claim. If you are responsible for directly paying the lawyer for any fees or costs, your lawyer must promptly inform you of that.

3.   Directing the Lawyer. If your policy, like most insurance policies, provides for the insurance company to control the defense of the lawsuit, the lawyer will be taking instructions from the insurance company. Under such policies, the lawyer cannot act solely on your instructions, and at the same time, cannot act contrary to your interests. Your preferences should be communicated to the lawyer.

4.   Litigation Guidelines. Many insurance companies establish guidelines governing how lawyers are to proceed in defending a claim. Sometimes those guidelines affect the range of actions the lawyer can take and may require authorization of the insurance company before certain actions are undertaken. You are entitled to know the guidelines affecting the extent and level of legal services being provided to you. Upon request, the lawyer or the insurance company should either explain the guidelines to you or provide you with a copy. If the lawyer is denied authorization to provide a service or undertake an action the lawyer believes necessary to your defense, you are entitled to be informed that the insurance company has declined authorization for the service or action.

5.   Confidentiality. Lawyers have a general duty to keep secret the confidential information a client provides, subject to limited exceptions. However, the lawyer chosen to represent you also may have a duty to share with the insurance company information relating to the defense or settlement of the claim. If the lawyer learns of information indicating that the insurance company is not obligated under the policy to cover the claim or provide a defense, the lawyer's duty is to maintain that information in confidence. If the lawyer cannot do so, the lawyer may be required to withdraw from the representation without disclosing to the insurance company the nature of the conflict of interest which has arisen. Whenever a waiver of the lawyer-client confidentiality privilege is needed, your lawyer has a duty to consult with you and obtain your informed consent. Some insurance companies retain auditing companies to review the billings and files of the lawyers they hire to represent policyholders. If the lawyer believes a bill review or other action releases information in a manner that is contrary to your interests, the lawyer should advise you regarding the

matter.

6.   Conflicts of Interest.   Most insurance policies state that the insurance company will provide a lawyer to represent your interests as well as those of the insurance company. The lawyer is responsible for identifying conflicts of interest and advising you of them. If at any time you believe the lawyer provided by the insurance company cannot fairly represent you because of conflicts of interest between you and the company (such as whether there is insurance coverage for the claim against you), you should discuss this with the lawyer and explain why you believe there is a conflict. If an actual conflict of interest arises that cannot be resolved, the insurance company may be required to provide you with another lawyer.

7.   Settlement. Many policies state that the insurance company alone may make a final decision regarding settlement of a claim, but under some policies your agreement is required. If you want to object to or encourage a settlement within policy limits, you should discuss your concerns with your lawyer to learn your rights and possible consequences. No settlement of the case requiring you to pay money in excess of your policy limits can be reached without your agreement, following full disclosure.

8.   Your Risk.   If you lose the case, there might be a judgment entered against you for more than the amount of your insurance, and you might have to pay it. Your lawyer has a duty to advise you about this risk and other reasonably foreseeable adverse results.

9.   Hiring Your Own Lawyer. The lawyer provided by the insurance company is representing you only to defend the lawsuit. If you desire to pursue a claim against the other side, or desire legal services not directly related to the defense of the lawsuit against you, you will need to make your own arrangements with this or another lawyer. You also may hire another lawyer, at your own expense, to monitor the defense being provided by the insurance company. If there is a reasonable risk that the claim made against you exceeds the amount of coverage under your policy, you should consider consulting another lawyer.

10.   Reporting Violations. If at any time you believe that your lawyer has acted in violation of your rights, you have the right to report the matter to The Florida Bar, the agency that oversees the practice and behavior of all lawyers in Florida. For information on how to reach The Florida Bar call (850) 561-5839 or you may access the Bar at www.FlaBar.org.

IF YOU HAVE ANY QUESTIONS ABOUT YOUR RIGHTS,

PLEASE ASK FOR AN EXPLANATION.
CERTIFICATE

The undersigned hereby certifies that this Statement of Insured Client's Rights has been provided to.....(name of insured/client(s))..... by .....(mail/hand delivery)..... at .....(address of insured/client(s) to which mailed or delivered, on
.....(date)......

[Signature of Attorney]

[Print/Type Name] Florida Bar No.:

(k) Imputation of Conflicts. While lawyers are associated in a firm, a prohibition in the foregoing subdivisions (a) through (i) that applies to any one of them shall apply to all of them.

Comment

Business transactions between client and lawyer

A lawyer's legal skill and training, together with the relationship of trust and confidence between lawyer and client, create the possibility of overreaching when the lawyer participates in a business, property, or financial transaction with a client. The requirements of subdivision (a) must be met even when the transaction is not closely related to the subject matter of the representation. The rule applies to lawyers engaged in the sale of goods or services related to the practice of law. See rule 4-5.7. It does not apply to ordinary fee arrangements between client and lawyer, which are governed by rule 4-1.5, although its requirements must be met when the lawyer accepts an interest in the client's business or other nonmonetary property as payment for all or part of a fee. In addition, the rule does not apply to standard commercial transactions between the lawyer and the client for products or services that the client generally markets to others, for example, banking or brokerage services, medical services, products manufactured or distributed by the client, and utilities services. In such transactions the lawyer has no advantage in dealing with the client, and the restrictions in subdivision (a) are unnecessary and impracticable. Likewise, subdivision (a) does not prohibit a lawyer from acquiring or asserting a lien granted by law to secure the lawyer's fee or expenses.

Subdivision (a)(1) requires that the transaction itself be fair to the client and that its essential terms be communicated to the client, in writing, in a manner that can be reasonably understood. Subdivision (a)(2) requires that the client also be advised, in writing, of the desirability of seeking the advice of independent legal counsel. It also requires that the client be given a reasonable opportunity to obtain such advice. Subdivision (a)(3) requires that the lawyer obtain the client's informed consent, in a writing signed by the client, both to the essential terms of the transaction and to the lawyer's role. When necessary, the lawyer should discuss both the material risks of the proposed transaction, including any risk presented by the lawyer's involvement, and the existence of reasonably available alternatives and should explain why the advice of independent legal counsel is desirable. See terminology (definition of informed consent).

The risk to a client is greatest when the client expects the lawyer to represent the client in the transaction itself or when the lawyer's financial interest otherwise poses a significant risk that the lawyer's representation of the client will be materially limited by the lawyer's financial interest in the transaction. Here the lawyer's role requires that the lawyer must comply, not only with the requirements of subdivision (a), but also with the requirements of rule 4-1.7. Under that rule, the lawyer must disclose the risks associated with the lawyer's dual role as both legal

adviser and participant in the transaction, such as the risk that the lawyer will structure the transaction or give legal advice in a way that favors the lawyer's interests at the expense of the client. Moreover, the lawyer must obtain the client's informed consent. In some cases, the lawyer's interest may be such that rule 4-1.7 will preclude the lawyer from seeking the client's consent to the transaction.

If the client is independently represented in the transaction, subdivision (a)(2) of this rule is inapplicable, and the subdivision (a)(1) requirement for full disclosure is satisfied either by a written disclosure by the lawyer involved in the transaction or by the client's independent counsel. The fact that the client was independently represented in the transaction is relevant in determining whether the agreement was fair and reasonable to the client as subdivision (a)(1) further requires.

Gifts to lawyers

A lawyer may accept a gift from a client, if the transaction meets general standards of fairness and if the lawyer does not prepare the instrument bestowing the gift. For example, a simple gift such as a present given at a holiday or as a token of appreciation is permitted. If a client offers the lawyer a more substantial gift, subdivision (c) does not prohibit the lawyer from accepting it, although such a gift may be voidable by the client under the doctrine of undue influence, which treats client gifts as presumptively fraudulent. In any event, due to concerns about overreaching and imposition on clients, a lawyer may not suggest that a substantial gift be made to the lawyer or for the lawyer's benefit, except where the lawyer is related to the client as set forth in subdivision (c). If effectuation of a substantial gift requires preparing a legal instrument such as a will or conveyance, however, the client should have the detached advice that another lawyer can provide and the lawyer should advise the client to seek advice of independent counsel. Subdivision (c) recognizes an exception where the client is related by blood or marriage to the donee or the gift is not substantial.

This rule does not prohibit a lawyer from seeking to have the lawyer or a partner or associate of the lawyer named as personal representative of the client's estate or to another potentially lucrative fiduciary position. Nevertheless, such appointments will be subject to the general conflict of interest provision in rule 4-1.7 when there is a significant risk that the lawyer's interest in obtaining the appointment will materially limit the lawyer's independent professional judgment in advising the client concerning the choice of a personal representative or other fiduciary. In obtaining the client's informed consent to the conflict, the lawyer should advise the client concerning the nature and extent of the lawyer's financial interest in the appointment, as well as the availability of alternative candidates for the position.

Literary rights

An agreement by which a lawyer acquires literary or media rights concerning the conduct of the representation creates a conflict between the interests of the client and the personal interests of the lawyer. Measures suitable in the representation of the client may detract from the publication value of an account of the representation. Subdivision (d) does not prohibit a lawyer representing a client in a transaction concerning literary property from agreeing that the lawyer's fee shall consist of a share in ownership in the property if the arrangement conforms to rule 4-1.5 and subdivision (a) and (i).

Financial assistance

Lawyers may not subsidize lawsuits or administrative proceedings brought on behalf of their clients, including making or guaranteeing loans to their clients for living expenses, because to do so would encourage clients to pursue lawsuits that might not otherwise be brought and because such assistance gives lawyers too great a financial stake in the litigation. These dangers do not warrant a prohibition on a lawyer advancing a client court costs and litigation expenses, including the expenses of diagnostic medical examination used for litigation purposes and the reasonable costs of obtaining and presenting evidence, because these advances are virtually indistinguishable from contingent fees and help ensure access to the courts. Similarly, an exception allowing lawyers representing indigent clients to pay court costs and litigation expenses regardless of whether these funds will be repaid is warranted.

Person paying for lawyer's services

Lawyers are frequently asked to represent a client under circumstances in which a third person will compensate the lawyer, in whole or in part. The third person might be a relative or friend, an indemnitor (such as a liability insurance company), or a co-client (such as a corporation sued along with one or more of its employees). Because third-party payers frequently have interests that differ from those of the client, including interests in minimizing the amount spent on the representation and in learning how the representation is progressing, lawyers are prohibited from accepting or continuing such representations unless the lawyer determines that there will be no interference with the lawyer's independent professional judgment and there is informed consent from the client. See also rule 4-5.4(d) (prohibiting interference with a lawyer's professional judgment by one who recommends, employs or pays the lawyer to render legal services for another).

Sometimes, it will be sufficient for the lawyer to obtain the client's informed consent regarding the fact of the payment and the identity of the third-party payer. If, however, the fee arrangement creates a conflict of interest for the lawyer, then the lawyer must comply with rule 4-1.7. The lawyer must also conform to the requirements of rule 4-1.6 concerning confidentiality. Under rule 4-1.7(a), a conflict of interest exists if there is significant risk that the lawyer's representation of the client will be materially limited by the lawyer's own interest in the fee arrangement or by the lawyer's responsibilities to the third-party payer (for example, when the third-party payer is a co-client). Under rule 4-1.7(b), the lawyer may accept or continue the representation with the informed consent of each affected client, unless the conflict is nonconsentable under that subdivision. Under rule 4-1.7(b), the informed consent must be confirmed in writing or clearly stated on the record at a hearing.

Aggregate settlements

Differences in willingness to make or accept an offer of settlement are among the risks of common representation of multiple clients by a single lawyer. Under rule 4-1.7, this is one of the risks that should be discussed before undertaking the representation, as part of the process of

obtaining the clients' informed consent. In addition, rule 4-1.2(a) protects each client's right to have the final say in deciding whether to accept or reject an offer of settlement and in deciding whether to enter a guilty or nolo contendere plea in a criminal case. The rule stated in this subdivision is a corollary of both these rules and provides that, before any settlement offer or plea bargain is made or accepted on behalf of multiple clients, the lawyer must inform each of them about all the material terms of the settlement, including what the other clients will receive or pay if the settlement or plea offer is accepted. See also terminology (definition of informed consent). Lawyers representing a class of plaintiffs or defendants, or those proceeding derivatively, must comply with applicable rules regulating notification of class members and other procedural requirements designed to ensure adequate protection of the entire class.

Acquisition of interest in litigation

Subdivision (i) states the traditional general rule that lawyers are prohibited from acquiring a proprietary interest in litigation. This general rule, which has its basis in common law champerty and maintenance, is subject to specific exceptions developed in decisional law and continued in these rules, such as the exception for reasonable contingent fees set forth in rule 4-1.5 and the exception for certain advances of the costs of litigation set forth in subdivision (e).

This rule is not intended to apply to customary qualification and limitations in legal opinions and memoranda.

Representation of insureds

As with any representation of a client when another person or client is paying for the representation, the representation of an insured client at the request of the insurer creates a special need for the lawyer to be cognizant of the potential for ethical risks. The nature of the relationship between a lawyer and a client can lead to the insured or the insurer having expectations inconsistent with the duty of the lawyer to maintain confidences, avoid conflicts of interest, and otherwise comply with professional standards. When a lawyer undertakes the representation of an insured client at the expense of the insurer, the lawyer should ascertain whether the lawyer will be representing both the insured and the insurer, or only the insured. Communication with both the insured and the insurer promotes their mutual understanding of the role of the lawyer in the particular representation. The Statement of Insured Client's Rights has been developed to facilitate the lawyer's performance of ethical responsibilities. The highly variable nature of insurance and the responsiveness of the insurance industry in developing new types of coverages for risks arising in the dynamic American economy render it impractical to establish a statement of rights applicable to all forms of insurance. The Statement of Insured Client's Rights is intended to apply to personal injury and property damage tort cases. It is not intended to apply to workers' compensation cases. Even in that relatively narrow area of insurance coverage, there is variability among policies. For that reason, the statement is necessarily broad. It is the responsibility of the lawyer to explain the statement to the insured. In particular cases, the lawyer may need to provide additional information to the insured.

Because the purpose of the statement is to assist laypersons in understanding their basic rights as clients, it is necessarily abbreviated. Although brevity promotes the purpose for which the statement was developed, it also necessitates incompleteness. For these reasons, it is specifically provided that the statement shall not serve to establish any legal rights or duties, nor create any presumption that an existing legal or ethical duty has been breached. As a result, the statement and its contents should not be invoked by opposing parties as grounds for disqualification of a lawyer or for procedural purposes. The purpose of the statement would be subverted if it could be used in such a manner.

The statement is to be signed by the lawyer to establish that it was timely provided to the insured, but the insured client is not required to sign it. It is in the best interests of the lawyer to have the insured client sign the statement to avoid future questions, but it is considered impractical to require the lawyer to obtain the insured client's signature in all instances.

Establishment of the statement and the duty to provide it to an insured in tort cases involving personal injury or property damage should not be construed as lessening the duty of the lawyer to inform clients of their rights in other circumstances. When other types of insurance are involved, when there are other third-party payors of fees, or when multiple clients are represented, similar needs for fully informing clients exist, as recognized in rules 4-1.7(c) and 4-1.8(f).

Imputation of prohibitions

Under subdivision (k), a prohibition on conduct by an individual lawyer in subdivisions (a) through (i) also applies to all lawyers associated in a firm with the personally prohibited lawyer. For example, 1 lawyer in a firm may not enter into a business transaction with a client of another member of the firm without complying with subdivision (a), even if the first lawyer is not personally involved in the representation of the client.

Amended: July 23, 1992, effective Jan. 1, 1993 (605 So.2d 252); April 25, 2002 (820 So.2d 210); May 20,
2004 (SC03-705) (875 So.2d 448); March 23, 2006, effective, May 22, 2006, (SC04-2246), (933 So.2d 417);
November 19, 2009, effective February 1, 2010 (SC08-1890) (34 Fla.L.Weekly S628a).

RULE 4-1.9 CONFLICT OF INTEREST; FORMER CLIENT

A lawyer who has formerly represented a client in a matter must not afterwards:

(a)   represent another person in the same or a substantially related matter in which that person's interests are materially adverse to the interests of the former client unless the former client gives informed consent;

(b)   use information relating to the representation to the disadvantage of the former client except as these rules would permit or require with respect to a client or when the information has become generally known; or

(c)   reveal information relating to the representation except as these rules would permit or require with respect to a client.

Comment

After termination of a client-lawyer relationship, a lawyer may not represent another client except in conformity with this rule. The principles in rule 4-1.7 determine whether the interests of the present and former client are adverse. Thus, a lawyer could not properly seek to rescind on behalf of a new client a contract drafted on behalf of the former client. So also a lawyer who has prosecuted an accused person could not properly represent the accused in a subsequent civil action against the government concerning the same transaction.

The scope of a "matter" for purposes of rule 4-1.9(a) may depend on the facts of a particular situation or transaction. The lawyer's involvement in a matter can also be a question of degree. When a lawyer has been directly involved in a specific transaction, subsequent representation of other clients with materially adverse interests clearly is prohibited. On the other hand, a lawyer who recurrently handled a type of problem for a former client is not precluded from later representing another client in a wholly distinct problem of that type even though the subsequent representation involves a position adverse to the prior client. Similar considerations can apply to the reassignment of military lawyers between defense and prosecution functions within the same military jurisdiction. The underlying question is whether the lawyer was so involved in the matter that the subsequent representation can be justly regarded as a changing of sides in the matter in question.

Matters are "substantially related" for purposes of this rule if they involve the same transaction or legal dispute, or if the current matter would involve the lawyer attacking work that the lawyer performed for the former client. For example, a lawyer who has previously represented a client in securing environmental permits to build a shopping center would be precluded from representing neighbors seeking to oppose rezoning of the property on the basis of environmental considerations; however, the lawyer would not be precluded, on the grounds of substantial relationship, from defending a tenant of the completed shopping center in resisting eviction for nonpayment of rent.

Lawyers owe confidentiality obligations to former clients, and thus information acquired by the lawyer in the course of representing a client may not subsequently be used by the lawyer to the disadvantage of the client without the former client's consent. However, the fact that a lawyer has once served a client does not preclude the lawyer from using generally known information about that client when later representing another client. Information that has been widely disseminated by the media to the public, or that typically would be obtained by any reasonably prudent lawyer who had never represented the former client, should be considered generally known and ordinarily will not be disqualifying. The essential question is whether, but for having represented the former client, the lawyer would know or discover the information.

Information acquired in a prior representation may have been rendered obsolete by the passage of time. In the case of an organizational client, general knowledge of the client's policies and practices ordinarily will not preclude a subsequent representation; on the other hand, knowledge of specific facts gained in a prior representation that are relevant to the matter in question ordinarily will preclude such a representation. A former client is not required to reveal the confidential information learned by the lawyer in order to establish a substantial risk that the lawyer has confidential information to use in the subsequent matter. A conclusion about the possession of such information may be based on the nature of the services the lawyer provided the former client and information that would in ordinary practice be learned by a lawyer providing such services.

The provisions of this rule are for the protection of clients and can be waived if the former client gives informed consent. See terminology.

With regard to an opposing party's raising a question of conflict of interest, see comment to rule 4-1.7. With regard to disqualification of a firm with which a lawyer is associated, see rule 4-1.10.

Amended July 23, 1992, effective Jan. 1, 1993 (605 So.2d 252); April 25, 2002 (820 So.2d 210); March 23,
2006, effective May 22, 2006 (SC04-2246), (933 So.2d 417); November 19, 2009, effective February 1, 2010
(SC08-1890) (34 Fla.L.Weekly S628a); amended May 29, 2014, effective June 1, 2014 (SC12-2234).

RULE 4-1.10 IMPUTATION OF CONFLICTS OF INTEREST; GENERAL RULE

(a)   Imputed Disqualification of All Lawyers in Firm. While lawyers are associated in a firm, none of them may knowingly represent a client when any 1 of them practicing alone would be prohibited from doing so by rule 4-1.7 or 4-1.9 except as provided elsewhere in this rule, or unless the prohibition is based on a personal interest of the prohibited lawyer and does not present a significant risk of materially limiting the representation of the client by the remaining lawyers in the firm.

(b)   Former Clients of Newly Associated Lawyer. When a lawyer becomes associated with a firm, the firm may not knowingly represent a person in the same or a substantially related matter in which that lawyer, or a firm with which the lawyer was associated, had previously represented a client whose interests are materially adverse to that person and about whom the lawyer had acquired information protected by rules 4-1.6 and 4-1.9(b) and (c) that is material to the matter.

(c)   Representing Interests Adverse to Clients of Formerly Associated Lawyer. When a lawyer has terminated an association with a firm, the firm is not prohibited from thereafter representing a person with interests materially adverse to those of a client represented by the formerly associated lawyer unless:

(1)   the matter is the same or substantially related to that in which the formerly associated lawyer represented the client; and

(2)   any lawyer remaining in the firm has information protected by rules 4-1.6 and 4-1.9(b) and (c) that is material to the matter.

(d)   Waiver of Conflict. A disqualification prescribed by this rule may be waived by the affected client under the conditions stated in rule 4-1.7.

(e)   Government Lawyers. The disqualification of lawyers associated in a firm with former or current government lawyers is governed by rule 4-1.11.

Comment

Definition of "firm"

With respect to the law department of an organization, there is ordinarily no question that the members of the department constitute a firm within the meaning of the Rules of Professional Conduct. However, there can be uncertainty as to the identity of the client. For example, it may not be clear whether the law department of a corporation represents a subsidiary or an affiliated corporation, as well as the corporation by which the members of the department are directly employed. A similar question can arise concerning an unincorporated association and its local affiliates.

Similar questions can also arise with respect to lawyers in legal aid. Lawyers employed in the same unit of a legal service organization constitute a firm, but not necessarily those employed in separate units. As in the case of independent practitioners, whether the lawyers should be treated as associated with each other can depend on the particular rule that is involved and on the specific facts of the situation.

Where a lawyer has joined a private firm after having represented the government, the situation is governed by rule 4-1.11(a) and (b); where a lawyer represents the government after having served private clients, the situation is governed by rule 4-1.11(c)(1). The individual lawyer involved is bound by the rules generally, including rules 4-1.6, 4-1.7, and 4-1.9.

Different provisions are thus made for movement of a lawyer from 1 private firm to another and for movement of a lawyer between a private firm and the government. The government is entitled to protection of its client confidences and, therefore, to the protections provided in rules 4-1.6, 4-1.9, and 4-1.11. However, if the more extensive disqualification in rule 4-1.10 were applied to former government lawyers, the potential effect on the government would be unduly burdensome. The government deals with all private citizens and organizations and thus has a much wider circle of adverse legal interests than does any private law firm. In these circumstances, the government's recruitment of lawyers would be seriously impaired if rule 4-1.10 were applied to the government. On balance, therefore, the government is better served in the long run by the protections stated in rule 4-1.11.

Principles of imputed disqualification

The rule of imputed disqualification stated in subdivision (a) gives effect to the principle of loyalty to the client as it applies to lawyers who practice in a law firm. Such situations can be considered from the premise that a firm of lawyers is essentially 1 lawyer for purposes of the rules governing loyalty to the client or from the premise that each lawyer is vicariously bound by the obligation of loyalty owed by each lawyer with whom the lawyer is associated. Subdivision
(a)   perates only among the lawyers currently associated in a firm. When a lawyer moves from 1 firm to another the situation is governed by subdivisions (b) and (c).

The rule in subdivision (a) does not prohibit representation where neither questions of client loyalty nor protection of confidential information are presented. Where 1 lawyer in a firm could not effectively represent a given client because of strong political beliefs, for example, but that lawyer will do no work on the case and the personal beliefs of the lawyer will not materially limit the representation by others in the firm, the firm should not be disqualified. On the other hand, if an opposing party in a case were owned by a lawyer in the law firm, and others in the firm would be materially limited in pursuing the matter because of loyalty to that lawyer, the personal disqualification of the lawyer would be imputed to all others in the firm.

The rule in subdivision (a) also does not prohibit representation by others in the law firm where the person prohibited from involvement in a matter is a nonlawyer, such as a paralegal or legal secretary. Such persons, however, ordinarily must be screened from any personal participation in the matter to avoid communication to others in the firm of confidential information that both the nonlawyers and the firm have a legal duty to protect. See terminology and rule 4-5.3.

Lawyers moving between firms

When lawyers have been associated in a firm but then end their association, however, the problem is more complicated. The fiction that the law firm is the same as a single lawyer is no longer wholly realistic. There are several competing considerations. First, the client previously represented must be reasonably assured that the principle of loyalty to the client is not compromised. Second, the rule of disqualification should not be so broadly cast as to preclude other persons from having reasonable choice of legal counsel. Third, the rule of disqualification should not unreasonably hamper lawyers from forming new associations and taking on new clients after having left a previous association. In this connection, it should be recognized that today many lawyers practice in firms, that many to some degree limit their practice to 1 field or another, and that many move from 1 association to another several times in their careers. If the concept of imputed disqualification were defined with unqualified rigor, the result would be radical curtailment of the opportunity of lawyers to move from 1 practice setting to another and of the opportunity of clients to change counsel.

Reconciliation of these competing principles in the past has been attempted under 2 rubrics. One approach has been to seek per se rules of disqualification. For example, it has been held that a partner in a law firm is conclusively presumed to have access to all confidences concerning all clients of the firm. Under this analysis, if a lawyer has been a partner in one law firm and then becomes a partner in another law firm, there is a presumption that all confidences known by a partner in the first firm are known to all partners in the second firm. This presumption might properly be applied in some circumstances, especially where the client has been extensively represented, but may be unrealistic where the client was represented only for limited purposes. Furthermore, such a rigid rule exaggerates the difference between a partner and an associate in modern law firms.

The other rubric formerly used for dealing with vicarious

disqualification is the appearance of impropriety and was proscribed in former Canon 9 of the Code of Professional Responsibility. This rubric has a two-fold problem. First, the appearance of impropriety can be taken to include any new client-lawyer relationship that might make a former client feel anxious. If that meaning were adopted, disqualification would become little more than a question of subjective judgment by the former client. Second, since "impropriety" is undefined, the term "appearance of impropriety" is question-begging. It therefore has to be recognized that the problem of imputed disqualification cannot be properly resolved either by simple analogy to a lawyer practicing alone or by the very general concept of appearance of impropriety.

A rule based on a functional analysis is more appropriate for determining the question of vicarious disqualification. Two functions are involved: preserving confidentiality and avoiding positions adverse to a client.

Confidentiality

Preserving confidentiality is a question of access to information. Access to information, in turn, is essentially a question of fact in particular circumstances, aided by inferences, deductions, or working presumptions that reasonably may be made about the way in which lawyers work together. A lawyer may have general access to files of all clients of a law firm and may regularly participate in discussions of their affairs; it should be inferred that such a lawyer in fact is privy to all information about all the firm's clients. In contrast, another lawyer may have access to the files of only a limited number of clients and participate in discussion of the affairs of no other clients; in the absence of information to the contrary, it should be inferred that such a lawyer in fact is privy to information about the clients actually served but not information about other clients.

Application of subdivisions (b) and (c) depends on a situation's particular facts. In any such inquiry, the burden of proof should rest upon the firm whose disqualification is sought.

Subdivisions (b) and (c) operate to disqualify the firm only when the lawyer involved has actual knowledge of relevant information protected by rules 4-1.6 and 4-1.9(b) and (c). Thus, if a lawyer while with 1 firm acquired no knowledge or information relating to a particular client of the firm and that lawyer later joined another firm, neither the lawyer individually nor the second firm is disqualified from representing another client in the same or a related matter even though the interests of the 2 clients conflict.

Independent of the question of disqualification of a firm, a lawyer changing professional association has a continuing duty to preserve confidentiality of information about a client formerly represented. See rules 4-1.6 and 4-1.9.

Adverse positions

The second aspect of loyalty to client is the lawyer's obligation to decline subsequent representations involving positions adverse to a former client arising in substantially related matters. This obligation requires abstention from adverse representation by the individual lawyer involved, but does not properly entail abstention of other lawyers through imputed disqualification. Hence, this aspect of the problem is governed by rule 4-1.9(a). Thus, if a lawyer left 1 firm for another, the new affiliation would not preclude the firms involved from continuing to represent clients with adverse interests in the same or related matters so long as the conditions of rule 4-1.10(b) and (c) concerning confidentiality have been met.

Rule 4-1.10(d) removes imputation with the informed consent of the affected client or former client under the conditions stated in rule 4-1.7. The conditions stated in rule 4-1.7 require the lawyer to determine that the representation is not prohibited by rule 4-1.7(b) and that each affected client or former client has given informed consent to the representation, confirmed in writing or clearly stated on the record. In some cases, the risk may be so severe that the conflict may not be cured by client consent. For a definition of informed consent, see terminology.

Where a lawyer is prohibited from engaging in certain transactions under rule 4-1.8, subdivision (k) of that rule, and not this rule, determines whether that prohibition also applies to other lawyers associated in a firm with the personally prohibited lawyer.

Amended July 23, 1992, effective Jan. 1, 1993 (605 So.2d 252); March 23, 2006, effective May 22, 2006
(SC04-2246), (933 So.2d 417); amended July 7, 2011, effective October 1, 2011 (SC10-1968) amended May
29, 2014, effective June 1, 2014 (SC12-2234).

RULE 4-1.18 DUTIES TO PROSPECTIVE CLIENT

(a)   Prospective Client. A person who discusses with a lawyer the possibility of forming a client-lawyer relationship with respect to a matter is a prospective client.

(b)   Confidentiality of Information. Even when no client-lawyer relationship ensues, a lawyer who has had discussions with a prospective client shall not use or reveal information learned in the consultation, except as rule 4-1.9 would permit with respect to information of a former client.

(c)   Subsequent Representation. A lawyer subject to subdivision (b) shall not represent a client with interests materially adverse to those of a prospective client in the same or a substantially related matter if the lawyer received information from the prospective client that could be used to the disadvantage of that person in the matter, except as provided in subdivision (d). If a lawyer is disqualified from representation under this rule, no lawyer in a firm with which that lawyer is associated may knowingly undertake or continue representation in such a matter, except as provided in subdivision (d).

(d)   Permissible Representation. When the lawyer has received disqualifying information as defined in subdivision (c), representation is permissible if:

(1)   both the affected client and the prospective client have given informed consent, confirmed in writing; or

(2)   the lawyer who received the information took reasonable measures to avoid exposure to more disqualifying information than was reasonably necessary to determine whether to represent the prospective client; and

(i)   the disqualified lawyer is timely screened from any participation in the matter and is apportioned no part of the fee therefrom; and

(ii)   written notice is promptly given to the prospective client.

Comment

Prospective clients, like clients, may disclose information to a lawyer, place documents or other property in the lawyer's custody, or rely on the lawyer's advice. A lawyer's discussions with a prospective client usually are limited in time and depth and leave both the prospective client and the lawyer free (and the lawyer sometimes required) to proceed no further. Hence, prospective clients should receive some but not all of the protection afforded clients.

Not all persons who communicate information to a lawyer are entitled to protection under this rule. A person who communicates information unilaterally to a lawyer, without any reasonable expectation that the lawyer is willing to discuss the possibility of forming a client- lawyer relationship, is not a "prospective client" within the meaning of subdivision (a).

It is often necessary for a prospective client to reveal information to the lawyer during an initial consultation prior to the decision about formation of a client-lawyer relationship. The lawyer often must learn such information to determine whether there is a conflict of interest with an existing client and whether the matter is one that the lawyer is willing to undertake. Subdivision (b) prohibits the lawyer from using or revealing that information, except as permitted by rule 4-1.9, even if the client or lawyer decides not to proceed with the representation. The duty exists regardless of how brief the initial conference may be.

In order to avoid acquiring disqualifying information from a prospective client, a lawyer considering whether to undertake a new matter should limit the initial interview to only such information as reasonably appears necessary for that purpose. Where the information indicates that a conflict of interest or other reason for non-representation exists, the lawyer should so inform the prospective client or decline the representation. If the prospective client wishes to retain the lawyer, and if consent is possible under rule 4-1.7, then consent from all affected present or former clients must be obtained before accepting the representation.

A lawyer may condition conversations with a prospective client on the person's informed consent that no information disclosed during the consultation will prohibit the lawyer from representing a different client in the matter. See terminology for the definition of informed consent. If the agreement expressly so provides, the prospective client may also consent to the lawyer's subsequent use of information received from the prospective client.

Even in the absence of an agreement, under subdivision (c), the lawyer is not prohibited from representing a client with interests adverse to those of the prospective client in the same or a substantially related matter unless the lawyer has received from the prospective client information that could be used to the disadvantage of the prospective client in the matter.

Under subdivision (c), the prohibition in this rule is imputed to other lawyers as provided in rule 4-1.10, but, under subdivision (d)(1), the prohibition and its imputation may be avoided if the lawyer obtains the informed consent, confirmed in writing, of both the prospective and affected clients. In the alternative, the prohibition and its imputation may be avoided if the conditions of subdivision (d)(2) are met and all disqualified lawyers are timely screened and written notice is promptly given to the prospective client. See terminology (requirements for screening procedures). Subdivision (d)(2)(i) does not prohibit the screened lawyer from receiving a salary or partnership share established by prior independent agreement, but that lawyer may not receive compensation directly related to the matter in which the lawyer is disqualified.

Notice, including a general description of the subject matter about which the lawyer was consulted, and of the screening procedures employed, generally should be given as soon as practicable after the need for screening becomes apparent.

The duties under this rule presume that the prospective client consults the lawyer in good faith. A person who consults a lawyer simply with the intent of disqualifying the lawyer from the matter, with no intent of possibly hiring the lawyer, has engaged in a sham and should not be able to invoke this rule to create a disqualification.

For the duty of competence of a lawyer who gives assistance on the merits of a matter to a prospective client, see rule 4-1.1. For a lawyer's duties when a prospective client entrusts valuables or papers to the lawyer's care, see chapter 5, Rules Regulating The Florida Bar.

Added March 23, 2006, effective May 22, 2006 (SC04-2246), (933 So.2d 417); Amended November 19, 2009,
    effective February 1, 2010 (SC08-1890) (34 Fla.L.Weekly S628a).

4-3. ADVOCATE
RULE 4-3.1 MERITORIOUS CLAIMS AND CONTENTIONS

A lawyer shall not bring or defend a proceeding, or assert or controvert an issue therein, unless there is a basis in law and fact for doing so that is not frivolous, which includes a good faith argument for an extension, modification, or reversal of existing law. A lawyer for the defendant in a criminal proceeding, or the respondent in a proceeding that could result in incarceration, may nevertheless so defend the proceeding as to require that every element of the case be established.

Comment

The advocate has a duty to use legal procedure for the fullest benefit of the client's cause, but also a duty not to abuse legal procedure. The law, both procedural and substantive, establishes the limits within which an advocate may proceed. However, the law is not always clear and never is static. Accordingly, in determining the proper scope of advocacy, account must be taken of the law's ambiguities and potential for change.

The filing of an action or defense or similar action taken for a client is not frivolous merely because the facts have not first been fully substantiated or because the lawyer expects to develop vital evidence only by discovery. What is required of lawyers, however, is that they inform themselves about the facts of their clients' cases and the applicable law and determine that they can make good faith arguments in support of their clients' positions. Such action is not frivolous even though the lawyer believes that the client's position ultimately will not prevail. The action is frivolous, however, if the lawyer is unable either to make a good faith argument on the merits of the action taken or to support the action taken by a good faith argument for an extension, modification, or reversal of existing law.

The lawyer's obligations under this rule are subordinate to federal or state constitutional law that entitles a defendant in a criminal matter to the assistance of counsel in presenting a claim or contention that otherwise would be prohibited by this rule.

Amended July 23, 1992, effective Jan. 1, 1993 (605 So.2d 252); Amended March 23, 2006, effective May 22,
    2006 (SC04-2246), (933 So.2d 417).

RULE 4-3.2 EXPEDITING LITIGATION

A lawyer shall make reasonable efforts to expedite litigation consistent with the interests of the client.

Comment

Dilatory practices bring the administration of justice into disrepute. Although there will be occasions when a lawyer may properly seek a postponement for personal reasons, it is not proper for a lawyer to routinely fail to expedite litigation solely for the convenience of the advocates. Nor will a failure to expedite be reasonable if done for the purpose of frustrating an opposing party's attempt to obtain rightful redress or repose. It is not a justification that similar conduct is often tolerated by the bench and bar. The question is whether a competent lawyer acting in good faith would regard the course of action as having some substantial purpose other than delay. Realizing financial or other benefit from otherwise improper delay in litigation is not a legitimate interest of the client.

Amended March 23, 2006, effective May 22, 2006 (SC04-2246), (933 So.2d 417).

RULE 4-3.3 CANDOR TOWARD THE TRIBUNAL

(a)   False Evidence; Duty to Disclose. A lawyer shall not knowingly:

(1)   make a false statement of fact or law to a tribunal or fail to correct a false statement of material fact or law previously made to the tribunal by the lawyer;

(2)   fail to disclose a material fact to a tribunal when disclosure is necessary to avoid assisting a criminal or fraudulent act by the client;

(3)   fail to disclose to the tribunal legal authority in the controlling jurisdiction known to the lawyer to be directly adverse to the position of the client and not disclosed by opposing counsel; or

(4)   offer evidence that the lawyer knows to be false. A lawyer may not offer testimony that the lawyer knows to be false in the form of a narrative unless so ordered by the tribunal. If a lawyer, the lawyer's client, or a witness called by the lawyer has offered material evidence and the lawyer comes to know of its falsity, the lawyer shall take reasonable remedial measures including, if necessary, disclosure to the tribunal. A lawyer may refuse to offer evidence that the lawyer reasonably believes is false.

(b)   Criminal or Fraudulent Conduct. A lawyer who represents a client in an adjudicative proceeding and who knows that a person intends to engage, is engaging, or has engaged in criminal or fraudulent conduct related to the proceeding shall take reasonable remedial measures, including, if necessary, disclosure to the tribunal.

(c)   Ex Parte Proceedings. In an ex parte proceeding a lawyer shall inform the tribunal of all material facts known to the lawyer that will enable the tribunal to make an informed decision, whether or not the facts are adverse.

Jason C. King

(d)   Extent of Lawyer's Duties. The duties stated in this rule continue beyond the conclusion of the proceeding and apply even if compliance requires disclosure of information otherwise protected by rule 4-1.6.

Comment

This rule governs the conduct of a lawyer who is representing a client in the proceedings of a tribunal. See terminology for the definition of "tribunal." It also applies when the lawyer is representing a client in an ancillary proceeding conducted pursuant to the tribunal's adjudicative authority, such as a deposition. Thus, for example, subdivision (a)(4) requires a lawyer to take reasonable remedial measures if the lawyer comes to know that a client who is testifying in a deposition has offered evidence that is false.

This rule sets forth the special duties of lawyers as officers of the court to avoid conduct that undermines the integrity of the adjudicative process. A lawyer acting as an advocate in an adjudicative proceeding has an obligation to present the client's case with persuasive force. Performance of that duty while maintaining confidences of the client is qualified by the advocate's duty of candor to the tribunal. Consequently, although a lawyer in an adversary proceeding is not required to present a disinterested exposition of the law or to vouch for the evidence submitted in a cause, the lawyer must not allow the tribunal to be misled by false statements of law or fact or evidence that the lawyer knows to be false.

Lawyers who represent clients in alternative dispute resolution processes are governed by the Rules of Professional Conduct. When the dispute resolution process takes place before a tribunal, as in binding arbitration (see terminology), the lawyer's duty of candor is governed by rule 4-3.3. Otherwise, the lawyer's duty of candor toward both the third-party neutral and other parties is governed by rule 4-4.1.

Representations by a lawyer

An advocate is responsible for pleadings and other documents prepared for litigation, but is usually not required to have personal knowledge of matters asserted therein, for litigation documents ordinarily present assertions by the client, or by someone on the client's behalf, and not assertions by the lawyer. Compare rule 4-3.1. However, an assertion purporting to be on the lawyer's own knowledge, as in an affidavit by the lawyer or in a statement in open court, may properly be made only when

230

the lawyer knows the assertion is true or believes it to be true on the basis of a reasonably diligent inquiry. There are circumstances where failure to make a disclosure is the equivalent of an affirmative misrepresentation. The obligation prescribed in rule 4-1.2(d) not to counsel a client to commit or assist the client in committing a fraud applies in litigation. Regarding compliance with rule 4-1.2(d), see the comment to that rule. See also the comment to rule 4-8.4(b).

Misleading legal argument

Legal argument based on a knowingly false representation of law constitutes dishonesty toward the tribunal. A lawyer is not required to make a disinterested exposition of the law, but must recognize the existence of pertinent legal authorities. Furthermore, as stated in subdivision (a)(3), an advocate has a duty to disclose directly adverse authority in the controlling jurisdiction that has not been disclosed by the opposing party. The underlying concept is that legal argument is a discussion seeking to determine the legal premises properly applicable to the case.

False evidence

Subdivision (a)(4) requires that the lawyer refuse to offer evidence that the lawyer knows to be false, regardless of the client's wishes. This duty is premised on the lawyer's obligation as an officer of the court to prevent the trier of fact from being misled by false evidence. A lawyer does not violate this rule if the lawyer offers the evidence for the purpose of establishing its falsity.

If a lawyer knows that the client intends to testify falsely or wants the lawyer to introduce false evidence, the lawyer should seek to persuade the client that the evidence should not be offered. If the persuasion is ineffective and the lawyer continues to represent the client, the lawyer must refuse to offer the false evidence. If only a portion of a witness's testimony will be false, the lawyer may call the witness to testify but may not elicit or otherwise permit the witness to present the testimony that the lawyer knows is false.

The duties stated in this rule apply to all lawyers, including defense counsel in criminal cases.

The prohibition against offering false evidence only applies if the lawyer knows that the evidence is false. A lawyer's reasonable belief that evidence is false does not preclude its presentation to the trier of fact.

The rule generally recognized is that, if necessary to rectify the situation, an advocate must disclose the existence of the client's deception to the court. Such a disclosure can result in grave consequences to the client, including not only a sense of betrayal but also loss of the case and perhaps a prosecution for perjury. But the alternative is that the lawyer cooperate in deceiving the court, thereby subverting the truth-finding process that the adversary system is designed to implement. See rule 4-1.2(d). Furthermore, unless it is clearly understood that the lawyer will act upon the duty to disclose the existence of false evidence, the client can simply reject the lawyer's advice to reveal the false evidence and insist that the lawyer keep silent. Thus, the client could in effect coerce the lawyer into being a party to fraud on the court.

Remedial measures

If perjured testimony or false evidence has been offered, the advocate's proper course ordinarily is to remonstrate with the client confidentially if circumstances permit. In any case, the advocate should ensure disclosure is made to the court. It is for the court then to determine what should be done--making a statement about the matter to the trier of fact, ordering a mistrial, or perhaps nothing. If the false testimony was that of the client, the client may controvert the lawyer's version of their communication when the lawyer discloses the situation to the court. If there is an issue whether the client has committed perjury, the lawyer cannot represent the client in resolution of the issue and a mistrial may be unavoidable. An unscrupulous client might in this way attempt to produce a series of mistrials and thus escape prosecution. However, a second such encounter could be construed as a deliberate abuse of the right to counsel and as such a waiver of the right to further representation. This commentary is not intended to address the situation where a client or prospective client seeks legal advice specifically about a defense to a charge of perjury where the lawyer did not represent the client at the time the client gave the testimony giving rise to the charge.

Refusing to offer proof believed to be false

Although subdivision (a)(4) only prohibits a lawyer from offering evidence the lawyer knows to be false, it permits the lawyer to refuse to offer testimony or other proof that the lawyer reasonably believes is false. Offering such proof may reflect adversely on the lawyer's ability to discriminate in the quality of evidence and thus impair the lawyer's effectiveness as an advocate.

A lawyer may not assist the client or any witness in offering false testimony or other false evidence, nor may the lawyer permit the client or any other witness to testify falsely in the narrative form unless ordered to do so by the tribunal. If a lawyer knows that the client intends to commit perjury, the lawyer's first duty is to attempt to persuade the client to testify truthfully. If the client still insists on committing perjury, the lawyer must threaten to disclose the client's intent to commit perjury to the judge. If the threat of disclosure does not successfully persuade the client to testify truthfully, the lawyer must disclose the fact that the client intends to lie to the tribunal and, per 4-1.6, information sufficient to prevent the commission of the crime of perjury.

The lawyer's duty not to assist witnesses, including the lawyer's own client, in offering false evidence stems from the Rules of Professional Conduct, Florida statutes, and caselaw.

Rule 4-1.2(d) prohibits the lawyer from assisting a client in conduct that the lawyer knows or reasonably should know is criminal or fraudulent.

Rule 4-3.4(b) prohibits a lawyer from fabricating evidence or assisting a witness to testify falsely.

Rule 4-8.4(a) prohibits the lawyer from violating the Rules of Professional Conduct or knowingly assisting another to do so.

Rule 4-8.4(b) prohibits a lawyer from committing a criminal act that reflects adversely on the lawyer's honesty, trustworthiness, or fitness as a lawyer.

Rule 4-8.4(c) prohibits a lawyer from engaging in conduct involving dishonesty, fraud, deceit, or misrepresentation.

Rule 4-8.4(d) prohibits a lawyer from engaging in conduct that is prejudicial to the administration of justice.

Rule 4-1.6(b) requires a lawyer to reveal information to the extent the lawyer reasonably believes necessary to prevent a client from committing a crime.

This rule, 4-3.3(a)(2), requires a lawyer to reveal a material fact to the tribunal when disclosure is necessary to avoid assisting a criminal or fraudulent act by the client, and 4- 3.3(a)(4) prohibits a lawyer from offering false evidence and requires the lawyer to take reasonable remedial measures when false material evidence has been offered.

Rule 4-1.16 prohibits a lawyer from representing a client if the representation will result in a violation of the Rules of Professional Conduct or law and permits the lawyer to withdraw from representation if the client persists in a course of action that the lawyer reasonably believes is criminal or fraudulent or repugnant or imprudent. Rule 4-1.16(c) recognizes that notwithstanding good cause for terminating representation of a client, a lawyer is obliged to continue representation if so ordered by a tribunal.

To permit or assist a client or other witness to testify falsely is prohibited by section 837.02, Florida Statutes (1991), which makes perjury in an official proceeding a felony, and by section 777.011, Florida Statutes (1991), which proscribes aiding, abetting, or counseling commission of a felony.

Florida caselaw prohibits lawyers from presenting false testimony or evidence. Kneale v. Williams, 30 So. 2d 284 (Fla. 1947), states that perpetration of a fraud is outside the scope of the professional duty of an attorney and no privilege attaches to communication between an attorney and a client with respect to transactions constituting the making of a false claim or the perpetration of a fraud. Dodd v. The Florida Bar, 118 So. 2d 17 (Fla. 1960), reminds us that "the courts are . . . dependent on members of the bar to . . . present the true facts of each cause . . . to enable the judge or the jury to [decide the facts] to which the law may be applied. When an

attorney . . . allows false testimony . . . [the attorney] . . . makes it impossible for the scales [of justice] to balance." See The Fla. Bar v. Agar, 394 So. 2d 405 (Fla. 1981), and The Fla. Bar v. Simons, 391 So. 2d 684 (Fla. 1980).

The United States Supreme Court in Nix v. Whiteside, 475 U.S. 157 (1986), answered in the negative the constitutional issue of whether it is ineffective assistance of counsel for an attorney to threaten disclosure of a client's (a criminal defendant's) intention to testify falsely.

Ex parte proceedings

Ordinarily, an advocate has the limited responsibility of presenting 1 side of the matters that a tribunal should consider in reaching a decision; the conflicting position is expected to be presented by the opposing party. However, in an ex parte proceeding, such as an application for a temporary injunction, there is no balance of presentation by opposing advocates. The object of an ex parte proceeding is nevertheless to yield a substantially just result. The judge has an affirmative responsibility to accord the absent party just consideration. The lawyer for the represented party has the correlative duty to make disclosures of material facts known to the lawyer and that the lawyer reasonably believes are necessary to an informed decision.

Amended: March 8, 1990 (557 So.2d 1368); July 23, 1992, effective Jan. 1, 1993 (605 So.2d 252); May 20,

2004 (SC03-705), (875 So.2d 448); November 19, 2009, effective February 1, 2010 (SC08-1890) (34 Fla.L.Weekly S628a).

RULE 4-3.4 FAIRNESS TO OPPOSING PARTY AND COUNSEL

A lawyer must not:

(a)   unlawfully obstruct another party's access to evidence or otherwise unlawfully alter, destroy, or conceal a document or other material that the lawyer knows or reasonably should know is relevant to a pending or a reasonably foreseeable proceeding;   nor counsel or assist another person to do any such act;

(b)   fabricate evidence, counsel or assist a witness to testify falsely, or offer an inducement to a witness, except a lawyer may pay a witness reasonable expenses incurred by the witness in attending or testifying at proceedings; a reasonable, noncontingent fee for professional services of an expert witness; and reasonable compensation to a witness for the time spent preparing for, attending, or testifying at proceedings;

(c)   knowingly disobey an obligation under the rules of a tribunal except for an open refusal based on an assertion that no valid obligation exists;

(d)   in pretrial procedure, make a frivolous discovery request or intentionally fail to comply with a legally proper discovery request by an opposing party;

(e)   in trial, state a personal opinion about the credibility of a witness unless the statement is authorized by current rule or case law, allude to any matter that the lawyer does not reasonably believe is relevant or that will not be supported by admissible evidence, assert personal

knowledge of facts in issue except when testifying as a witness, or state a personal opinion as to the justness of a cause, the culpability of a civil litigant, or the guilt or innocence of an accused;

(f)   request a person other than a client to refrain from voluntarily giving relevant information to another party unless the person is a relative or an employee or other agent of a client, and it is reasonable to believe that the person's interests will not be adversely affected by refraining from giving such information;

(g)   present, participate in presenting, or threaten to present criminal charges solely to obtain an advantage in a civil matter; or

(h)   present, participate in presenting, or threaten to present disciplinary charges under these rules solely to obtain an advantage in a civil matter.

Comment

The procedure of the adversary system contemplates that the evidence in a case is to be marshalled competitively by the contending parties. Fair competition in the adversary system is secured by prohibitions against destruction or concealment of evidence, improperly influencing witnesses, obstructive tactics in discovery procedure, and the like.

Documents and other items of evidence are often essential to establish a claim or defense. Subject to evidentiary privileges, the right of an opposing party, including the government, to obtain evidence through discovery or subpoena is an important procedural right. The exercise of that right can be frustrated if relevant material is altered, concealed, or destroyed. Applicable law in many jurisdictions makes it an offense to destroy material for the purpose of impairing its availability in a pending proceeding or one whose commencement can be foreseen. Falsifying evidence is also generally a criminal offense. Subdivision (a) applies to evidentiary material generally, including computerized information.

With regard to subdivision (b), it is not improper to pay a witness's expenses or to compensate an expert witness on terms permitted by law. The common law rule in most jurisdictions is that it is improper to pay an occurrence witness any fee for testifying and that it is improper to pay an expert witness a contingent fee.

Previously, subdivision (e) also proscribed statements about the credibility of witnesses. However, in 2000, the Supreme Court of Florida entered an opinion in Murphy v. International Robotic Systems, Inc., 766 So. 2d 1010 (Fla. 2000), in which the court allowed counsel in closing argument to call a witness a "liar" or to state that the witness "lied."

There the court stated: "First, it is not improper for counsel to state during closing argument that a witness 'lied' or is a 'liar,' provided such characterizations are supported by the record." Murphy, id., at 1028. Members of the bar are advised to check the status of the law in this area.

Subdivision (f) permits a lawyer to advise employees of a client to refrain from giving information to another party, for the employees may identify their interests with those of the client. See also rule 4-4.2.

Amended July 23, 1992, effective Jan. 1, 1993 (605 So.2d 252); Oct. 20, 1994 (644 So.2d 282); Sept. 24, 1998,
effective Oct. 1, 1998 (718 So.2d 1179); October 6, 2005, effective Jan. 1, 2006 (SC05-206), (916 So.2d 655);
amended May 29, 2014, effective June 1, 2014 (SC12-2234).

4-4. TRANSACTIONS WITH PERSONS OTHER THAN CLIENTS RULE 4-4.1 TRUTHFULNESS IN STATEMENTS TO OTHERS

In the course of representing a client a lawyer shall not knowingly:

(a)   make a false statement of material fact or law to a third person; or

(b)   fail to disclose a material fact to a third person when disclosure is necessary to avoid assisting a criminal or fraudulent act by a client, unless disclosure is prohibited by rule 4-1.6.

Comment

Misrepresentation

A lawyer is required to be truthful when dealing with others on a client's behalf, but generally has no affirmative duty to inform an opposing party of relevant facts. A misrepresentation can occur if the lawyer incorporates or affirms a statement of another person that the lawyer knows is false. Misrepresentations can also occur by partially true but misleading statements or omissions that are the equivalent of affirmative false statements.   For dishonest conduct that does not amount to a false statement or for misrepresentations by a lawyer other than in the course of

Jason C. King

representing a client, see rule 4-8.4.

Statements of fact

This rule refers to statements of fact. Whether a particular statement should be regarded as one of fact can depend on the circumstances. Under generally accepted conventions in negotiation, certain types of statements ordinarily are not taken as statements of material fact. Estimates of price or value placed on the subject of a transaction and a party's intentions as to an acceptable settlement of a claim are ordinarily in this category, and so is the existence of an undisclosed principal except where nondisclosure of the principal would constitute fraud. Lawyers should be mindful of their obligations under applicable law to avoid criminal and tortious misrepresentation.

Crime or fraud by client

Under rule 4-1.2(d), a lawyer is prohibited from counseling or assisting a client in conduct that the lawyer knows is criminal or fraudulent. Subdivision (b) states a specific application of the principle set forth in rule 4-1.2(d) and addresses the situation where a client's crime or fraud

takes the form of a lie or misrepresentation. Ordinarily, a lawyer can avoid assisting a client's crime or fraud by withdrawing from the representation. Sometimes it may be necessary for the lawyer to give notice of the fact of withdrawal and to disaffirm an opinion, document, affirmation or the like. In extreme cases, substantive law may require a lawyer to disclose information relating to the representation to avoid being deemed to have assisted the client's crime or fraud. If the lawyer can avoid assisting a client's crime or fraud only by disclosing this information, then under subdivision (b) the lawyer is required to do so, unless the disclosure is prohibited by rule 4-1.6.

Amended July 23, 1992, effective Jan. 1, 1993 (605 So.2d 252); amended March 23, 2005, effective May 22, 2006 (SC04-2246), (933 So.2d 417) (The court conformed the rule to the ABA model rule which was different from the proposal.

4-6. PUBLIC SERVICE
RULE 4-6.1 PRO BONO PUBLIC SERVICE

(a)   Professional Responsibility. Each member of The Florida Bar in good standing, as part of that member's professional responsibility, should

(1) render pro bono legal services to the poor and (2) participate, to the extent possible, in other pro bono service activities that directly relate to the legal needs of the poor. This professional responsibility does not apply to members of the judiciary or their staffs or to government lawyers who are prohibited from performing legal services by constitutional, statutory, rule, or regulatory prohibitions. Neither does this professional responsibility apply to those members of the bar who are retired, inactive, or suspended, or who have been placed on the inactive list for incapacity not related to discipline.

(b)   Discharge of the Professional Responsibility to Provide Pro Bono Legal Service to the Poor. The professional responsibility to provide pro bono legal services as established under this rule is aspirational rather than mandatory in nature. The failure to fulfill one's professional responsibility under this rule will not subject a lawyer to discipline. The professional responsibility to provide pro bono legal service to the poor may be discharged by:

(1)   annually providing at least 20 hours of pro bono legal service to the poor; or

(2)   making an annual contribution of at least $350 to a legal aid organization.

(c)   Collective Discharge of the Professional Responsibility to Provide Pro Bono Legal Service to the Poor. Each member of the bar should strive to individually satisfy the member's professional responsibility to provide pro bono legal service to the poor. Collective satisfaction of this professional responsibility is permitted by law firms only under a collective satisfaction plan that has been filed previously with the circuit pro bono committee and only when providing pro bono legal service to the poor:

(1)   in a major case or matter involving a substantial expenditure of time and resources; or

(2)   through a full-time community or public service staff; or

(3)   in any other manner that has been approved by the circuit pro bono committee in the circuit in which the firm practices.

(d)   Reporting Requirement. Each member of the bar shall annually report whether the member has satisfied the member's professional responsibility to provide pro bono legal services to the poor. Each member shall report this information through a simplified reporting form that is made a part of the member's annual membership fees statement. The form will contain the following categories from which each member will be allowed to choose in reporting whether the member has provided pro bono legal services to the poor:

(1)   I have personally provided   hours of pro bono legal services;

(2)   I have provided pro bono legal services collectively by: (indicate type of case and manner in which service was provided);

(3)   I have contributed $to: (indicate organization to which funds were provided);

(4)   I have provided legal services to the poor in the following special manner: (indicate manner in which services were provided); or

(5)   I have been unable to provide pro bono legal services to the poor this year; or

(6)   I am deferred from the provision of pro bono legal services to the poor because I am: (indicate whether lawyer is: a member of the judiciary or judicial staff; a government lawyer prohibited by statute, rule, or regulation from providing services; retired, or inactive).

The failure to report this information shall constitute a disciplinary offense under these rules.

(e)   Credit Toward Professional Responsibility in Future Years.   In the event that more than 20 hours of pro bono legal service to the poor are provided and reported in any 1 year, the hours in excess of 20 hours may be carried forward and reported as such for up to 2 succeeding years for the purpose of determining whether a lawyer has fulfilled the professional responsibility to provide pro bono legal service to the poor in those succeeding years.

(f)   Out-of-State Members of the Bar.   Out-of-state members of the bar may fulfill their professional responsibility in the states in which they practice or reside.

Comment

Pro bono legal service to the poor is an integral and particular part of a lawyer's pro bono public service responsibility. As our society has become one in which rights and responsibilities are increasingly defined in legal terms, access to legal services has become of critical importance. This is true for all people, be they rich, poor, or of moderate means. However, because the legal problems of the poor often involve areas of basic need, their inability to obtain legal services can have dire consequences. The vast unmet legal needs of the poor in Florida have been recognized by the Supreme Court of Florida and by several studies undertaken in Florida over the past two decades. The Supreme Court of Florida has further recognized the necessity of finding a solution to the problem of providing the poor greater access to legal service and the unique role of lawyers in our adversarial system of representing and defending persons against the actions and conduct of governmental entities, individuals, and nongovernmental entities. As an officer of the court, each member of The Florida Bar in good standing has a professional responsibility to provide pro bono legal service to the poor. Certain lawyers, however, are prohibited from performing legal services by constitutional, statutory, rule, or other regulatory prohibitions. Consequently, members of the judiciary and their staffs, government lawyers who are prohibited from performing legal services by constitutional, statutory, rule, or regulatory prohibitions, members of the bar who are retired, inactive, or suspended, or who have been placed on the inactive list for incapacity not related to discipline are deferred from participation in this program.

In discharging the professional responsibility to provide pro bono legal service to the poor, each lawyer should furnish a minimum of twenty hours of pro bono legal service to the poor annually or contribute $350 to a legal aid organization. "Pro bono legal service" means legal service rendered without charge or expectation of a fee for the lawyer at the time the service commences. Legal services written off as bad debts do not qualify as pro bono service. Most pro bono service should involve civil proceedings given that government must provide indigent representation in most criminal matters. Pro bono legal service to the poor is to be provided not only to those persons whose household incomes are below the federal poverty standard but also to those persons frequently referred to as the "working poor." Lawyers providing pro bono legal service on their own need not undertake an investigation to determine client eligibility. Rather, a good faith determination by the lawyer of client eligibility is sufficient. Pro bono legal service to the poor need not be provided only through legal services to individuals; it can also be provided through legal services to charitable, religious, or educational organizations whose overall mission and activities are designed predominately to address the needs of the poor. For example, legal service to organizations such as a church, civic, or community service organizations relating to a project seeking to address the problems of the poor would qualify.

While the personal involvement of each lawyer in the provision of pro bono legal service to the poor is generally preferable, such personal involvement may not always be possible or produce the ultimate desired result, that is, a significant maximum increase in the quantity and quality of legal service provided to the poor. The annual contribution alternative recognizes a lawyer's professional responsibility to provide financial assistance to increase and improve the delivery of legal service to the poor when a lawyer cannot or decides not to provide legal service to the poor through the contribution of time. Also, there is no prohibition against a lawyer contributing a combination of hours and financial support. The limited provision allowing for

collective satisfaction of the 20-hour standard recognizes the importance of encouraging law firms to undertake the pro bono legal representation of the poor in substantial, complex matters requiring significant expenditures of law firm resources and time and costs, such as class actions and post-conviction death penalty appeal cases, and through the establishment of full-time community or public service staffs. When a law firm uses collective satisfaction, the total hours of legal services provided in such substantial, complex matters or through a full-time community or public service staff should be credited among the firm's lawyers in a fair and reasonable manner as determined by the firm.

The reporting requirement is designed to provide a sound basis for evaluating the results achieved by this rule, reveal the strengths and weaknesses of the pro bono plan, and to remind lawyers of their professional responsibility under this rule. The fourth alternative of the reporting requirements allows members to indicate that they have fulfilled their service in some manner not specifically envisioned by the plan.

The 20-hour standard for the provision of pro bono legal service to the poor is a minimum. Additional hours of service are to be encouraged. Many lawyers will, as they have before the adoption of this rule, contribute many more hours than the minimum. To ensure that a lawyer receives credit for the time required to handle a particularly involved matter, this rule provides that the lawyer may carry forward, over the next 2 successive years, any time expended in excess of 20 hours in any 1 year.

Former Rule 4-6.1 deleted June 23, 1993, effective Oct. 1, 1993. New Rule 4- 6.1 adopted June 23, 1993, eff.

Oct. 1, 1993 (630 So.2d 501). Amended Sept. 24, 1998, effective Oct. 1, 1998 (718 So.2d 1179).

RULE 4-6.5 VOLUNTARY PRO BONO PLAN

(a)   Purpose. The purpose of the voluntary pro bono attorney plan is to increase the availability of legal service to the poor. The following operating plan has as its goal the improvement of the availability of legal services to the poor and the expansion of present pro bono legal service programs. The following operating plan was implemented to accomplish this purpose and goal.

(b)   Standing Committee on Pro Bono Legal Service. The president-elect of The Florida Bar is responsible for appointing a standing committee on pro bono legal service to the poor.

(1)   Composition of the Standing Committee.   The standing committee consists of no more than 25 members and include, but not be limited to:

(A)   5 members of the board of governors The Florida Bar, 1 of whom is the chair or a member of the access to the legal system committee of the board of governors;

(B)   5 past or current directors of The Florida Bar Foundation;

(C)   1 trial judge and 1 appellate judge;

(D)   2 representatives of civil legal assistance providers;

(E)   2 representatives from local and statewide voluntary bar associations;

(F)   2 public members, 1 of whom shall be a representative of the poor;

(G)   the president or designee of the Board of Directors of Florida Legal Services,
Inc.; and

(H)   1 representative of the out-of-state division of The Florida Bar.

(2)   Responsibilities of the Standing Committee.   The standing

committee will:

(A)   identify, encourage, support, and assist statewide and local pro bono projects and activities;

(B)   receive reports from circuit committees submitted on standardized forms developed by the standing committee;

(C)   review and evaluate circuit court pro bono plans;

(D)   beginning in the first year in which individual attorney pro bono reports are due, submit an annual report as to the activities and results of the pro bono plan to the board of governors of The Florida Bar, The Florida Bar Foundation, and to the Supreme Court of Florida;

(E)   present to the board of governors of The Florida Bar and to the Supreme Court of Florida any suggested changes or modifications to the pro bono rules.

(c)   Circuit Pro Bono Committees. There will be 1 circuit pro bono committee in each of the judicial circuits of Florida. In each judicial circuit the chief judge of the circuit, or the chief judge's designee, shall appoint and convene the initial circuit pro bono committee and the committee will appoint its chair.

(1)   Composition of Circuit Court Pro Bono Committee. Each circuit pro bono committee is composed of:

(A)   the chief judge of the circuit or the chief judge's designee;

(B)   to the extent feasible, 1 or more representatives from each voluntary bar association, including each federal bar association, recognized by The Florida Bar and 1 representative from each pro bono and legal assistance provider in the circuit, which representatives are nominated by the association or provider; and

(C)   at least 1 public member and at least 1 client-eligible member, which members are nominated by the other members of the circuit pro bono committee.

Governance and terms of service are determined by each circuit pro bono committee. Replacement and succession members are appointed by the chief judge of the circuit or the chief judge's designee, upon nomination by the association, the provider organization or the circuit pro bono committee, as the case may be, as deemed appropriate or necessary to ensure an active circuit pro bono committee in each circuit.

(2)   Responsibilities of Circuit Pro Bono Committee. The circuit pro bono committee will:

(A)   prepare in written form a circuit pro bono plan after evaluating the needs of the circuit and making a determination of present available pro bono services;

(B)   implement the plan and monitor its results;

(C)   submit an annual report to The Florida Bar standing committee;

(D)   use current legal assistance and pro bono programs in each circuit, to the extent possible, to implement and operate circuit pro bono plans and provide the necessary coordination and administrative support for the circuit pro bono committee;

(E)   encourage more lawyers to participate in pro bono activities by preparing a plan that provides for various support and educational services for participating pro bono attorneys, which, to the extent possible, should include:

(i)   intake, screening, and referral of prospective clients;

(ii)   matching cases with individual attorney expertise, including the establishment of specialized panels;

(iii)   resources for litigation and out-of-pocket expenses for pro bono cases;

(iv)   legal education and training for pro bono attorneys in specialized areas of law useful in providing pro bono legal service;

(v)   the availability of consultation with attorneys who have expertise in areas of law with respect to which a volunteer lawyer is providing pro bono legal service;

(vi)   malpractice insurance for volunteer pro bono lawyers with respect to their pro bono legal service;

(vii)   procedures to ensure adequate monitoring and follow-up for assigned cases and to measure client satisfaction; and

(viii)   recognition of pro bono legal service by lawyers.

(d)   Suggested Pro Bono Service Opportunities. The following are suggested pro bono service opportunities that should be included in each circuit plan:

(1)   representation of clients through case referral;

(2)   interviewing of prospective clients;

(3)   participation in pro se clinics and other clinics in which lawyers provide advice and counsel;

(4)   acting as co-counsel on cases or matters with legal assistance providers and other pro bono lawyers;

(5)   providing consultation services to legal assistance providers for case reviews and evaluations;

(6)   participation in policy advocacy;

(7)   providing training to the staff of legal assistance providers and other volunteer pro bono attorneys;

(8)   making presentations to groups of poor persons regarding their rights and obligations under the law;

(9)   providing legal research;

(10)   providing guardian ad litem services;

(11)   providing assistance in the formation and operation of legal entities for groups of poor persons; and

(12)   serving as a mediator or arbitrator at no fee to the client-eligible party.

Added June 23, 1993, effective Oct. 1, 1993 (630 So.2d 501); Amended December 20, 2007, effective March
1, 2008 (978 So.2d 91); amended May 29, 2014, effective June 1, 2014

(SC12-2234).

RULE 4-8.4 MISCONDUCT

A lawyer shall not:

(a)   violate or attempt to violate the Rules of Professional Conduct, knowingly assist or induce another to do so, or do so through the acts of another;

(b)   commit a criminal act that reflects adversely on the lawyer's honesty, trustworthiness, or fitness as a lawyer in other respects;

(c)   engage in conduct involving dishonesty, fraud, deceit, or misrepresentation, except that it shall not be professional misconduct for a lawyer for a criminal law enforcement agency or regulatory agency to advise others about or to supervise another in an undercover investigation, unless prohibited by law or rule, and it shall not be professional misconduct for a lawyer employed in a capacity other than as a lawyer by a criminal law enforcement agency or regulatory agency to participate in an undercover investigation, unless prohibited by law or rule;

(d)   engage in conduct in connection with the practice of law that is prejudicial to the administration of justice, including to knowingly, or through callous indifference, disparage, humiliate, or discriminate against litigants, jurors, witnesses, court personnel, or other lawyers on any basis, including, but not limited to, on account of race, ethnicity, gender, religion, national origin, disability, marital status, sexual orientation, age, socioeconomic status, employment, or physical characteristic;

(e)   state or imply an ability to influence improperly a government agency or official or to achieve results by means that violate the Rules of Professional Conduct or other law;

(f)   knowingly assist a judge or judicial officer in conduct that is a violation of applicable rules of judicial conduct or other law;

(g)   fail to respond, in writing, to any official inquiry by bar counsel or a disciplinary agency, as defined elsewhere in these rules, when bar counsel or the agency is conducting an investigation into the lawyer's conduct. A written response shall be made:

(1)   within 15 days of the date of the initial written investigative

inquiry by bar counsel, grievance committee, or board of governors;

(2)   within 10 days of the date of any follow-up written investigative inquiries by bar counsel, grievance committee, or board of governors;

(3)   within the time stated in any subpoena issued under these Rules Regulating The Florida Bar (without additional time allowed for mailing);

(4)   as provided in the Florida Rules of Civil Procedure or order of the referee in matters assigned to a referee; and

(5)   as provided in the Florida Rules of Appellate Procedure or order of the Supreme Court of Florida for matters pending action by that court.

Except as stated otherwise herein or in the applicable rules, all times for response shall be calculated as provided elsewhere in these Rules Regulating The Florida Bar and may be extended or shortened by bar counsel or the disciplinary agency making the official inquiry upon good cause shown.

Failure to respond to an official inquiry with no good cause shown may be a matter of contempt and processed in accordance with rule 3-7.11(f) of these Rules Regulating The Florida Bar.

(h)   willfully refuse, as determined by a court of competent jurisdiction, to timely pay a child support obligation; or

(i)   engage in sexual conduct with a client or a representative of a client that exploits or adversely affects the interests of the client or the lawyer-client relationship.

If the sexual conduct commenced after the lawyer-client relationship was formed it shall be presumed that the sexual conduct exploits or adversely affects the interests of the client or the lawyer-client relationship. A lawyer may rebut this presumption by proving by a preponderance of the evidence that the sexual conduct did not exploit or adversely affect the interests of the client or the lawyer-client relationship.

The prohibition and presumption stated in this rule do not apply to a lawyer in the same firm as another lawyer representing the client if the lawyer involved in the sexual conduct does not personally provide legal services to the client and is screened from access to the file concerning the legal representation.

Comment

Lawyers are subject to discipline when they violate or attempt to violate the Rules of Professional Conduct, knowingly assist or induce another to do so, or do so through the acts of another, as when they request or instruct an agent to do so on the lawyer's behalf. Subdivision (a), however, does not prohibit a lawyer from advising a client concerning action the client is legally entitled to take, provided that the client is not used to indirectly violate the Rules of Professional Conduct.

Many kinds of illegal conduct reflect adversely on fitness to practice law, such as offenses involving fraud and the offense of willful failure to file an income tax return. However, some kinds of offense carry no such implication. Traditionally, the distinction was drawn in terms of offenses involving "moral turpitude." That concept can be construed to include offenses

concerning some matters of personal morality, such as adultery and comparable offenses, that have no specific connection to fitness for the practice of law. Although a lawyer is personally answerable to the entire criminal law, a lawyer should be professionally answerable only for offenses that indicate lack of those characteristics relevant to law practice. Offenses involving violence, dishonesty, or breach of trust or serious interference with the administration of justice are in that category. A pattern of repeated offenses, even ones of minor significance when considered separately, can indicate indifference to legal obligation.

A lawyer may refuse to comply with an obligation imposed by law upon a good faith belief that no valid obligation exists. The provisions of rule 4-1.2(d) concerning a good faith challenge to the validity, scope, meaning, or application of the law apply to challenges of legal regulation of the practice of law.

Subdivision (c) recognizes instances where lawyers in criminal law enforcement agencies or regulatory agencies advise others about or supervise others in undercover investigations, and provides an exception to allow the activity without the lawyer engaging in professional misconduct. The exception acknowledges current, acceptable practice of these agencies. Although the exception appears in this rule, it is also applicable to rules 4-4.1 and 4-4.3. However, nothing in the rule allows the lawyer to engage in such conduct if otherwise prohibited by law or rule.

Subdivision (d) of this rule proscribes conduct that is prejudicial to the administration of justice. Such proscription includes the prohibition against discriminatory conduct committed by a lawyer while performing duties in connection with the practice of law. The proscription extends to any characteristic or status that is not relevant to the proof of any legal or factual issue in dispute. Such conduct, when directed towards litigants, jurors, witnesses, court personnel, or other lawyers, whether based on race, ethnicity, gender, religion, national origin, disability, marital status, sexual orientation, age, socioeconomic status, employment, physical characteristic, or any other basis, subverts the administration of justice and undermines the public's confidence in our system of justice, as well as notions of equality. This subdivision does not prohibit a lawyer from representing a client as may be permitted by applicable law, such as, by way of example, representing a client accused of committing discriminatory conduct.

Lawyers holding public office assume legal responsibilities going beyond those of other citizens. A lawyer's abuse of public office can suggest an inability to fulfill the professional role of attorney. The same is true of abuse of positions of private trust such as trustee, executor, administrator, guardian, or agent and officer, director, or manager of a corporation or other organization.

A lawyer's obligation to respond to an inquiry by a disciplinary agency is stated in subdivision (g) of this rule and subdivision (h)(2) of rule 3-7.6. While response is mandatory, the lawyer may deny the charges or assert any available privilege or immunity or interpose any disability that prevents disclosure of a certain matter. A response containing a proper invocation thereof is sufficient under the Rules Regulating The Florida Bar. This obligation is necessary to ensure the proper and efficient operation of the disciplinary system.

Subdivision (h) of this rule was added to make consistent the treatment of attorneys who fail to pay child support with the treatment of other professionals who fail to pay child support, in accordance with the provisions of section 61.13015, Florida Statutes. That section provides for the suspension or denial of a professional license due to delinquent child support payments after all other available remedies for the collection of child support have been exhausted. Likewise, subdivision (h) of this rule should not be used as the primary means for collecting child support, but should be used only after all other available remedies for the collection of child support have been exhausted. Before a grievance may be filed or a grievance procedure initiated under this subdivision, the court that entered the child support order must first make a finding of willful refusal to pay. The child support obligation at issue under this rule includes both domestic

(Florida) and out-of-state (URESA) child support obligations, as well as arrearages.

Subdivision (i) proscribes exploitation of the client or the lawyer-client relationship by means of commencement of sexual conduct. The lawyer-client relationship is grounded on mutual trust. A sexual relationship that exploits that trust compromises the lawyer-client relationship. Attorneys have a duty to exercise independent professional judgment on behalf of clients. Engaging in sexual relationships with clients has the capacity to impair the exercise of that judgment.

Sexual conduct between a lawyer and client violates this rule, regardless of when the sexual conduct began when compared to the commencement of the lawyer-client relationship, if the sexual conduct exploits the lawyer-client relationship, negatively affects the client's interest, creates a conflict of interest between the lawyer and client, or negatively affects the exercise of the lawyer's independent professional judgment in representing the client.

Subdivision (i) creates a presumption that sexual conduct between a lawyer and client exploits or adversely affects the interests of the client or the lawyer-client relationship if the sexual conduct is entered into after the lawyer-client relationship begins. A lawyer charged with a violation of this rule may rebut this presumption by a preponderance of the evidence that the sexual conduct did not exploit the lawyer-client relationship, negatively affect the client's interest, create a conflict of interest between the lawyer and client, or negatively affect the exercise of the lawyer's independent professional judgment in representing the client.

For purposes of this rule, a "representative of a client" is an agent of the client who supervises, directs, or regularly consults with the organization's lawyer concerning a client matter or has authority to obligate the organization with respect to the matter, or whose act or omission in connection with the matter may be imputed to the organization for purposes of civil or criminal liability.

Amended: July 23, 1992, effective Jan. 1, 1993 (605 So.2d 252); July 1, 1993 (621 So.2d 1032); July 1, 1993,
effective. Jan. 1, 1994 (624 So.2d 720); Feb. 9, 1995 (649 So.2d 868); July 20, 1995 (658 So.2d 930); Sept. 24,
1998, effective Oct. 1, 1998 (718 So.2d 1179); Feb. 8, 2001 (795 So.2d 1); May 20, 2004 (SC03-705), 875
So.2d 448); December 8, 2005, the Supreme Court of Florida issued a

revised version of its original October 6, 2005 opinion adopting this amendment, effective January 1, 2006 (SC05-206) (2005 WL 2456201), (916 So.2d

655); Amended March 23, 2006, effective May 22, 2006 (SC04-2246), (933 So.2d 417); Amended November

19, 2009, effective February 1, 2010 (SC08-1890) (34 Fla.L.Weekly S628a).

RULES REGULATING TRUST ACCOUNTS 5-1. GENERALLY RULE 5-1.1 TRUST ACCOUNTS

(a)   Nature of Money or Property Entrusted to Attorney.

(1)   Trust Account Required; Commingling Prohibited. A lawyer shall hold in trust, separate from the lawyer's own property, funds and property of clients or third persons that are in a lawyer's possession in connection with a representation. All funds, including advances for fees, costs, and expenses, shall be kept in a separate bank or savings and loan association account maintained in the state where the lawyer's office is situated or elsewhere with the consent of the client or third person and clearly labeled and designated as a trust account. A lawyer may maintain funds belonging to the lawyer in the trust account in an amount no more than is reasonably sufficient to pay bank charges relating to the trust account.

(2)   Compliance With Client Directives. Trust funds may be separately held and maintained other than in a bank or savings and loan association account if the lawyer receives written permission from the client to do so and provided that written permission is received before maintaining the funds other than in a separate account.

(3)   Safe Deposit Boxes. If a member of the bar uses a safe deposit box to store trust funds or property, the member shall advise the institution in which the deposit box is located that it may include property of clients or third persons.

(b)   Application of Trust Funds or Property to Specific Purpose. Money or other property entrusted to an attorney for a specific purpose, including advances for fees, costs, and expenses, is held in trust and must be applied only to that purpose. Money and other property of clients coming into the hands of an attorney are not subject to counterclaim or setoff for attorney's fees, and a refusal to account for and deliver over such property upon demand shall be deemed a conversion.

(c)   Liens Permitted. This subchapter does not preclude the retention of money or other property upon which the lawyer has a valid lien for services nor does it preclude the payment of agreed fees from the proceeds of transactions or collection.

(d)   Controversies as to Amount of Fees. Controversies as to the amount of fees are not grounds for disciplinary proceedings unless the amount demanded is clearly excessive, extortionate, or fraudulent. In a controversy alleging a clearly excessive, extortionate, or fraudulent fee, announced willingness of an attorney to submit a dispute as to the amount of a fee to a competent tribunal for determination may be considered in any determination as to intent or in mitigation of discipline; provided, such willingness shall not preclude admission of any other relevant admissible evidence relating to such controversy, including evidence as to the withholding of funds or property of the client, or to other injury to the client occasioned by such controversy.

(e)   Notice of Receipt of Trust Funds; Delivery; Accounting. Upon receiving funds or other property in which a client or third person has an interest, a lawyer shall promptly notify the

client or third person.   Except as stated in this rule or otherwise permitted by law or by agreement with the client, a lawyer shall promptly deliver to the client or third person any funds or other property that the client or third person is entitled to receive and, upon request by the client or third person, shall promptly render a full accounting regarding such property.

(f)   Disputed Ownership of Trust Funds.   When in the course of representation a lawyer is in possession of property in which 2 or more persons (1 of whom may be the lawyer) claim interests, the property shall be treated by the lawyer as trust property, but the portion belonging to the lawyer or law firm shall be withdrawn within a reasonable time after it becomes due unless the right of the lawyer or law firm to receive it is disputed, in which event the portion in dispute shall be kept separate by the lawyer until the dispute is resolved. The lawyer shall promptly distribute all portions of the property as to which the interests are not in dispute.

(g)   Interest on Trust Accounts (IOTA) Program.

(1)   Definitions. As used herein, the term:

(A)   "Nominal or short term" describes funds of a client or third person that, pursuant to subdivision (3), below, the lawyer has determined cannot earn income for the client or third person in excess of the costs to secure the income.

(B)   "Foundation" means The Florida Bar Foundation, Inc..

(C)   "IOTA account" means an interest or dividend-bearing trust account benefiting The Florida Bar Foundation established in an eligible institution for the deposit of nominal or short-term funds of clients or third persons.

(D) "Eligible Institution" means any bank or savings and loan association authorized by federal or state laws to do business in Florida and insured by the Federal Savings and Loan Insurance Corporation, or any successor insurance corporation(s) established by federal or state laws, or any open-end investment company registered with the Securities and Exchange Commission and authorized by federal or state laws to do business in Florida, all of which must meet the requirements set out in subdivision (5), below.

(E) "Interest or dividend-bearing trust account" means a federally insured checking account or investment product, including a daily financial institution repurchase agreement or a money market fund. A daily financial institution repurchase agreement must be fully collateralized by, and an open-end money market fund must consist solely of, United States Government Securities. A daily financial institution repurchase agreement may be established only with an eligible institution that is deemed to be "well capitalized" or "adequately capitalized" as defined by applicable federal statutes and regulations. An open- end money market fund must hold itself out as a money market fund as defined by applicable federal statutes and regulations under the Investment Company Act of 1940, and have total assets of at least $250 million. The funds covered by this rule shall be subject to withdrawal upon request and without delay.

(2) Required Participation. All nominal or short-term funds belonging to clients or third persons that are placed in trust with any member of The Florida Bar practicing law from an office or other business location within the state of Florida shall be deposited into one or more IOTA accounts, unless the funds may earn income for the client or third person in excess of the costs incurred to secure the income, except as provided elsewhere in this chapter. Only trust funds that are nominal or short term shall be deposited into an IOTA account. The member shall certify annually, in writing, that the member is in compliance with, or is exempt from, the provisions of this rule.

(3) Determination of Nominal or Short-Term Funds. The lawyer shall exercise good faith judgment in determining upon receipt whether the funds of a client or third person are nominal or short term. In the exercise of this good faith judgment, the lawyer shall consider such factors as:

(A) the amount of a client's or third person's funds to be held by the lawyer or law firm;

(B)   the period of time such funds are expected to be held;

(C)   the likelihood of delay in the relevant transaction(s) or proceeding(s);

(D)   the cost to the lawyer or law firm of establishing and maintaining an interest- bearing account or other appropriate investment for the benefit of the client or third person; and

(E)   minimum balance requirements and/or service charges or fees imposed by the eligible institution.

The determination of whether a client's or third person's funds are nominal or short term shall rest in the sound judgment of the lawyer or law firm. No lawyer shall be charged with ethical impropriety or other breach of professional conduct based on the exercise of such good faith judgment.

(4)   Notice to Foundation.   Lawyers or law firms shall advise the Foundation, at Post Office Box 1553, Orlando, Florida 32802-1553, of the establishment of an IOTA account for funds covered by this rule.   Such notice shall include: the IOTA account number as assigned by the eligible institution; the name of the lawyer or law firm on the IOTA account; the eligible institution name; the eligible institution address; and the name and Florida Bar attorney number of the lawyer, or of each member of The Florida Bar in a law firm, practicing from an office or other business location within the state of Florida that has established the IOTA account.

(5)   Eligible Institution Participation in IOTA.   Participation in the IOTA program is voluntary for banks, savings and loan associations, and investment companies.   Institutions that choose to offer and maintain IOTA accounts must meet the following requirements:

(A)   Interest Rates and Dividends. Eligible institutions shall maintain IOTA accounts which pay the highest interest rate or dividend generally available from the institution to its non-IOTA account customers when IOTA accounts meet or exceed the same minimum balance or other account eligibility qualifications, if any.

(B)   Determination of Interest Rates and Dividends. In determining the highest interest rate or dividend generally available from the institution to its non-IOTA accounts in compliance with subdivision (5)(A), above, eligible institutions may consider factors, in addition to the IOTA account balance, customarily considered by the institution when setting interest rates or dividends for its customers, provided that such factors do not discriminate between IOTA accounts and accounts of non-IOTA customers, and that these factors do not include that the account is an IOTA account.

(C)   Remittance and Reporting Instructions. Eligible institutions shall:

(i)   calculate and remit interest or dividends on the balance of the deposited funds, in accordance with the institution's standard practice for non-IOTA account customers, less reasonable service charges or fees, if any, in connection with the deposited funds, at least quarterly, to the Foundation;

(ii)   transmit with each remittance to the Foundation a statement showing the name of the lawyer or law firm from whose IOTA account the remittance is sent, the lawyer's or law firm's IOTA account number as assigned by the institution, the rate of interest applied, the period for which the remittance is made, the total interest or dividend earned during the remittance period, the amount and description of any service charges or fees assessed during the remittance period, and the net amount of interest or dividend remitted for the period; and

(iii)   transmit to the depositing lawyer or law firm, for each remittance, a statement showing the amount of interest or dividend paid to the Foundation, the rate of interest applied, and the period for which the statement is made.

(6)   Small Fund Amounts. The Foundation may establish procedures for a lawyer or law firm to maintain an interest-free trust account for client and third-person funds that are nominal or short term when their nominal or short-term trust funds cannot reasonably be expected to produce or have not produced interest income net of reasonable eligible institution service charges or fees.

(7)   Confidentiality and Disclosure. The Foundation shall protect the confidentiality of information regarding a lawyer's or law firm's trust account obtained by virtue of this rule. However, the Foundation shall, upon an official written inquiry of The Florida Bar made in the course of an investigation conducted under these Rules Regulating The Florida Bar, disclose requested relevant information about the location and account numbers of lawyer or law firm trust accounts.

(h)   Interest on Funds That Are Not Nominal or Short-Term. A lawyer who holds funds for a client or third person and who determines that the funds are not nominal or short-term as defined elsewhere in this subchapter shall not receive benefit from interest on funds held in trust.

(i)   Unidentifiable Trust Fund Accumulations and Trust Funds Held for Missing Owners. When an attorney's trust account contains an unidentifiable accumulation of trust funds or property, or trust funds or property held for missing owners, such funds or property shall be so designated. Diligent search and inquiry shall then be made by the attorney to

determine the beneficial owner of any unidentifiable accumulation or the address of any missing owner.   If the beneficial owner of an unidentified accumulation is determined, the funds shall be properly identified as the lawyer's trust property.   If a missing beneficial owner is located, the trust funds or property shall be paid over or delivered to the beneficial owner if the owner is then entitled to receive the same.   Trust funds and property that remain unidentifiable and funds or property that are held for missing owners after being designated as such shall, after diligent search and inquiry fail to identify the beneficial owner or owner's address, be disposed of as provided in applicable Florida law.

(j)   Disbursement Against Uncollected Funds.   A lawyer generally may not use, endanger, or encumber money held in trust for a client for purposes of carrying out the business of another client without the permission of the owner given after full disclosure of the circumstances. However, certain categories of trust account deposits are considered to carry a limited and acceptable risk of failure so that disbursements of trust account funds may be made in reliance on such deposits without disclosure to and permission of clients owning trust account funds subject to possibly being affected.   Except for disbursements based upon any of the 6 categories of limited-risk uncollected deposits enumerated below, a lawyer may not disburse funds held for a client or on behalf of that client unless the funds held for that client are collected funds.   For purposes of this provision, "collected funds" means funds deposited, finally settled, and credited to the lawyer's trust account.   Notwithstanding that a deposit made to the lawyer's trust account has not been finally settled and credited to the account, the lawyer may disburse funds from the trust account in reliance on such deposit:

(1)   when the deposit is made by certified check or cashier's check;

(2)   when the deposit is made by a check or draft representing loan proceeds issued by a federally or state-chartered bank, savings bank, savings and loan association, credit union, or other duly licensed or chartered institutional lender;

(3)   when the deposit is made by a bank check, official check, treasurer's check, money order, or other such instrument issued by a bank, savings and loan association, or credit union when the lawyer has reasonable and prudent grounds to believe the instrument will clear and constitute collected funds in the lawyer's trust account within a reasonable period of time;

(4)   when the deposit is made by a check drawn on the trust account of a lawyer licensed to practice in the state of Florida or on the escrow or trust account of a real estate broker licensed under applicable Florida law when the lawyer has a reasonable and prudent belief that the deposit will clear and constitute collected funds in the lawyer's trust account within a reasonable period of time;

(5)   when the deposit is made by a check issued by the United States, the State of Florida, or any agency or political subdivision of the State of Florida;

(6)   when the deposit is made by a check or draft issued by an insurance company, title insurance company, or a licensed title insurance agency authorized to do business in the state of Florida and the lawyer has a reasonable and prudent belief that the instrument will clear and constitute collected funds in the trust account within a reasonable period of time.

A lawyer's disbursement of funds from a trust account in reliance on deposits that are not
yet collected funds in any circumstances other than those set forth above, when it results in funds of other clients being used, endangered, or encumbered without authorization, may be grounds for a finding of professional misconduct. In any event, such a disbursement is at the risk of the lawyer making the disbursement. If any of the deposits fail, the lawyer, upon obtaining knowledge of the failure, must immediately act to protect the property of the lawyer's other clients. However, if the lawyer accepting any such check personally pays the amount of any failed deposit or secures or arranges payment from sources available to the lawyer other than trust account funds of other clients, the lawyer shall not be considered guilty of professional misconduct.

(k)   Overdraft Protection Prohibited. An attorney shall not authorize overdraft protection for any account that contains trust funds.

Comment

A lawyer must hold property of others with the care required of a professional fiduciary. This chapter requires maintenance of a bank or savings and loan association account, clearly labeled as a trust account and in which only client or third party trust funds are held.

Securities should be kept in a safe deposit box, except when some other form of safekeeping is warranted by special circumstances.

All property that is the property of clients or third persons should be kept separate from the lawyer's business and personal property and, if money, in 1 or more trust accounts, unless requested otherwise in writing by the client. Separate trust accounts may be warranted when administering estate money or acting in similar fiduciary capacities.

A lawyer who holds funds for a client or third person and who determines that the funds are not nominal or short-term as defined elsewhere in this subchapter should hold the funds in a separate interest-bearing account with the interest accruing to the benefit of the client or third person unless directed otherwise in writing by the client or third person.

Lawyers often receive funds from which the lawyer's fee will be paid. The lawyer is not required to remit to the client funds that the lawyer reasonably believes represent fees owed. However, a lawyer may not hold funds to coerce a client into accepting the lawyer's contention. The disputed portion of the funds must be kept in a trust account and the lawyer should suggest means for prompt resolution of the dispute, such as arbitration.   The undisputed portion of the funds shall be promptly distributed.

Third parties, such as a client's creditors, may have lawful claims against funds or other property in a lawyer's custody. A lawyer may have a duty under applicable law to protect such third-party claims against wrongful interference by the client. When the lawyer has a duty under applicable law to protect the third-party claim and the third-party claim is not frivolous under applicable law, the lawyer must refuse to surrender the property to the client until the claims are resolved.   However, a lawyer should not unilaterally assume to arbitrate a dispute between the client and the third party, and, where appropriate, the lawyer should consider the possibility of

depositing the property or funds in dispute into the registry of the applicable court so that the matter may be adjudicated.

The Supreme Court of Florida has held that lawyer trust accounts may be the proper target of garnishment actions. See Arnold, Matheny and Eagan, P.A. v. First American Holdings, Inc., 982 So.2d 628 (Fla. 2008).

The obligations of a lawyer under this chapter are independent of those arising from activity other than rendering legal services. For example, a lawyer who serves only as an escrow agent is governed by the applicable law relating to fiduciaries even though the lawyer does not render legal services in the transaction and is not governed by this rule.

Each lawyer is required to be familiar with and comply with the Rules Regulating Trust Accounts as adopted by the Supreme Court of Florida.

Money or other property entrusted to a lawyer for a specific purpose, including advances for fees, costs, and expenses, is held in trust and must be applied only to that purpose. Money and other property of clients coming into the hands of a lawyer are not subject to counterclaim or setoff for attorney's fees, and a refusal to account for and deliver over such property upon demand shall be a conversion. This does not preclude the retention of money or other property upon which a lawyer has a valid lien for services or to preclude the payment of agreed fees from the proceeds of transactions or collections.

Advances for fees and costs (funds against which costs and fees are billed) are the property of the client or third party paying same on a client's behalf and are required to be maintained in trust, separate from the lawyer's property. Retainers are not funds against which future services are billed. Retainers are funds paid to guarantee the future availability of the lawyer's legal services and are earned by the lawyer upon receipt. Retainers, being funds of the lawyer, may not be placed in the client's trust account.

The test of excessiveness found elsewhere in the Rules Regulating The Florida Bar applies to all fees for legal services including retainers, nonrefundable retainers, and minimum or flat fees.

Amended July 20, 1989, effective Oct. 1, 1989 (547 So.2d 117); Oct. 10, 1991, effective Jan. 1, 1992 (587

So.2d 1121); July 23, 1992, effective Jan. 1, 1993 (605 So.2d 252); July 1, 1993 (621 So.2d 1032); July 20,

1995 (658 So.2d 930); April 24, 1997 (692 So.2d 181); June 14, 2001, effective July 14, 2001 (797 So.2d 551);

April 25, 2002 (820 So.2d 210); May 20, 2004 (SC03-705) (875 So.2d 448); March 23, 2006, effective May

22, 2006 (SC04-2246), (933 So.2d 417); December 20, 2007, effective March 1, 2008 (SC06-736), (978 So.2d

91); November 19, 2009, effective February 1, 2010 (SC08-1890) (34 Fla.L.Weekly S628a); amended July 7,

2011, effective October 1, 2011 (SC10-1968).

RULE 5-1.2 TRUST ACCOUNTING RECORDS AND PROCEDURES

(a)　Applicability. The provisions of these rules apply to all trust funds received or disbursed by members of The Florida Bar in the course of their professional practice of law as members of The Florida Bar except special trust funds received or disbursed by a lawyer as guardian, personal representative, receiver, or in a similar capacity such as trustee under a

specific trust document where the trust funds are maintained in a segregated special trust account and not the general trust account and where this special trust position has been created, approved, or sanctioned by law or an order of a court that has authority or duty to issue orders pertaining to maintenance of such special trust account. These rules apply to matters in which a choice of laws analysis indicates that such matters are governed by the laws of Florida.

As set forth in this rule, "lawyer" denotes a person who is a member of The Florida Bar or otherwise authorized to practice in any court of the state of Florida. "Law firm" denotes a lawyer or lawyers in a private firm who handle client trust funds.

(b)　Minimum Trust Accounting Records. Records may be maintained in their original format or stored in digital media as long as the copies include all data contained in the original documents and may be produced when required. The following are the minimum trust accounting records that must be maintained:

(1)　a separate bank or savings and loan association account or accounts in the name of the lawyer or law firm and clearly labeled and designated as a "trust account";

(2)   original or clearly legible copies of deposit slips if the copies include all data on the originals and, in the case of currency or coin, an additional cash receipts book, clearly identifying the date and source of all trust funds received and the client or matter for which the funds were received;

(3)   original canceled checks or clearly legible copies of original canceled checks for all funds disbursed from the trust account, all of which must:

(A)   be numbered consecutively

(B)   include all endorsements and all other data and tracking information, and

(C)   clearly identify the client or case by number or name in the memo area of the check;

(4)   other documentary support for all disbursements and transfers from the trust account including records of all electronic transfers from client trust accounts, including:

(A)   the name of the person authorizing the transfer;

(B)   the name of the recipient;

(C)   confirmation from the banking institution confirming the number of the trust account from which money is withdrawn; and

(D)   the date and time the transfer was completed;

(5)   original or clearly legible digital copies of all records regarding all wire transfers into or out of the trust account, which at a minimum must include the receiving and sending financial institutions' ABA routing numbers and names, and the receiving and sending account holder's

name, address and account number. If the receiving financial institution processes through a correspondent or intermediary bank, then the records must include the ABA routing number and name for the intermediary bank. The wire transfer information must also include the name of the client or matter for which the funds were transferred or received, and the purpose of the wire transfer, (e.g., "payment on invoice 1234" or "John Doe closing").

(6)   a separate cash receipts and disbursements journal, including columns for receipts, disbursements, transfers, and the account balance, and containing at least:

(A)   the identification of the client or matter for which the funds were received, disbursed, or transferred;

(B)   the date on which all trust funds were received, disbursed, or transferred;

(C)   the check number for all disbursements; and

(D)   the reason for which all trust funds were received, disbursed, or transferred;

(7)   a separate file or ledger with an individual card or page for each client or matter, showing all individual receipts, disbursements, or transfers and any unexpended balance, and containing:

(A)   the identification of the client or matter for which trust funds were received, disbursed, or transferred;

(B)   the date on which all trust funds were received, disbursed, or transferred;

(C)   the check number for all disbursements; and

(D)   the reason for which all trust funds were received, disbursed, or transferred;

(8)   all bank or savings and loan association statements for all trust accounts.

(c)   Responsibility of Lawyers for Firm Trust Accounts and Reporting.

(1)   Every law firm with more than 1 lawyer must have a written plan in place for supervision and compliance with this rule for each of the firm's trust account(s), which plan must be disseminated to each lawyer in the firm. The written plan must include the name(s) of the lawyer(s) who sign trust account checks for the law firm, the name(s) of the lawyer(s) who are

responsible for reconciliation of the law firm's trust account(s) monthly and annually and the name(s) of the lawyer(s) who are responsible for answering any questions that lawyers in the firm may have about the firm's trust account(s). This written plan must be updated and re-issued to each lawyer in the firm whenever there are material changes to the plan, such as a change in the lawyer(s) signing trust account checks and/or reconciliation of the firm's trust account(s).

(2)   Every lawyer is responsible for that lawyer's own actions regarding trust account funds subject to the requirements of chapter 4 of these rules. Any lawyer who has actual knowledge

that the firm's trust account(s) or trust accounting procedures are not in compliance with chapter 5 may report the noncompliance to the managing partner or shareholder of the lawyer's firm. If the noncompliance is not corrected within a reasonable time, the lawyer must report the noncompliance to staff counsel for the bar if required to do so pursuant to the reporting requirements of chapter 4.

(d)   Minimum Trust Accounting Procedures. The minimum trust accounting procedures that must be followed by all members of The Florida Bar (when a choice of laws analysis indicates that the laws of Florida apply) who receive or disburse trust money or property are as follows:

(1)   The lawyer is required to make monthly:

(A)   reconciliations of all trust bank or savings and loan association accounts, disclosing the balance per bank, deposits in transit, outstanding checks identified by date and check number, and any other items necessary to reconcile the balance per bank with the balance per the checkbook and the cash receipts and disbursements journal; and

(B)   a comparison between the total of the reconciled balances of all trust accounts and the total of the trust ledger cards or pages, together with specific descriptions of any differences between the 2 totals and reasons for the differences.

(2)   The lawyer is required to prepare an annual detailed list identifying the balance of the unexpended trust money held for each client or matter.

(3)   The above reconciliations, comparisons, and listings must be retained for at least 6 years.

(4)   The lawyer or law firm must authorize, at the time the account is opened, and request any bank or savings and loan association where the lawyer is a signatory on a trust account to notify Staff Counsel, The Florida Bar, 651 East Jefferson Street, Tallahassee, Florida 32399- 2300, in the event the account is overdrawn or any trust check is dishonored or returned due to insufficient funds or uncollected funds, absent bank error.

(5)   The lawyer must file with The Florida Bar between June 1 and August 15 of each year a trust accounting certificate showing compliance with these rules on a form approved by the board of governors. If the lawyer fails to file the trust accounting certificate, the lawyer will be deemed a delinquent member and ineligible to practice law.

(e)   Electronic Wire Transfers. Authorized electronic transfers from a lawyer or law firm's trust account are limited to:

(1)   money required to be paid to a client or third party on behalf of a client;

(2)   expenses properly incurred on behalf of a client, such as filing fees or payment to third parties for services rendered in connection with the representation;

(3)   money transferred to the lawyer for fees which are earned in connection with the representation and which are not in dispute; or

(4)   money transferred from one trust account to another trust account.

(f)   Record Retention. A lawyer or law firm that receives and disburses client or third- party funds or property must maintain the records required by this chapter for 6 years subsequent to the final conclusion of each representation in which the trust funds or property were received.

(g)   Audits. Any of the following are cause for The Florida Bar to order an audit of a trust account:

(1)   failure to file the trust account certificate required by rule 5-1.2(c)(5);

(2)   return of a trust account check for insufficient funds or for uncollected funds, absent bank error;

(3)   filing of a petition for creditor relief on behalf of a lawyer;

(4)   filing of felony charges against a lawyer;

(5)   adjudication of insanity or incompetence or hospitalization of a lawyer under The Florida Mental Health Act;

(6)   filing of a claim against a lawyer with the Clients' Security Fund;

(7)   when requested by the chair or vice chair of a grievance committee or the board of governors; or

(8)   upon court order; or

(9)   upon entry of an order of disbarment, on consent or otherwise.

(h)   Cost of Audit.   Audits conducted in any of the circumstances enumerated in this rule will be at the cost of the lawyer audited only when the audit reveals that the lawyer was not in substantial compliance with the trust accounting requirements. It will be the obligation of any lawyer who is being audited to produce all records and papers concerning property and funds held in trust and to provide such explanations as may be required for the audit. Records of general accounts are not required to be produced except to verify that trust money has not been deposited in them. If it has been determined that trust money has been deposited into a general account, all of the transactions pertaining to any firm account will be subject to audit.

(i)   Failure to Comply With Subpoena for Trust Accounting Records. Failure of a member to timely produce trust accounting records will be considered as a matter of contempt and process in the manner provided in subdivision (d) and (f) of rule 3-7.11, Rules Regulating The Florida Bar.

Amended Oct. 10, 1991, effective Jan. 1, 1992 (587 So.2d 1121); July 23, 1992, effective Jan. 1, 1993 (605
So.2d 252); July 17, 1997 (697 So.2d 115); April 25, 2002 (820 So.2d 210); July 3, 2003 (850 So.2d 499);

May 20, 2004 (SC03-705) (875 So.2d 448); November 19, 2009, effective February 1, 2010 (SC08-1890) (34
Fla.L.Weekly S628a). Amended April 12, 2012, effective July 1, 2012 (SC10-1967); amended May 29, 2014,

effective June 1, 2014 (SC12-2234).

FLORIDA BAR DISCIPLINE STATISTICS

Type of Action	Fiscal Year				
	09-10	**10-11**	**11-12**	**12-13**	**13-14**
Disbarments	92	84	103	53	61
Suspensions	153	179	149	95	129
Public Reprimands	46	49	41	28	61
Disciplinary Resignations	0	1	0	0	0
Disciplinary Revocations					40
Admonishments	60	39	40	21	44
Probations	39	52	46	33	51

Note:

The Florida Bar changed the discipline statistics table beginning in 2013-14 to reflect recent amendments to The Florida Bar Rules of Discipline. Attorneys facing disciplinary charges can now petition for a disciplinary revocation, which is tantamount to a disbarment. Additionally, an emergency suspension now serves as a formal complaint based on the misconduct alleged in the petition for emergency suspension. Before the rule change, the Bar was required to seek discipline in addition to the emergency suspension. Under the new rule, the emergency suspension is temporary and will eventually be superseded by further discipline.

www.ingramcontent.com/pod-product-compliance
Lightning Source LLC
Chambersburg PA
CBHW051856170526
45168CB00001B/127